DATE			

41

GENOCIDE IN BOSNIA

**Number One
Eastern European Studies
Stjepan Meštrović, Series Editor**

GENOCIDE IN BOSNIA
The Policy of "Ethnic Cleansing"

Norman Cigar

Texas A&M University Press
College Station

Library of Congress Cataloging-In-Publication Data

Cigar, Norman L.
    Genocide in Bosnia : the policy of "ethnic cleansing" by
Norman Cigar ; foreword by Stjepan Meštrović — 1st ed.
        p.   cm. — (Eastern European studies ; no. 1)
    Includes bibliographical references and index.
    ISBN 0-89096-638-9 (alk. paper)
    1. Yugoslav War, 1991– —Atrocities. 2. Yugoslav War,
1991– —Bosnia and Hercegovina. 3. Muslims—Bosnia and
Hercegovina—History—20th century. 4. Bosnia and Hercegovina—Ethnic relations. I. Title.
DR1313.7.A85C54 1995
949.702'4—dc20   94–32948
                                                                          CIP

To my mother and father
for a lifetime of support and encouragement.

Zemlja naša

Sve od Broda do Mostara,
pobijena naša raja.
Pobijena il' prognana
i po svijetu razaslana.
Do juče smo skupa bili,
zlo i dobro, sve, dijelili.
A sada nas protjeraše,
iz te Bosne, zemlje naše.

Our Land

Everywhere from Brod to Mostar,
Our folk are vanquished,
Vanquished or exiled,
And scattered around the world.
Until yesterday, we lived together,
Sharing all, both the good and bad.
Now they banish us
From Bosnia, from our own land.

Sanita Isović,
refugee in Germany,
BiH Ekskluziv,
November 19, 1993

Contents

Contents

12. Heading for the End-State:
The Continuing Humanitarian Dilemma

Illustrations

Foreword

The genocide that has been occurring in Bosnia-Herzegovina since 1992 demands national attention. Incidents of these atrocities have involved European, American, and Islamic interests; they have taken place in the heart of Europe which had promised never to tolerate such a bloodbath again; they have paralyzed mechanisms set up to prevent such genocide, from the UN Charter to the NATO mandate; and they have been monitored, observed, and documented in progress. In this pioneering book, the first scholarly treatise on genocide in Bosnia-Herzegovina, Norman Cigar casts a harsh spotlight on this issue. He analyzes with sensitivity, insight, and scrupulous documentation the horrors of Bosnia-Herzegovina that have taken place even as the West has passively stood by.

In a thoroughly objective manner, Cigar discusses and documents the implementation of the Serbian policy of genocide from the points of view of the Serbs, Muslims, and Croats as well as the major powers outside the Balkans, including the Americans, French, and British. He tackles the most widely used rationalization used for understanding this case of genocide, that it stems from "tribal" and "historical" hatreds among the peoples of the former Yugoslavia. And he proves with no uncertainties that this philosophical stance is blatantly false. The truth is that the Belgrade regime, headed by Serbian President Slobodan Milošević planned carefully and supported completely the genocide unleashed in Bosnia-Herzegovina by his apprentice, the suspected war-criminal, Radovan Karadžić.

Foreword

Cigar concludes with a searing set of questions concerning the stability of Europe and of the rest of the world. Much like the way the international community's tolerance of genocide against the Armenians at the beginning of the twentieth century, Japan's invasion of Manchuria, and Mussolini's invasion of Ethiopia paved the way for Hitler's crimes, a dangerous state of moral disorder is being established by the West's refusal to respond to Serbian genocide toward the Bosnians.

Cigar's book is simultaneously a scholarly treatise on contemporary genocide as well as an example of social criticism. Its theme echoes Karl Jasper's theory of metaphysical guilt: those who are present at the murder of innocents, without risking their lives to prevent it, are guilty in a way not adequately conceived legally, politically, or morally. Similarly, Cigar contends that because of widespread media coverage devoted to genocide in Bosnia-Herzegovina, much of the world has witnessed these crimes.

This book raises profound and disturbing questions about preventing genocide, in Bosnia now and elsewhere in the future, and evokes provocative responses about our moral responsibility.

Stjepan G. Meštrović
General Editor

Acknowledgments

The author would like to thank Stjepan Meštrović, who generously took time to provide continuous encouragement and valuable advice throughout the writing and editing of this book; James Sadkovich, who offered many insights and numerous useful suggestions on an early draft; and Milan Vego, whose broad regional expertise served as a welcome sounding board for ideas.

GENOCIDE IN BOSNIA

CROATIA

SLOVENIA

Sava

• Prijedor

• Bihać

Brčko

Bijeljina •

• Banja Luka

Sava

• Tuzla

BOSNIA-HERZEGOVINA

Zvornik •

SERBIA

• Jajce

Bratunac •

• Travnik

Srebrenica •

SARAJEVO ★

Višegrad •

Goražde •

Drina

Foča •

• Mostar

• Grude

Gacko •

Montenegro

Trebinje •

Adriatic Sea

ALB.

1. Genocide

The Terms of Reference

The Muslim community of the former Yugoslav republic of Bosnia-Herzegovina has been the victim of what can be termed, by any accepted legal and moral measure, genocide. The intent of this book is to seek an understanding of the roots and dynamics of this process and to assess its human and political impact. As of this writing, the situation is still sorting itself out, but whatever agreement takes hold and whatever geopolitical configuration ultimately emerges will not erase the fact that genocide has occurred. Even if a rump Bosnian state emerges as a result of partition, the consequences of genocide will not be reversed, and the Muslims will likely remain vulnerable. Indeed, many of the dilemmas which have faced the world community in dealing with genocide in Bosnia-Herzegovina will continue not only there but elsewhere in the region.

The focus here is on the Muslims, although others, notably the Croatians, but Serbs too, have also been the target of atrocities in Bosnia-Herzegovina. The intent is not to minimize the suffering of any victims. However, the unique ideological aspects of the anti-Muslim campaign, the sheer numbers of the Muslims affected, and the extent of their suffering warrant a specific examination of that community's victimization. The assault on the Muslim community has happened essentially at the hands of their Serbian neighbors, whose intent was clearly to find a total solution; that is, to remove the Muslims from the land by whatever means feasible. Killings, torture, rape, and deportation, often carried out in a strikingly gruesome manner, have occurred on a scale not seen in Europe since World War II. Genocide in the former Yugoslavia has been disturbing not only for its destabilizing effect on regional affairs but also for the intrinsic tragedy that such a development represents in moral terms. The resurgence of genocide is all the more distressing in that this was a part of history which the West believed it had put firmly behind.

The key question, of course, is how such a seemingly senseless course of events could befall Europe. How could anyone bring himself to participate in, approve of, or ignore such a human tragedy, particularly with the sad experience of the Jewish holocaust etched in people's memories? As with other social phenomena, it is probably not realistic to look for a single factor as motivation for all the perpetrators, since ultimate explanations may be elusive, lying in the realm of human psychology and in age-old questions of morality. What are more amenable to analysis, however, are the intellectual, political, and social components which served to generate and sustain that process.

This study contends that the genocide—or ethnic cleansing, as it has been commonly known—that befell the Muslims of Bosnia-Herzegovina was not simply the unintentional and unfortunate by-product of combat or civil war. Rather, it was a rational policy, the direct and planned consequence of conscious policy decisions taken by the Serbian establishment in Serbia and Bosnia-Herzegovina. This policy was implemented in a deliberate and systematic manner as part of a broader strategy intended to achieve a well-defined, concrete, political objective, namely, the creation of an expanded, ethnically pure Greater Serbia.

A related contention is that international reaction was largely ineffective in either preventing genocide or in reversing its actual results, and that, despite a display of good intentions, more could have been done to stem the genocide. Moreover, the implications of the international community's failure to arrest this victimization are bound to be reflected in an erosion of the moral barriers and political sanctions believed to have been established in society since World War II. In real terms, this attitude is likely to result in continued political instability not only in the former Yugoslavia but also beyond its borders in the region. At the same time, the specter of ethnic cleansing in multiethnic societies around the globe will become increasingly real if other would-be perpetrators also come to view this ideology as a successful and accepted political model.

Crossing the Boundary into Genocide

Extensive literature exists on the phenomenon of genocide in general and on the holocaust in particular. One of its main objectives has been to analyze the variables that may trigger or facilitate this process.[1] Although each scenario is unique, genocide is most likely to occur if the perpetrators regard it as a rational, cost-effective strategy in pursuit of broader, concrete objectives. For this attitude to develop, however, the appropriate values and perspective that are conducive to genocide need to shift significantly, if they are not already in harmony. Top-down leadership and official legitimization were key factors for Bosnia-Herzegovina, and they are considerably more significant as a motivating force than history or tradition.

The existence of a heterogenous population, by itself, does not lead to or explain genocide, despite the alluringly simple attractiveness of such a view. For example, one American government briefer, pointing to a map showing the variegated communal patchwork in Yugoslavia, concluded, as if the map were self-evident, "That explains it all!" Bosnia-Herzegovina's population (44 percent Muslims, 31 percent Serbs, and 17 percent Croatians, according to the 1991 census) was conspicuously intertwined across the republic's territory. However, polities with even greater ethnic diversity than Yugoslavia or Bosnia-Herzegovina—not least of which is the United States—exist in many places around the world without genocide occurring. Even in situations where tensions among ethnic or religious communities may be acute, escalation to genocide is not automatic. Most often, such friction is translated into political competition, as in South Africa, even if the atmosphere becomes very intense or results in protracted violence. Even in wartime, genocide need not be an accompanying component. Nor are ethnic groups in the former Yugoslavia so inherently warped by nature or by a culture of violence that genocide is an almost inevitable outcome.[2] Some policy makers subscribed to the view that the general "irrationality" supposedly ingrained in the region could serve as an explanation for events.[3] However, recourse to this point of departure is not a valid substitute for serious analysis.

Nationalism too is not synonymous with genocide nor is it necessarily its cause. Certainly, not all nationalisms are the same, and those having such an extremist tinge are, fortunately, the exception. Many groups, again including Americans, would not take a backseat to anyone in terms of being nationalist, either in the past or present. However, the likelihood of

American nationalism degenerating into state-sanctioned genocide is remote, even under the pressures of a war. What, then, serves as a catalyst or facilitator in vaulting such competition, or conflict, across the threshold into genocide?

The Centrality of Leadership

One element—and perhaps the key element—in the emergence of genocide is leadership. One must examine how the elite in a society channel the competition, or conflict, among ethnic communities, whether within a single state or across international boundaries. Genocide in Bosnia-Herzegovina was neither a spontaneous expression of communal hatreds, extending back over a millennium, nor was it a primeval popular emotion, which the Serbian leadership could not control. On the contrary, in seeking to develop a vehicle for its own acquisition and consolidation of power, the Serbian elite (both governmental and non-governmental) found it necessary to engage in a systematic and intensive campaign in order to create a nationalist movement and to exacerbate intercommunal relations to the extent that genocide could be made plausible.

Although most societies contain extremist elements, with crises or war often arousing considerable popular passions, relatively few descend into genocide. In the United States and Great Britain, for example, popular sentiments against the Germans in both World Wars and against the Japanese in World War II were quite extreme and often expressed in crude terminology that bordered racist stereotyping. The fundamental difference, however, between that situation and the development of genocide is that, instead of further inflaming these tendencies, the leadership wisely moderated such emotions before they crossed a threshold of no return. By not legitimizing these excesses, leadership prevented their implementation.

If, however, a political establishment exploits and magnifies existing inchoate sentiments to an extreme degree, or even generates them *ex nihilo*, to mobilize support for its own policies or position of power, competition or conflict is more likely to degenerate into genocide. Not only can the leadership's control of a political infrastructure facilitate the effective mobilization of popular passions, but the legal authorities' influence can also provide an essential dimension of legitimacy to justify, and even require, support of and participation in any activities they may decree necessary.

The Preparatory Phase—Building Legitimacy

Another element in the emergence of genocide is a preparatory phase, an important step for the mobilization of support and even more so for the development of legitimacy to execute the policy later. The preparatory phase preceding the breakup of Yugoslavia was crucial, as it established a moral, legal, and institutional framework within which genocide could occur during the subsequent implementation phase. To understand the situation in Bosnia-Herzegovina, one must first study Serbia's political system from the preceding decade. One must comprehend the developments that created the environment and the legitimacy needed to impel a sufficient portion of the population to implement or acquiesce to a policy of genocide.

The Legal Framework for Analysis

How does one recognize genocide? Does the plight of the Muslims in Bosnia-Herzegovina qualify as genocide? Although each case differs, international precedents and existing agreements on war crimes and crimes against humanity provide enough common characteristics to provide an appropriate working definition and a framework by which to judge this and other cases. Within these parameters, there is little doubt that genocide indeed exists in Bosnia-Herzegovina.

The Nuremberg Tribunal Charter

The Nuremberg Tribunal Charter was drafted in 1945 with the establishment of the Nuremberg tribunal. Article 6 (c) and (d) of that charter define war crimes and crimes against humanity:

(c) War crimes: Namely, violations of the laws and customs of war. Such violations shall include, but not be limited to, murder, ill-treatment or deportation to slave labor or for any other purpose of civilian population of or in occupied territory, murder or ill-treatment of prisoners of war or persons on the seas, killing of hostages, plunder of public or private property, wanton destruction of cities, towns, or villages, or devastation not justified by military necessity.

(d) Crimes against humanity: Namely, murder, extermination, enslavement, deportation, and other inhumane acts committed against any civilian population, before or during the war, or persecutions on political, racial, or religious grounds in execution of or in connection with any crime within the jurisdiction of the Tribunal, whether or not in violation of the domestic law of the country where perpetrated.[4]

The United Nations Convention

In the United Nations' Convention on the Prevention and Punishment of the Crime of Genocide, dated December 11, 1946, Article II defines the following as genocide:

Any of the following acts committed with intent to destroy, in whole or in part, a national, ethnical, racial, or religious group, as such:
  a. Killing members of the group;
  b. Causing serious bodily or mental harm to members of the group;
  c. Deliberately inflicting on the group conditions of life calculated to bring about its physical destruction in whole or in part;
  d. Imposing measures intended to prevent births within the group;
  e. Forcibly transferring children of the group to another group.

Article II specifies which actions within this scope are punishable: (*a*) genocide, (*b*) conspiracy to commit genocide, (*c*) direct and public incitement to commit genocide, (*d*) attempt to commit genocide, (*e*) complicity in genocide.

Specific intent, though a key aspect of legal proceedings in criminal law, is difficult to prove in most circumstances involving genocide, as perpetrators are often anxious to conceal their actions. Scholars have proposed, instead, that the destruction of a group by "purposive action" be sufficient to qualify an act as genocide. Neither is the complete destruction of a group required for violence to qualify as genocide, as this act would develop by degrees along a continuum.[5]

Documenting Genocide in Bosnia-Herzegovina

From the standpoint of source material, the situation in Bosnia-Herzegovina has differed in several ways from other cases of genocide. Unlike the case of Nazi Germany, for example, the international community does not control a defeated state's documents, the sites where war crimes have been perpetrated, or captured key personnel who will be interrogated. However, thanks to the current fluid situation in Bosnia-Herzegovina, immediate access by representatives of foreign governments, the United Nations, and relief and humanitarian agencies, and many victims' own accounts have provided abundant and compelling evidence.[6] Perhaps the most striking difference from previous occurrences of genocide has been the unprecedented coverage in the media by determined reporters, such as *Newsday*'s Roy Gutman, whose riveting dispatches from the field earned a Pulitzer Prize in 1993.[7]

Table 1

Population Losses during and Immediately after World War II (in thousands)

	Serbs	Croats	Muslims	Others
In All of Yugoslavia				
Kočović	487	207	86	234
Žerjavić	530	192	103	202
In Bosnia-Herzegovina Only				
Kočović	209	79	75	19
Žerjavić	170	66	78	14

SOURCES: Although the two most reliable assessments of wartime population losses from all causes, based on a comparison of pre- and post-war population registers, were done independently, they agree to a great degree. One study was conducted by Serb scholar Bogoljub Kočović, *Žrtve drugog svetskog rata u Jugoslaviji* (*The Victims of World War II in Yugoslavia*) (London: Libra Books, 1985), pp. 102, 174, 182. The second study was done by Croatian scholar Vladimir Žerjavić and published by the Yugoslav Society for the Study of Victims and Zagreb's Jewish Community in *Gubici stanovništva Jugoslavije u drugom svjetskom ratu* [*Yugoslavia's Population Losses during World War II*] (Zagreb: Jugoslavensko Viktimološko Društvo, 1989), pp. 61, 82. Of course, not all those killed were victims of ethnic strife; in some cases, Croatians also killed fellow-Croatians and Serbs killed fellow-Serbs, for ideological reasons, while members of all communities died at the hands of Axis forces.

Additionally, television's vivid images, seen by millions of viewers around the world, made this the first case of genocide being televised as it was actually taking place.

As in similar situations with large-scale population shifts and inaccessible areas, the exact number of victims is difficult to determine, especially during an ongoing process. By all measures, however, the numbers appear to be staggering. Figures released by the Bosnian government in early 1994 included over 140,000 dead or missing and over 160,000 wounded. Since entire regions were inaccessible, these numbers are likely to be only partial totals, with actual figures probably closer to the 200,000 mark. In addition, almost two million people have been forced to flee abroad or to other parts of the country. The overwhelming majority of victims have been civilians, killed either deliberately or in the crossfire, although substantial numbers of people have also been killed in combat.

Even if one takes the low figure of 140,000 dead as a total for the two years since large-scale fighting began in April, 1992, the number would equal between 37 and 43 percent of the total population loss of Bosnia-

Herzegovina over the four years of World War II (table 1). In addition, one should also consider the other types of victims, mostly Muslims and Croatians, who have either fled to refuge abroad or become displaced elsewhere within Bosnia-Herzegovina. These types of victims exist in far greater numbers than during World War II, and many of them may be at continuing risk from the effects of partition and deteriorating living conditions. Altogether, the republic's potential population losses, as well as the level of destruction, may be comparable to those from World War II.

2. The Historical Context

Analytical Tool or Straitjacket?

History has provided a powerful, and often determining, reference point for dealing with the crisis in the former Yugoslavia. Commonly, observers have promoted the view that the conflict is little more than a continuation of endemic communal strife in the area, and that history has been the principal, if not exclusive, genesis of today's events. Typically, one analyst commented that the situation consisted "only [of] rekindled generations of hatred and atrocities the Serbs, Croats, and Muslims have inflicted on each other since the beginning of history.[1] Even scholars have often adopted this framework for analysis, with one concluding that "today's horrors are woven from strands of nothing less than the entire tapestry of history since the sixth century Slavic invasion of the Balkans." As a solution, based on this emphasis on historical causality, he proposed a fanciful academic healing mechanism, consisting of the "establishment of a unique, continuous conference of Serbian, Croatian, Muslim, and other historians," with the vital mediation of "Western experts."[2]

Of perhaps greater import is that many influential civilian and military decision makers also accepted this historicist paradigm, and by doing so, they contributed to shaping their approach as if dealing with a millennium of unremitting ethnic strife. Those who used this premise as a starting point included most of the top civilian policy makers in the West, as well as many military leaders involved in the problem. Once the European Union's mediator, Lord David Owen, had this assumption fixed in his mind, it remained his overriding paradigm. Asked even in mid-1994 why finding a solution in

Bosnia-Herzegovina seemed so difficult, he still attributed the problem to history—"these characters are locked in history."[3] Often, this attitude was to be the basis of an approach that combined pity with a sense of moral superiority. For many, such as U.S. Army Lt. Gen. Barry McCaffrey, then the assistant to the chairman of the Joint Chiefs of Staff, the local people had not only had "long experience of ethnic hatred," but, apparently, that reaction was all one could expect of them, for they were merely "three distinct tribal groupings," as he condescendingly called them when he testified in the Senate.[4]

Furthermore, the understanding of history as it was used to inform policy was often shallow at best and, more often than not, distorted. Characteristically, the ranking Republican on the Senate Committee on Armed Services, Sen. John Warner, was a prominent opponent of stronger measures in Bosnia-Herzegovina. In hearings on the Yugoslav crisis, he buttressed his case by noting that "my own research . . . indicates that . . . these people have fought each other for not hundreds of years, but thousands of years for religious, ethnic, cultural differences." Turning to the Joint Chiefs of Staff's top intelligence officer and unaware of possible internal contradictions in his own analysis, he continued: "So my question to you, Admiral: As we continuously search in our own minds why, why, why, this killing and rape and pillage, is there any answer? Are there any answers to why these people, who live peaceably side by side, intermarry, go to the same churches [sic], held an international sports event [the 1984 Winter Olympics] in Sarajevo, why is it that they fall upon themselves periodically, and have done this for a thousand years?" The reply he received was equally vacuous: "Sir, I wish I had the answer to your question. . . . But there is certainly a history, going back, at least into my study of the problem, as far back as the thirteenth century, of constant ethnic and religious fighting among and between these groups."[5]

History, of course, has helped to form the background against which recent events have taken place and can help us understand them. However, history has not been, as some have suggested, the deterministic factor. One cannot explain today's developments, much less the occurrence of genocide, simply by taking a mechanistic linear view of such a milestone as, say, the 1389 Battle of Kosovo, in which the Ottomans defeated the medieval Serbian state. This battle, however, has been perceived by many Western observers as the root of an enduring Serbian-Islamic struggle and, ostensibly, the mainspring of the current situation.

Instead, history, as an ideological club, as opposed to the actual chronological record and its scholarly study, in recent times has been a highly malleable quantity, with its greatest utility as a potential mobilization vehicle for political objectives. As Serbia's leader, Slobodan Milošević, remarked perceptively in his watershed speech commemorating the six hundredth anniversary of the Battle of Kosovo: "Today, it is difficult to say what is true and what is legend about the Battle of Kosovo. Today, that is not even important."[6] As he had stressed the previous year, what are uppermost instead are current, hard-headed, interests. He claimed: "Hearkening back to history, in fact, is not the basis upon which to carry out our mobilization. To be sure, history provides an obligation to us to mobilize. However, the main incentive for the mobilization of all the Yugoslav peoples and minorities is their present condition and especially the future."[7]

Relegating today's events solely to insoluble centuries-old atavistic dilemmas shrouded in the dawn of time implicitly assumes that a solution will always be elusive and that it is pointless to seek one. Although superficially attractive, this idea was often only a convenient rationalization for shrugging one's shoulders and doing nothing. History, however, neither dooms one to a repetition of the past nor to immobilism. In the case of Yugoslavia, moreover, such blanket evaluations are misleading, because interethnic relations have been far from static over time, with fluid communal alliances common. Even in recent times, communal relations have been fairly adaptable rather than fixed in following a stereotypical pattern of unalloyed Christian-Muslim vendettas. Often, on the contrary, the alleged innate hatreds have been of recent invention as a useful tool for national mobilization and the legitimization of power by specific elites.

History and Conventional Wisdom: Assessing the Record

Significantly, all three communities in Bosnia-Herzegovina lived for centuries in relative harmony. At most, one can trace a genuine penchant for genocide only as far back as the appearance of a modern nationalist movement in Serbia during the nineteenth century.

The Ottoman Period

Islamic-Christian coexistence, not genocide against the Serbs, was the rule during the five hundred years of Ottoman presence. Bosnia, which came under Ottoman control in the fifteenth and sixteenth centuries, provided a relatively tolerant environment for the times. In fact, Jews forced to flee the

Inquisition in Spain settled in Ottoman Sarajevo, while the indigenous Catholic community in Bosnia was granted a formal charter guaranteeing the freedom to practice its religion after the Ottoman conquest. At the same time, most of the interior of the Balkans enjoyed relatively healthy economic development and, until the eighteenth century, a degree of stability and security probably comparable to most contemporary west European states.

As is true of virtually all of Europe's peoples, Bosnia's Muslims are an amalgam of various ethnic origins, although the overwhelming majority was drawn from the local Catholic and Bogomil Christian population, who converted in phases over three centuries while retaining their original Croatian language. In no way are they a foreign community, despite the common Serbian practice of calling them Turks. Although, alternatively, many Serbian nationalists claim that today's Muslims are of Serbian origin, there is little evidence of Serbs or other Orthodox peoples having converted to Islam in significant numbers as they moved into Bosnia-Herzegovina on the heels of the Ottoman conquest.[8] Serbian nationalists, including the Serbian Orthodox Church hierarchy, however, have been prone to make sweeping statements about the unacknowledged or unconscious Serbian ethnicity of most of their neighbors. Thus, they maintain that most of today's Croatians—both in Croatia and Bosnia-Herzegovina—are also Serbs who allegedly converted to Catholicism, that the Macedonians are southern Serbs, and even that most Albanians are forcibly assimilated Serbs. Some leading nationalists today still maintain that large tracts of Hungary, Rumania, Bulgaria, Albania, and Greece are also ethnically Serbian.

For most of this period, it was the Catholic Hapsburgs and Venetians, not the Serbs and other Orthodox peoples, who were involved in destructive wars with the Muslim Ottomans along the marches of their competing empires. However, divisions were never as clear-cut along religious lines as one might think for individual and even group relations. To take but one example from the late seventeenth century, the two most prominent Croatian noblemen, Petar Zrinski and Fran Krsto Frankopan, together with a good deal of the rest of the Croatian nobility, sought to trade Hapsburg for Ottoman suzerainty but were thwarted and executed before they could carry out their plan. In return for switching sovereigns, the Croatian nobles were to have been given dominion over all Croatian lands—both those then under the Hapsburgs and those already under the Ottomans—which would henceforth have been united and have enjoyed autonomy under the Ottoman Sultan.[9]

14

The Orthodox communities during much of this period were outright allies of the Ottoman state in its campaigns against the Christian powers. At the Battle of Nicopolis in 1396, for example, the vassal Serbian ruler and army were instrumental in the Ottomans' defeat of a united Christian army, thus definitively opening up the Balkans to Ottoman rule. Serbian troops were also key in saving the Ottoman state from Tamerlane's onslaught at the battle of Ankara in 1402. Similarly, the *martelozi*, Orthodox military auxiliaries, were significant in helping the Ottomans raid Christian territory and defend the Ottoman borders. Only later did such militias switch sides to become Hapsburg mercenaries, as the regional balance of power shifted away from the Ottomans. The Orthodox Church itself developed into an administrative adjunct of the Ottoman state, helping the latter to govern the Christians at the local level. In a move designed to weaken the Greek patriarch in Istanbul, the Ottomans in 1557 had even reestablished the Serbian Orthodox Church as an institution independent from the jurisdiction of the Greek Orthodox Church.

As a protected *millet,* or autonomous religious and juridical entity within the Ottoman state, the Orthodox community also expanded noticeably by the amount of territory it inhabited during the centuries of Ottoman rule. Not only the Serbs, but also various other Orthodox groups—such as Vlachs, Greeks, Albanians, and other smaller communities—spread as mercenaries or immigrants from their original lands into present-day Bosnia-Herzegovina, Croatia, Northern Serbia, and Vojvodina. In Bosnia-Herzegovina, large-scale Serbian and other Orthodox immigration continued into modern times. Especially significant was the 1813–17 epidemic, in which many Muslim peasants perished and were replaced by Orthodox peasants from Montenegro.[10] Today's Serbs who live outside of Serbia proper—the Prečani Serbs ("those on the other side [of the Drina River]")—are the descendants of not only these Serbian settlers and the probably more numerous non-Serbian Orthodox immigrants but also of the converts to Orthodoxy from the local Catholic and Bogomil population. These Orthodox communities eventually assimilated over the centuries and today constitute Bosnia-Herzegovina's Serbian community.

After Bosnia-Herzegovina came under Hapsburg tutelage in 1878, all three religious communities coexisted in relative harmony. Paradoxically, as Catholic-Islamic tensions in the Balkans faded in the nineteenth century, in the wake of improving Ottoman-Hapsburg relations, Muslim-Orthodox tensions flared up. A basic motive appears to have been the course of the emerging Balkan nationalist movements. This development was linked to the socioeconomic changes that were occurring throughout the Ottoman Empire and that often expressed themselves in revolt against local misrule. As in other Christian areas of the Empire, but in contrast to predominantly Muslim regions, in Serbia this political ferment eventually assumed a militant religious-nationalist hue. The local notables sought to use this new development as a way to differentiate themselves both from the officially Islamic Ottoman polity and from sectors in the local elite willing to work within the Ottoman system. Adopting such a confrontational policy served to legitimize the new elite's leadership role in society as well as to mobilize popular support for the elite's goals and emerging political aspirations. This new spirit of revolt against the Ottoman state eventually led to the establishment of an independent Serbian state based on a new nationalist ideology.[11]

The Vision of a Greater Serbia

A NEW IDEOLOGY. If there were one overriding modern historical factor whose legacy has had a continuing impact on current political developments affecting all these ethnic groups, it would be the quest for a Greater Serbia. This quest developed as a core element of Serbian nationalist ideology with the emergence of an independent Serbia in the nineteenth century. Given its particular focus on territorial control coterminous with the national-religious community, this ideology has been a pivotal force for policy prescription, as domestic political legitimacy could henceforth be expressed as an obligation to gather all Serbs, wherever and however many they be, into a single nation-state.

The accompanying notion of ethnic exclusivity at the heart of this new nationalism inevitably raised the dilemma of what to do with non-Serbian communities. In practical terms, the Serbian state sought to assimilate other communities if they were Orthodox. If they were Muslim, the state sought to cleanse them if they impeded progress or if they were unwilling to foreswear their faith to assimilate. In the course of modern Serbian nation-building, the Muslims—because of their location—were to become a particularly vulnerable community, as Serbia expanded and developed a tradition that made ethnic cleansing an acceptable part of the process.

TERRITORIAL EXPANSION AS NATION-BUILDING. After gaining its autonomy and then independence, Serbia continued to expand during the nineteenth century. In the territories acquired during this phase, the Muslims were forced to convert, leave, or be liquidated.[12] By the end of the nineteenth century, the Kingdom of Serbia had been largely cleansed of native Muslims and of the Turkish minority. The problem reemerged, however, after the Balkan Wars of 1912–13, when Serbia was able to seize and annex two predominantly Islamic provinces from the hapless Ottoman Empire: Kosovo and the Sandžak, as well as Macedonia, which had a large Muslim Albanian community.[13]

THE FIRST YUGOSLAVIA. The advent of World War I allowed the Muslim issue in the newly acquired territories to be placed on the back burner; but the problem for Serbian nationalists was compounded with the projected formation of Yugoslavia after World War I and the expected inclusion of Bosnia-Herzegovina in the newly created state. Asked in 1917 about his plans for Bosnia, Stojan Protić, leader of the Serbian Popular Radical Party and Yugoslavia's future first prime minister, admitted to Croatian politicians: "Leave that to us. We have the solution for Bosnia. . . . When our army crosses the Drina, we will give the Turks [local Muslims] twenty-four hours, or even forty-eight hours, of time to return to their ancestral religion. Those who do not wish to do so are to be cut down, as we did in Serbia earlier."

Responding to protests by the startled Croatian leaders present, Protić conceded that he did not insist necessarily that all of the Muslims who did not convert be killed, but, he added: "There can no longer be any Turks [Muslims] in Bosnia. They can flee across the Sava [River, into Croatia], or wherever."[14] Although wiser heads prevailed at the time, significant numbers of Muslims were nevertheless pressured into emigrating in the period after World War I.[15]

Montenegro, many of whose inhabitants also consider themselves Serbs, has followed a parallel path of expansion, sharing in the annexation of Albanian-inhabited areas, part of the coastline, and part of the Sandžak in the 1870s, and seizing additional lands during the Balkan Wars of 1912–13. In 1945, Montenegro completed its expansion by annexing the Boka Kotorska coastline from Croatia and the Herceg-Novi coastline and other territories from Bosnia-Herzegovina.

With the collapse of the Hapsburg Empire and the establishment of Yugoslavia in 1918, all Serbs were united in a single state. Soon, subsequent hegemony by the Serbs and the resulting discontent among virtually all other national communities with second-class status led to chronic instability and growing hostility between Serbs and non-Serbs. Pressure on the Muslims, in particular, continued, and, when Bosnia-Herzegovina was temporarily split in 1933 in a reshuffle of internal borders, Yugoslav President Milan Srškić explained that he had done so "because of the Turks [Muslims]. I cannot stand to see minarets in Bosnia; they must disappear."[16] By the late 1930s, encouraged by the prevailing acceptance of intolerance in many parts of Europe, the situation had deteriorated to the point that plans were drafted for the mass expulsion of Yugoslavia's largely Muslim Albanians, plans which were derailed only by the advent of World War II. The atmosphere of estrangement prevalent among the non-Serbs in interwar Yugoslavia, predictably, was instrumental in the latter's rapid disintegration under the German onslaught in April, 1941.

World War II

World War II was a watershed in interethnic relations in Yugoslavia, particularly to the degree that it gave rise to genocide, with its huge toll of victims serving more recently as a rallying cry for all communities.

In 1941 both Croatia and Serbia established Fascist states allied to Germany. In addition to the pro-Axis Serbian state created in Belgrade, other Serbian nationalists also organized the Chetnik movement, whose focus was to establish a Greater Serbia under Serbia's royal family. The Chetnik leadership was headed by Draža Mihailović, a Serbian officer who had gone underground after Yugoslavia's defeat by the Germans. By June, 1941, Chetnik leaders had drafted a formal policy document calling for a "Homogeneous Serbia," based on the premise that the Serbs "must fulfill their historic mission." The plan envisaged a "Greater Serbia" extending over present-day Bosnia-Herzegovina, Montenegro, Macedonia, Kosovo, Vojvodina, most of Croatia, northern (and possibly all of) Albania, and parts of Bulgaria, Romania, and Hungary as well as Serbia proper.

Recognizing that the Serbs would be in the minority in most of these areas, the planners proposed "cleansing the lands of all non-Serb elements."[17] Operational orders provided by Mihailović, such as one sent to his field commanders on December 20, 1941, spelled out the Chetniks' intent toward to the Muslims:

Point 4. To cleanse the state territory of all national minorities and anti-national elements.
Point 5. To create a direct, continuous, border between Serbia and Montenegro, and

between Serbia and Slovenia, by cleansing the Sandžak of the Muslim inhabitants and Bosnia of the Muslim and Croatian inhabitants.[18]

This objective was clarified in further instructions sent by Mihailović's headquarters to the commander of the Second Sarajevo Chetnik Brigade. They read in part: "It should be made clear to everyone that, after the war or when the time becomes appropriate, we will complete our task and that no one except the Serbs will be left in Serbian lands. Explain this to [our] people and ensure that they make this their priority. You cannot put this in writing or announce it publicly, because the Turks [Muslims] would hear about it too, and this must not be spread around by word of mouth."[19]

The Chetniks' extremist counterparts on the Croatian side, the Ustaše, tried to implement a similarly brutal exclusivist ethnic program against the Serbs. They established a Croatian state extending over Croatia and Bosnia-Herzegovina, arguing that until 1945 most Slavic Muslims, notwithstanding the development of a distinct culture, identified themselves as Muslim Croatians.

The Muslims, given their pivotal position in Bosnia-Herzegovina, became a primary target of mass killings by the Serbian Chetniks as the latter sought to execute their plan for a Greater Serbia. Retaliation soon followed, with many Muslims joining the Ustaše to protect themselves or to exact revenge.

Tito's Communist Partisans (whose members came from all ethnic groups) joined in the killings and atrocities, spurred more by ideological rather than by ethnic motivation. The Serbs, Muslims, and Croatians became at the same time victims and perpetrators—though, of course, usually not the same individuals in both cases—in the ethnic and ideological strife that characterized the period. The Germans and Italians fueled the conflicts for their own ends. An estimated one million people perished in Yugoslavia from all causes during World War II. This number was approximately split between Serbs and non-Serbs, of which one third were in Bosnia-Herzegovina (table 1).

The Aftermath—The Second Yugoslavia

AN UNSTABLE POLITY. Although the defeat of the Chetniks by the Communists in World War II prevented the fulfillment of the Serbian nationalist program, as a compromise intended to buttress his new government, the Croatian-born Tito granted Serbia control over several areas in which non-

Serbs were a majority of the population: Kosovo, Vojvodina, and the Sandžak. In addition, the Serbs were given a disproportionate share of posts in the federal bureaucracy, military, diplomatic corps, economic infrastructure, judicial system, and Communist Party—a situation which prevailed until the breakup of Yugoslavia.[20]

Among the other ethnic groups in Yugoslavia, the alienation and suspicion, which resulted from what they perceived as Serbian attempts to dominate the reestablished Yugoslav state, caused much of the political gridlock that had befallen the country by the 1980s. The passing away of Tito's generation of leaders, committed to a vision of a Communist Yugoslavia, removed a significant element of coercion and opened the way toward democracy and change. At the same time, the withering of authoritarianism would have inevitably led to calls to redress the inequality and, potentially, to efforts to dissolve Yugoslavia. This possibility aroused deep concern among many Serbs who saw a potential loss of status and privilege on an individual and communal basis. However, it also offered an opportunity. New elites could attempt to use this tension to carve out a greater role for themselves in the shifting structure of power within society, as existing forms of political legitimacy frayed and anxieties escalated.

REVIVING TESTED GOALS. It was in this post-Tito period of transition that earlier attempts to create a Greater Serbia reacquired their attractiveness as a political tool. They also represented a ready-made nationalist ideology with a familiar symbology available for exploitation. Moreover, one of the more enduring results of Serbia's modern nationalist record had been the establishment of a blueprint, a proven methodology for ethnic cleansing to which future generations of nationalists could look back, if they so desired. To the extent that this framework provided a tested road-map for nationalists, recent historical experience may be viewed as a facilitator, more so than as an ineluctable cause, of the current genocide in Bosnia-Herzegovina.

Although the nationalist program, as it reemerged, came to parallel the goals and methods in many ways of earlier plans and solutions, a repetition of earlier excesses was in no way an automatic inevitability. Neither was regression to past patterns a spontaneous development. Rather, it was the result of a deliberate policy choice. In fact, despite friction between Serbs and non-Serbs in the political and economic spheres in the post-war period, and often clear discrimination against Islam in particular, ethnic groups in Yugoslavia, including Bosnia-Herzegovina, had managed to coexist without overt violence for over a generation (with the exception of periodic crackdowns against Kosovo's Albanian community). The reason for this coexistence was not that the old parties from World War II were being held barely at bay by the Titoist system's strong hand. Nor was it the result of a general amnesia attributable supposedly to the fact that "the civil war's existence was deliberately suppressed" by Tito, as Lord David Owen and others have maintained.[21] Quite the opposite, the civil war had become a recurring theme of much of the government's post-war propaganda and official historiography, albeit as viewed through an official lens, and the terms Chetnik and Ustaša were distributed liberally to tar anyone who would not support the new system.

In fact, the transformation in interethnic relations needed for the mass mobilization of the Serbs in support of a more confrontational relationship, including vis-à-vis the Muslims, was neither spontaneous nor unavoidable. Instead, a preparatory phase, marked by an intensive and methodical top-down political and information campaign in the 1980s, was required to change the value system of an entire generation of Serbs.

3. The Preparatory Phase

Paving the Road to Genocide

The period preceding Yugoslavia's disintegration is significant in that it served as the preparatory phase to the slide into genocide. It prepared the ideology, the machinery, and what Thompson and Quets call the "prevailing moral ambiance" that were to make ethnic cleansing possible. Although long-term factors—such as religion, history, or culture—may have provided the backdrop for the resurgence of Serbian nationalism in the 1980s, they would not have been enough to generate open warfare, much less the genocide that was to follow.

The Need for an Ideology

For genocide, the development of an ideology is especially significant insofar as a guide and justification are needed. As sociologist Leo Kuper stresses, "At least when operating collectively, they [perpetrators of genocide] need an ideology to legitimate their behavior, for without it they would have to see themselves and one another as what they really are—common thieves and murderers."[1] In the present case, a redefinition and legitimation of national goals was required, within a convincing intellectual framework, which could motivate strata of the population beyond the small number of psychopaths and opportunists found in most societies. Also required was the creation of a suitable and effective political structure, led by a new or transformed elite, which could implement this agenda.

Initially, Serbian intellectuals, outside the official government circles, with the backing of the Serbian Orthodox Church, took the lead in developing the nationalist agenda in the early 1980s, following Tito's death. It was only with the rise of Milošević's own power within Serbia's League of Communists—as the ruling Serbian Communist Party was called—and his adoption of the nationalist program, that the full weight of the government also became engaged in this effort. Ultimately, Milošević and his government, who came to dominate this process, must bear the greatest blame for what was to happen in Bosnia-Herzegovina. However, the moral and intellectual support which Serbian opposition parties, the intellectual community along the entire ideological spectrum, and the Serbian Orthodox Church hierarchy provided made it considerably easier for Milošević to persuade the masses to back even the most extreme options. To that extent, they too must share fully in this responsibility.

The Serbian Memorandum—A *Defining Moment*

If one is to look within this preparatory phase for a defining moment and a traceable catalyst to the recent series of events in Bosnia-Herzegovina, it is most likely to be found in the *Serbian Memorandum,* drafted in 1986 by the Serbian Academy of Arts and Sciences. The *Memorandum* was penned by Serbia's leading intellectuals, who envisioned a greater role for themselves in society. Many of them subsequently did become key political figures. This document crystallized the revival among Serbian intellectuals of earlier nationalist goals.

The *Memorandum* proclaimed in no uncertain terms that the earlier quest for a Greater Serbia retained its validity and thereby defined the nation's legitimate political agenda. The manifesto maintained that the "national question" of the Serbian people had been thwarted by the Communists at the end of World War II, since "it [the Serbian people] did not get its own state like other peoples." The only solution to ensure the very "existence and development" of the Serbs, according to the *Memorandum,* was the "territorial unity of the Serbian people," to be achieved by uniting all the Serbs in a single Serbian national state. As the *Memorandum* expressed it, "the establishment of the full national integrity of the Serbian people, regardless of which republic or province it inhabits, is its historic and democratic right."[2]

23

Predictably, most of the Communists then in power in Belgrade reacted with hostility to this agenda of creating a Greater Serbia, since they viewed it as a point of no return toward communal violence. In an address at Belgrade University on October 30, 1986, Ivan Stambolić, Serbia's president and a reformist Communist, stated that the "so-called Memorandum is not new. It is the old chauvinist concern for the fate of the Serbian cause with the well-known formula that the Serbs win the wars but lose the peace. . . . In short, the so-called Memorandum, more precisely and with an easy conscience, could be entitled 'In Memoriam' for Yugoslavia, Serbia, Socialism, self-management, equality, brotherhood, and unity. . . . Essentially, it is diametrically opposed to the interests of the Serbs throughout Yugoslavia."[3]

Coming at a time of impending change and uncertainty, the *Memorandum* seemed to answer the need for a national strategy blueprint for Serbia. However, it also set the stage for the outbreak of violence, since its implementation was bound to threaten the fundamental security of Yugoslavia's other national communities. Unless the latter accepted the *Memorandum's* implications passively—an unlikely scenario—it could only be put into effect through the use of force.

Shaping the Intellectual Atmosphere

The new wave of Serbian nationalism in the 1980s, not surprisingly, turned its attention against all those communities which, by their physical presence, were seen to stand in the way of the goal of creating a Greater Serbia. In particular, the new nationalism included as a key component an uncompromising hostility—spearheaded by Serbia's intellectual elite—directed against the Muslim community, which, because of its size and location, was central in determining whether or not Bosnia-Herzegovina would become part of a Greater Serbia. Although it was the Albanian community, most of which is also Muslim, which had been the principal target initially, the strong anti-Islamic component of the attacks launched by Belgrade also served to prepare the groundwork for the time when the primary focus of effort was to shift against the Muslims of Bosnia-Herzegovina and the Sandžak.

Well before the actual breakup of Yugoslavia, influential figures in Serbia had begun to shape a stereotypical image of Muslims as alien, inferior, and a threat to all that the Serbs held dear. This perception was Orientalism taken in a broad sense and writ large. Orientalism, studied by Edward Said in his pioneer work on the phenomenon, is a remarkably stark and implication-laden division into "them" and "us."[4] This discourse spanned much of the Serbian national elite, including leading intellectuals, political figures, and clergymen, and its impact was to extend to all strata of society. To a great extent, the need to portray Muslims according to this pattern was a response to the needs of certain political goals, which the Muslims, and other non-Serbs, by their very presence, obstructed. That is, by reifying and isolating the entire Muslim community, any steps subsequently taken against Muslims in pursuit of Belgrade's political goals would acquire legitimacy and popular support.

Vuk Drašković, author of several controversial best-sellers, such as the evocatively titled novel, *Nož* (*Knife*), which was first published in 1982 and reprinted several times, was perhaps the most popular and influential individual in developing such stereotypes early. Set largely against the background of World War II, the Muslim characters in *Nož* appear mostly as treacherous, cold-blooded murderers. What is more, *Nož* contains an explicit denial of the Muslims' existence as a legitimate community. According to Drašković's central story line, Muslims are supposedly really only descendants of Serbs who had converted centuries earlier, thereby betraying their own nation. In the book, Muslim characters stand out starkly against the virtuous and long-suffering Serbs. This portrayal also includes the wartime Chetniks, who are all depicted with considerable sympathy.

Such messages about the Muslims eventually were to become commonplace in Serbia's popular and scholarly literature, while the Serbian media denigrated Islam openly and gratuitously, often in terms approaching racism. Drašković himself continued to propagate these ideas in other writings and speeches. He lashed out vehemently at the "fury of offensive and intolerant Islam in Bosnia, Kosovo, the Sandžak, and Herzegovina, . . . [at] the vampire-like resurgence of the tradition of the Shariah [religious law], and . . . the strategy of *jihad* [holy war] with the goal of creating an Islamic state in the Balkans."[5]

That the written word during this phase already had a concrete negative influence can be gauged from the effect it had on the future commander of the militia—the Serbian Guard—that Drašković established later. As the future commander admitted in the late 1980s, "I beat up many Muslims and Croatians on vacation in Cavtat because of his [Drašković's] *Nož*. Reading that book, I would see red, I would get up, select the biggest fellow on the beach, and smash his teeth."[6]

Serbian nationalists appeared to be especially irked by the good relations between the Catholic and Islamic communities and periodically sought to sow discord instead. When one of the largest mosques in Europe was inaugurated in Zagreb in 1988 for Croatia's Muslim community, for example, an article in the glossy Serbian nationalist publication *Duga* took Croatia to task. Asking rhetorically what medieval Zagreb's bishops or the seventeenth century Croatian commander Nikola Zrinski, who had fought against the Ottomans, would have thought, the periodical adduced the mosque as proof that Croatia had failed to keep out Islam. The mocking language of the article and the accompanying photo of the backsides of Muslims bowing for prayer were clearly intended to be insulting.[7]

Overall, Muslims, as well as Croatians, were depicted routinely as virtually non-people, essentially being labeled—with little historical basis—as Serbs who had converted to Islam or to Catholicism, respectively, but who were lacking consciousness of their very roots and identity. The Serbian media also sought to sensitize the Macedonians to the alleged threat posed by Islam, thereby hoping to win an ally in what was already being represented as a struggle.[8]

Some Serbian intellectuals went even further and interjected a clear tinge of racism into their arguments. One of them, Dragoš Kalajić, dismissed Bosnia's Muslims as "not belonging to the European family of nations," since their music, *inter alia,* is, according to him, "an unconscious and spontaneous expression of the semi-Arab subculture," the result of a "genetic predetermination and penchant." Speaking of the origin of the Muslims in Yugoslavia, he claimed that "during five centuries, in satisfying their sexual impulses . . . the Ottoman armies and administrators—drawn from the Near Eastern and North African bazaars—created a distinct semi-Arab ethnic group."

As a result of their purported "desert origins" and of a "special gene of the Ottoman soldiery," Yugoslavia's Muslims allegedly exhibit a long list of inherited character flaws, such as propensity to theft, a lack of ethics, laziness, authoritarianism, a "neo-primitive lust for power," and even discomfort with wearing European clothing. Local Muslims, he continued, are supposedly incapable of ruling themselves, since, like their "desert ancestors" they will only use "nomadic-robber means." When in power, local Muslims, according to Kalajić, will plunder, "not in the least showing any of the shame which is characteristic for a European in a similar situation." Moreover, "simply put, the semi-Arab is not capable of understanding the essence of one of the basic traits of the European, namely the institution of

the uniqueness of personal freedom which is fundamentally above any col-
lectivity." His conclusion was that in light of this alien Muslim peril, ultimately force could be the only solution, or, as he put it, "What is needed is
the general mobilization of European energies, and a supranational, supra-
religious, supraideological union of Europeans. . . . What is also needed is a
qualitative increase in the readiness of those Yugoslav systems that have
been maintained, such as the State Security and the JNA [Army]." To add
insult to injury and to reinforce the Muslim stereotypes, the article featured
an illustration of a scantily clad belly dancer.[9]

Other nationalists had recourse to the discipline of abnormal psychology
to portray the Muslims. Psychiatrist Jovan Rašković—subsequently a leading figure in the Serbs' secessionist movement in Croatia—believed that,
based on his clinical observations, the key to understanding the Muslims was
"their anal fixation." This behavior, allegedly, stemmed from the preoccupa-
tion with ritual cleanliness found in their religious law and supposedly
warped their character so that they were markedly aggressive and exces-
sively materialistic.[10]

Serbia's Orientalists—The Scholarly Reassurance

In a narrower sense, Serbia's Orientalists, scholars specializing in the study
of Islam, have also been a key factor in this process by providing an academic armature to the campaign against Islam since the 1980s. By interpret-
ing the Muslim community with a blending—and bending—of scholarship
and political rhetoric, they have contributed significantly to making hostility
toward the Muslims intellectually respectable among broad strata of the
Serbian population, particularly because of these scholars' frequent presence in the mass media. At the very least, such academics, as the recognized
subject matter experts, crystallized and reinforced generalized stereotypes
toward Islam and provided a putatively scholarly justification for any measures the government might take against the Muslims. Much as the Orientalists of an earlier colonial era had done, their Serbian counterparts supported the national political interests in relation to the objects of their study,
but seldom has the linkage been so immediate and so destructive as in the
case of Bosnia-Herzegovina.

In general, Serbian scholars taxed Islam and Muslims with being retro-
grade and a threat to modern civilization, both in general terms and to
Serbia specifically. Miroljub Jevtić, a political scientist and specialist on
Islam at Belgrade University, was perhaps the most active proponent of such

ideas. He claimed that Islamic "fundamentalists," a label he applied freely to any Muslim, are little more than a reflection of the "darkness of the past." They understand "slavery and equality, not the way a civilized person does, but rather the way their God understands it." According to Jevtić, "Islam is opposed to any just relations, tolerance, dialogue or 'coexistence,'" and, in fact, the Qur'an and Shariah allegedly permit the "destruction of those who have another religion." Supposedly, Islam mandates the banning of tourism, sports, and going to cafes where alcohol is served, thus inevitably leading to xenophobia and to "100 percent segregation." He asks rhetorically, "If you cannot eat, drink, be buried in the same cemetery or marry a neighbor of another faith, what then can you do?"[11] Since clearly not all Muslims in Bosnia-Herzegovina are religiously observant (including many who had been members of the Communist Party), Jevtić was forced to stretch his definition of fundamentalism to one of "secular Islamic fundamentalism" and "Communist Islam" in order to encompass anyone and everyone who is in any way a Muslim.[12]

According to Jevtić, in a book devoted to studying the concept of *jihad,* or holy war, this phenomenon is an inseparable part of Islam everywhere and at all times. In Yugoslavia, although at the time he was writing there was no military activity at all, he insisted that a quieter, but no less dangerous, form of *jihad* was being waged. Taking guidance from "international Islamic organizations, which, thanks to great financial resources, are striving to conquer the world," Yugoslavia's Muslims were allegedly using such tactics as a "high birthrate, the building of mosques, and pressure on non-Muslims." He claimed that "on the basis of detailed reports, it is clear that this strategy is much more effective in attaining its goal without creating an uproar."[13]

Behind every action by the Muslims lay an alleged master plan to undermine Serbia. According to Jevtić, Serbia's Muslim minority served as a bridgehead for the "complete Islamization of Serbia." When Belgrade's Muslim community, for example, requested land for a cemetery for its members, Jevtić responded: "From land for the dead, the next step is to conquer land for the living. They will then seek a mosque, fully legitimately, but then, around the mosque, they will seek land on which to settle Muslims. Then, it will not be long before non-Muslims will leave, initially voluntarily but later under pressure. . . . What is planned is to settle Muslims in those areas, and to then step up the birthrate in order to achieve numerical superiority gradually."

28

As his ultimate argument, he pointed to a somewhat hollow object lesson, namely what he saw as the decline in the nightlife of the Pigalle adult entertainment district in Paris after North African Muslims had settled there. Viewed in this light, even the request for a cemetery, he concluded, was an "enormous political issue." Serbia, in fact, is only part of a broader Islamic plan to reconquer lost territories not only in the Balkans but also on the Iberian Peninsula, according to Jevtić.[14] Translating such dire assessments into concrete terms, Jevtić warned without any basis in fact that there were moves afoot to repatriate over a million Muslims who had settled in Turkey when they had been forced to leave the Sandžak in earlier times. "What would happen to Serbia if people who [now] have a Turkish consciousness were to move back here?" he asked, seeking to elicit alarm in his audience.[15]

Another strand of the Orientalists' campaign focused on the idea that Muslims belonged to an alien religion and culture, and as a corollary, they somehow had less legitimacy to live in Bosnia-Herzegovina than did the Serbs, although it is the Muslims who are native there and the Serbs who are the newcomers. Professor Darko Tanasković, an expert on Islamic studies at Belgrade University, concluded that "many [in Serbia] still view [Islam] as foreign, and also as hostile."[16] Jevtić, similarly, stressed an interpretation of the Muslims of Bosnia-Herzegovina as traitors. He claimed: "Those who accepted Islam accepted the conquerors de facto as their brothers and the crimes of the latter as their own. That means that their own hands are also covered with the blood of their own ancestors, the former Bosnian non-Muslim population." By converting to Islam, they had destroyed "Christian Bosnia" and "caused the Ottomans to rule over Christian Bosnia for a long time." Apparently anything that could be used to criticize the Muslims was fair game, even the accusation that they had betrayed "Stjepan Tomašević, the last Catholic Bosnian king," hardly someone for whom a Serbian nationalist would ordinarily show much concern.

Ruing the renewed religious Islamic activity and piety in Bosnia-Herzegovina, Jevtić argued that "not a single normal country would tolerate that a religious community actively publicize and popularize an occupier [the Ottomans] who covered this land in [mourning] black."[17] "It is well known," he continued, "that Serbia, by means of its struggle, liberated our portion of the Balkans from the Caliphate, and it is therefore not surprising that Serbophobia is highly developed among fundamentalist Muslims."[18] Well before the current upheaval, Jevtić was already proposing that Islam was the "most significant threat to Yugoslavia, even more significant than. . . . Serbian-Croatian relations."[19]

The Serbian Orthodox Church—Dispensing Moral Absolution

The Serbian Orthodox Church also played a key role in forming the moral atmosphere surrounding the Muslim issue. Although its influence in society had weakened under Communist rule after 1945, by the late 1980s it was beginning to regain part of its lost position as a moral force which could shape popular attitudes among its followers. Stressing the overlap of national and religious identity, the Church hierarchy cast the subsequent war as a religious experience. The Church viewed this stance not only as an opportunity to promote the spiritual interests of Serbian Orthodoxy but also as a springboard to vault the Church to greater prominence in the political arena and to expand the number of its committed followers, thanks to its leadership on the issue. Even when emphasizing spiritual interests in its preaching, these ideas have often been expressed in temporal terms. For example, territorial expansion was deemed legitimate even at the expense of other communities, such as the Muslims, who stood in the way of control over what the Church claimed were Serbian lands.

Rather than stemming confrontational tendencies among the communities in the former Yugoslavia, the Serbian Orthodox Church contributed significantly to their exacerbation, as putting an issue into religious terms has often raised the conflict to a high emotional pitch. Although remaining largely in the background initially, the Church hierarchy contributed in highlighting the threat from Islam and in delegitimizing Islam's very presence as valid. Reflecting a commonly held view, then-Serbian Orthodox Abbot Atanasije—later a bishop and leading activist in politics—helped set Islam apart as something alien. He categorized the walls built around Albanian houses as a sign that Muslims were not liberated, adding that the "roots of that [practice] go deeply. There are walls around houses from Baghdad to Bihać [in Western Bosnia]. . . . It would be an understatement to call that primitivism."[20] Likewise, in an interview in 1989, the Serbian Orthodox metropolitan of Zagreb-Ljubljana, Jovan Pavlović, had blithely characterized Islam as aggressive.[21]

In this early phase of propaganda, the Orthodox Church media also frequently carried anti-Islamic material, with an emphasis on an alleged threat. One article, written by a priest from Bosnia-Herzegovina, claimed that "for the last few decades we [Serbs] have also become known for being the target of sudden pressure of *jihad* from fundamentalist Islam."[22] Writing in the Orthodox Church's official organ, *Glas Crkve,* in 1991—while Yugoslavia was still in existence—a Serb academic likewise openly promoted the creation of a Greater Serbia. He proceeded from an assessment that "Serbia and its people find themselves between two powerful religious internationals [Islam and Catholicism]. . . . In a state such as this, the national and ethnic survival of the Serbs is in great danger." He saw as the only salvation a new national strategy whose "essence must be the expression of an exclusively Serbian nationalist ideology. . . . A new and up-to-date *Načertanije* [the nineteenth century political program for an enlarged Serbian state] must set out clearly and unambiguously the borders for the new Serbian state . . . [and] it must defend our people [living] in other states. Serbia, as a state, must of necessity be formed within its ethnic boundaries, and no one has the right to make concessions or to betray national interests." He added, Bosnian Serb political circles were already taking the initiative in establishing a consensus on just such a plan for a new, expanded Serbia.[23]

At times, Church representatives descended to metaphors of disease to address the Muslim community. In late 1991, in lashing out against the alleged Islamic inspiration of articles in a Sarajevo newspaper, a Serbian Orthodox cleric wrote in the official Church organ about the "malignant disease of the authors of these texts and of those at whose orders they write." Labeling the latter "Fascist-fundamentalists," he rhetorically asked the Muslim population in Bosnia-Herzegovina to decide "whether this disease has been contained or whether it has infected the majority of its organism." Moreover, he suggested menacingly that "instead of a condemnation or a tit for tat, the Serbs must help the Muslims to cure or excise that rather naive tumor from their breasts."[24] Such discourse is characteristic of a process of dehumanization related to genocide and is especially significant, for, as Thompson and Quets point out, "One element [in dehumanization] is the denigration of out-groups either as subhuman or by metaphors of disease. There is a consensus that this [type of defamation] provides moral license for general destruction."[25]

In practical terms, the Church also provided an early haven and public forum for nationalists when they were still dissidents, as opponents to the ruling Communist regime. Thus, many of Drašković's most inflammatory articles appeared first in *Glas Crkve,* an official Church journal. The Church subsequently also copublished his collected works, which were promoted in *Glas Crkve* with testimonials in the accompanying ads, proclaiming his books to be "literature which gives birth to the great spiritual movement of renewal and rebirth among the Serbs."

The Church, in its own way, also contributed to making force a morally acceptable means to use in Bosnia-Herzegovina in rejecting peaceful solutions. Shortly before the outbreak of violence there, for example, an article in *Pravoslavlje,* an official Church publication, seemed to encourage the Serbs to view conflict in positive terms and took a clear stand against what it condemned as pacifism and defeatism. Stressing that the Serbs were engaged in a veritable struggle between good and evil, the author of the article argued that "such [Serbian] partisans of peace help the evil forces that are opposed to God (and by the same token to humanity), and they are the champions of treason and defeat. In our present Armageddon, they are on the side of the destructive Gog and Magog (the mythical personifications of enslavement and tyranny). *The basis for such a practice and theory of peace most often is cowardly egoism"* [emphasis in the original]. Summing up his exhortation, he portrayed war as a religious experience for the Serbs, assuring his audience that "self-sacrificing struggle for the purpose of bringing about this [state of] righteousness is a highly creative impulse and a contribution to the fulfillment of God's and mankind's goals against evil and oppression as part of the universal plan of salvation."[26]

Creating the Machinery for Genocide

The Rise of the Red-Brown-Black Symbiosis

Despite increasing intolerance and agitation, the *Memorandum* might have languished had it not been for Milošević. Sensing the decay of Communism as a legitimizing tool for power throughout the Eastern Bloc, Milošević sought instead to harness and develop further the nationalist sentiments which non-government Serbian elites were generating, with the intention of mobilizing support for his own political power. Thanks to Milošević, Serbia's Communists were to forge a marriage of convenience with the non-Communist secular nationalists and with the Serbian Orthodox Church, a Red-Brown-Black symbiosis, which was to provide the initial impetus and structure for Serbian nationalism.

It was Milošević who not only brought the nationalists into the political mainstream but who also provided the machinery in the form of a political organization, media and financial assets, and the military muscle that transformed inchoate sentiments into a concrete state program.[27] Without his contribution, the efforts by Serbian nationalists, for all their vehemence, would probably not have been enough to trigger and sustain the subsequent violence and genocide.

Instead of promoting an atmosphere for coexistence and peaceful solutions, the campaigns in the state-controlled media and the direct political activity which Milošević and his faction within the Party unleashed played a significant part in fueling and agitating Serbian fear and hatred. At the same time, the cult of a strong unquestionable leader and the idealization of violence, which Milošević encouraged as part of his rise to power, must also be viewed as significant contributing factors to the subsequent high level of victims and destruction. Milošević's speeches, as well as the strong-arm methods his enforcers used to intimidate and overpower political rivals, set the moral tone early for intercommunal relations and made violence appear to be an acceptable and natural means of political interaction.[28]

Milošević and his hard-line faction were able to gain power within the Serbian League of Communists over more moderate rivals by December, 1987, in large part by developing and playing the nationalist card. His most effective method was to intimidate rivals using his control of the media and violent street rallies, which were sustained initially by the Serbian nationalist backlash in Kosovo, where Serbian influence had eroded during the preceding decade. Significantly, convincing documentation shows that the entire process, from the original appearance of Serbian protests in Kosovo through the subsequent series of political machinations, was orchestrated and managed by Milošević and his faction.[29] Once secure in Serbia, he proceeded throughout 1988 and 1989 to finance and organize more street violence to consolidate Serbia's hold over the autonomous provinces of Vojvodina and Kosovo—as well as his own personal power base. His supporters succeeded in overthrowing the moderate Communist leadership in Vojvodina and the pliant Albanian leadership in Kosovo, and, for all intents and purposes, when Serbia ratified a new constitution in July, 1990, the two provinces' traditional autonomy was completely quashed. In Montenegro mob pressure was also successful in bringing hard-line pro-Milošević nationalists to power.

Milošević's consolidation of power accelerated the momentum of the nationalist campaign by throwing the full force of the state behind the *Memorandum*'s agenda. Serbia's state-run media proceeded to unleash an unprecedented barrage of attacks against other communities and, as part of the government's new tilt, provided an open forum for the intellectuals to conduct a sustained campaign in favor of the nationalist program. As part of his effort to solidify popular opinion on his behalf, Milošević encouraged the Serbs to focus their wrath, in particular, against those ethnic groups who stood in the way of fulfilling the *Memorandum*'s goals. The official campaign emphasized such themes as the World War II killing of Serbs and the need for protection from an alleged renewed present-day danger of their becoming victims of genocide.

In relation to the Muslims, by the late 1980s, the nationalist and the state-controlled media was full of sensationalized features highlighting massacres of Serbs by Muslim Ustaše during World War II and emphasizing suggestions that the same threat had reemerged. The Muslims, duly designated as one of the principal threats, increasingly became an object of political activity by the Serbs. Throughout 1988 and 1989, Serbian nationalist rallies organized by Milošević focused on the Muslims as a target. These rallies included slogans such as "Oh Muslims, you black crows, Tito is no longer around to protect you!" "We love you Slobodan [Milošević] because you hate the Muslims!" and "I'll be first, who'll be second, to drink some Turkish [Muslim] blood?"[30] Perhaps most unsettling were the demands that "we want arms," voiced at such staged rallies.[31]

Moreover, in an emotionally charged speech at Gazimestan on June 28, 1989, on the six hundredth anniversary of the Battle of Kosovo, Milošević had signaled his government's intention to extend the nationalist agenda beyond Serbia's borders. When coupled with active measures being undertaken in neighboring republics, his emphasis that the "Serbs have always liberated themselves and, when they had the chance, also helped others to liberate themselves" seemed to commit Serbia to a forcible redrawing of Yugoslavia's long-established internal borders in pursuit of "liberating" the Serbs outside of Serbia, as the *Memorandum* had preached. Without the subsequent provocation, encouragement, and direct massive financial, political, and eventually military support from Serbia, however, it is unlikely that Bosnia-Herzegovina's Serbs would have moved toward secession, much less engaged in genocide against their neighbors.

Serbian Nationalists: The Transition from Word to Action

At the same time, Milošević promoted the reemergence of various Chetnik political organizations, which had been banned since 1945. Most of them quickly set up their own militias, armed and financed by the Belgrade authorities, and soon constituted the mainstream of the nationalist movement. To be sure, the Muslims were not the only target of the Serbian neo-nationalist movement as it gathered momentum. Attacks against the Muslims, moreover, varied in intensity over time, as the Serbian media and the political apparatus alternated the focus of effort on each of Yugoslavia's communities in turn, as dictated by the immediate political need. At any one time, the targets were the Albanians, the Slovenes, the Muslims, the Croatians, or the Macedonians, and the process suggested a degree of coordination beyond coincidence.

Within this framework of phased escalation against all of the non-Serb communities, Serbian intellectuals intensified their anti-Islamic outlook as they shifted from academic work into political action, with Milošević's blessing. The noted author Dobrica Ćosić—also widely reputed as the father of the *Memorandum,* and later president of Yugoslavia—continued to insist, for example, that the Serbs in Bosnia-Herzegovina were threatened by the Muslims, while the Belgrade media did its best through a concerted campaign to convince the Serbian community in Bosnia-Herzegovina that this was actually so. In Bosnia-Herzegovina nationalist rallies, staged with the help of demonstrators bussed in from Serbia and organized with the support of the Serbian government, had become common by the late 1980s. Ominously, in order to mobilize support for such goals, nationalists from Serbia undertook a tour through Bosnia-Herzegovina with the reputed remains of Prince Lazar (the Serbian ruler killed at the Battle of Kosovo in 1389). This display was accompanied by a proclamation warning enemies of the "bloodied and long-suffering Serbs" that "we will do our utmost to crush their race and descendants so completely that history will not even remember them."[32]

Drašković, for his part, drafted the manifesto for the Serbian Popular Renewal (Srpska Narodna Obnova—SNO), one of the most strident of the new nationalist organizations. Denying that the Muslims were anything but forcibly converted Serbs whose Muslim identity had been artificially invented by Tito, and railing against the threat of "militant Islamic fundamentalism," the manifesto called for a Greater Serbia, which would include Bosnia-Herzegovina.[33] Mirko Jović, leader of the SNO and of its White Eagles militia, moreover, underlined that "we are not only interested in Serbia, but in a Christian, Orthodox Serbia, with no mosques or unbelievers."[34] Drašković, taking an additional practical step, openly promoted a map showing revised borders and extensive Muslim-inhabited areas to be incorporated under Serbian control.

Here, too, the Serbian Orthodox Church played a role beyond merely providing its blessing to the nationalist agenda. In practical terms, for example, warlord Željko Ražnatović (Arkan), whose gunmen were later accused of some of the worst war crimes in Bosnia-Herzegovina, received initial help "above all," as he acknowledged subsequently, from the Serbian Orthodox Church in organizing, financing, and arming his militia.[35]

By the late 1980s, incidents against Serbia's Muslim minority had begun to multiply as the hostility took an increasingly concrete form. For Belgrade's Muslim community, these activities ranged from spray painting of its mosque with Serbian nationalist symbols to the mosque's attempted firebombing in December, 1988.[36] The Serbian press criticized the building of what it saw as too many new mosques and warned that those built without a hard-to-get permit were technically illegal (or "wild," as the media called them), and liable to be demolished. In the Sandžak in 1989, the authorities ordered the demolition of the minaret of a recently constructed mosque. Although the demolition had to be postponed, as even the convicts charged with the task refused to do it, the incident led to the dismissal of the tolerant local officials, who had not up to then strictly enforced the existing prohibitions against the building of mosques in the area. This action heightened Muslim fears in general.[37]

In Bosnia-Herzegovina itself, the 1983 trial of Alija Izetbegović and other Muslim intellectuals in Sarajevo on the charge of "fundamentalism," although legally and morally indefensible, reflected the Communist government's desire to crack down to prevent the development of any elements in society beyond its control, rather than indicating a nationalist-motivated initiative per se. At the time, Serbian nationalists were still, by and large, dissidents at odds with the ruling Communist Party and enjoyed influence with only a limited audience. As part of the Communist regime's desire for balance, several Serb nationalists were also arrested at the time of the Izetbegović trial and charged with being Chetniks.

However, by the time a criminal case was brought against the Muslim directors of the Agrokomerc agribusiness complex in the Bihać area in 1987 and 1988, Serbian nationalists had injected themselves into the political mainstream in collaboration with the rising Milošević. The new relationship was reflected in the direction that the politically driven Agrokomerc affair took. The charge against the defendants of financial malfeasance was combined with those of "counterrevolutionary endangerment to the social order" and of "fundamentalism." The case was accompanied by the widespread participation of Serbian nationalists in a sweeping anti-Islam propaganda assault, which fed a perception that the Muslim community was being targeted as a whole with a broader political agenda in mind.

To be sure, the growing intolerance before the outbreak of war also was aimed against other non-Serbs, in addition to the Muslims. Indicative of the deteriorating general atmosphere was a telling incident in October, 1990, on Belgrade's trendy pedestrian mall, a well-known venue for local artists and musicians. When Gypsy musicians tried to perform there, toughs in Chetnik uniforms drove them away, with the justification that there is "no place for Gypsy music here" and that the mall was located on a "Serbian Chetnik street."[38]

Nevertheless, the anti-Muslim antipathy carried with it a particular intensity, given the assumed obstacle they represented to the Serbian polity. Serbian politicians threatened the Muslim community overtly if the latter decided to stand in the way of the Serbian agenda. In a landmark October, 1991 session of the Bosnia-Herzegovina Parliament, basic issues about the republic's future were discussed. On that occasion, the Bosnian Serbs' Montenegrin-born leader, Radovan Karadžić, warned that the Muslim community would "disappear from the face of the Earth" if the latter were to "opt for war." That is, these dire consequences were inevitable if they decided for independence of a united Bosnia-Herzegovina rather than agreeing to Bosnian Serb proposals for annexation to the rump Yugoslavia or to partition along lines proposed by Karadžić. Questioned on this statement a short time later, he amplified that the "Muslims are the most threatened. They are the most threatened not only in the physical sense, and I did not think that they might disappear only physically; rather, this is also the beginning of the end of their existence as a nation."[39]

4. The Responsibility Dilemma

Did the Muslims Have an Option?

Western observers have often placed a large part of the responsibility on the Muslims themselves for the concatenation of events in Bosnia-Herzegovina that led to their genocide. In essence, this attitude tacitly placed a portion of the blame on the victim.

Where Did the Responsibility Lie?

According to this view, the proximate cause of what befell the Muslims was the latter's pursuit of Bosnia-Herzegovina's independence after a positive vote in the February 29, 1992 referendum.[1] After this, the Serbs, allegedly not wishing to stop being part of Yugoslavia or to become a minority in another state, took up arms, with the help of their fellow-Serbs from the neighboring rump Yugoslavia. Implicitly, based on this premise, had the Muslims acted with greater self-restraint and remained within the rump Yugoslavia (already shorn of Slovenia and Croatia, and eventually also of Macedonia), they would not have become victims of ethnic cleansing. A related strand of conventional wisdom is the foreign-recognition-as-precipitant theory. According to this view, without the "premature" recognition of Bosnia-Herzegovina's independence by the European Community (the EC, later renamed the European Union, or EU) and the United States in April, 1992, somehow there would have been no fighting and no ethnic cleansing.

What was especially significant was that even such influential participants in the subsequent mediating process as Lord David Owen, representative of the EU, apparently operated from that basis. As he noted in an interview well into the process: "The problem was the setting up of a dominant Muslim government, since that would cause a civil war. Everyone warned against that. The cause of this war was the disregarding of the wishes of the large minorities, the Serbs and the Croatians. Many expected this war but, despite that, the world insisted on recognizing Bosnia-Herzegovina."[2] Proponents of these views included other influential players, such as Lord Carrington, the EU's initial special mediator, who, in an interview in August, 1992, disclosed that he had adamantly opposed recognition based on that rationale. Even some otherwise sophisticated observers of international affairs continued to hold to this view despite subsequent events. For example, political commentator Stephen S. Rosenfeld claimed long after the fact that the "unilateral declaration of independence . . . by Bosnia" was the "triggering event . . . without which this whole tragedy might have been averted." While not exculpating the Serbs for their subsequent actions, he nevertheless concluded that "the original sin was committed not by Serbs but against Serbs."[3] This position became a mainstay of the Serb case as well, with the head of the Serbian Orthodox Church, Patriarch Pavle, still claiming in 1994 that the West was guilty for what happened in Bosnia-Herzegovina. According to him, everything would have gone smoothly, since the three sides "had agreed to divide Bosnia into three states, but then the West had recognized a unitary state."[4]

Foreclosing Other Options

REJECTING COMPROMISE. The process of the Muslims' victimization was set in motion well before Bosnia-Herzegovina had declared its independence and can be traced back to at least the anti-Islamic campaign in Serbia in the 1980s. The anti-Islamic rhetoric genuinely reflected a plan of action. Karadžić himself had delineated his goal openly as the establishment of a Greater Serbia—a goal that was incompatible with the status quo—before Bosnia-Herzegovina had held its referendum for independence. In an interview published in January, 1992, for example, after being questioned on what the Serbian strategy was, Karadžić asserted: "There is no longer any retreat. We will fight." When asked "How far?", he replied "[We will fight] until we achieve Karadjordje's objective of uniting all the Serbs and until we complete his struggle."[5] As he also admitted in an unguarded moment in

Table 2

Rump Yugoslavia's Ethnic Profile (in thousands, 1991 Census)

	Serbs	Non-Serbs
Rump Yugoslavia (Serbia and Montenegro)	6356 (61.5%)	3982 (38.5%)
Bosnia-Herzegovina	1363 (31.3%)	2991 (69.7%)
Greater Serbia (Serbia, Montenegro, and Bosnia-Herzegovina)	7719 (52.5%)	6973 (47.5%)

SOURCES: "Stanovništvo: Koliko nas ima?" ("Population: How Many of Us Are There?"), *Vojska*, Apr. 29, 1993, pp. 24–25; and Leksikografski Zavod Miroslav Krleža, *Republic of Croatia and Republic of Bosnia and Herzegovina Ethnic Map* (Zagreb, [1992]). The envisioned addition of the territories subsequently occupied in Croatia would have eroded the proportion of Serbs in a Greater Serbia even further. The Serbs only numbered about 51 percent of the population in what came to be known as the Krajina, and even less if Serbian forces had been able to seize other areas in Croatia, which they claimed. If Macedonia were also annexed, as most Serbian nationalists would prefer, the percentage of Serbs in a Greater Serbia would be even smaller, as Serbs comprise only 2.1 percent of Macedonia's 2 million inhabitants. Furthermore, the non-Serbian minorities in Serbia are probably underestimated, with the Gypsies especially grossly undercounted. Typically, for one section of Belgrade, where 355 Gypsies were officially registered in 1981, estimates of actual numbers ranged between 10 and 15,000 (see Milan Milošević, "Živeti kao sav ostali svet," ("To Live Like the Rest of the World"), *NIN*, Jan. 16, 1983, p. 14.

January, 1992: "There is no return to a united Bosnia-Herzegovina. The time has come for the Serbian people to organize itself as a totality, without regard to the administrative [existing] borders."[6] Dobrica Ćosić, shortly before becoming president of rump Yugoslavia, likewise, openly disclosed that "peace in Bosnia-Herzegovina cannot be preserved by recognizing that republic's Communist [existing] borders," or the "internal administrative borders," as he also called them.[7]

Given the Serbs' goal of creating a Greater Serbia, an ambition shared by the entire spectrum of the Serbian establishment, the Muslim problem would have had to have been dealt with in a decisive manner sooner rather than later. The annexation of Bosnia-Herzegovina with its nearly two million Muslims would have meant a specter of a Greater Serbia in which the Serbs would become a minority within a few years—taking into account the Muslims and Albanians of Serbia and Montenegro, as well as other minorities such as the Hungarians, Croatians, and Gypsies (table 2).

Indicative of Serbian plans was the outline sketched out in December, 1991, by Drašković, who had become the flamboyant leader of the more liberal wing of the Chetnik movement. In his vision of what a Greater Serbia within a revamped Yugoslavia would be like, he equated the status that the more numerous Serbs should have to that of a commercial firm in the West, where "if someone has 51 percent of the capital, he is the owner."[8] Given such a perspective, even within Serbian opposition circles, non-Serb communities, and especially the Muslims, inevitably would have faced a bleak and dangerous future in a rump Yugoslavia no matter how they reacted. For a state emphasizing national cohesiveness, there could be little room in such a polity for non-Serbs, and the Muslims would likely as not have been pushed out even if Bosnia-Herzegovina had not decided in favor of independence and had acquiesced instead to absorption into a Greater Serbia.

Even areas which have remained within Yugoslavia have not been spared ethnic cleansing, although up to now the pace has been far less dramatic than in Bosnia-Herzegovina. In Vojvodina, for example, where there was, and is, no conceivable threat to the Serbs, the Hungarian, Croatian, Ukrainian, and Slovak minorities have been under intense pressure to leave. They have been the targets of discrimination and verbal and physical attacks. This treatment has also been the lot of the Muslims in the Sandžak and the Albanians and Croatians in Kosovo.

With the anti-Muslim atmosphere already being created in the preparatory phase, the likelihood was high that pressure on the Muslims would have taken an extreme form no matter what the latter did. Earlier instances of violence against the Muslims in Serbian history were revalidated and portrayed to the public as acceptable and even as praiseworthy and necessary. This attitude even found its way into scholarly literature. An academic work published in 1989 on the anniversary of the Battle of Kosovo applauded and justified the policy of massacre by which Danilo Njegoš, the eighteenth century ruler and Orthodox bishop of Montenegro, had eliminated the Muslims from Montenegro. With the parallels to the present situation all too apparent, the book's author judged:

Turks [local Muslims] had been the very symbol of all that is evil in this world, Satan's seed. . . . Njegoš's sense of justice and righteousness, however, was highly developed . . . [as] only that of an Orthodox ruler could be. Thus, he could liquidate without mercy the Turks, as the embodiment of evil and injustice. Those heads [of the Muslims] reminded him and his subjects daily that one can and one must struggle against evil, and that that is the greatest Christian and human duty. To struggle

41

against evil was Njegoš's duty toward God. He sought revenge, revenge without mercy. . . . For Njegoš, revenge was a holy, divine, act! Yes, he was in favor of peace and love among people, but only among people; that did not apply to beasts with human faces.[9]

Such sentiments were shared by political figures as well. Characteristically, throughout the ensuing war, Karadžić carried with him and often referred to the works of his favorite author, Njegoš, who had extolled the violent eradication of all traces of the Muslim presence.

Perhaps of greatest significance, Milošević's stance offered little hope for a peaceful outcome. Speaking in the Serbian Parliament in April, 1991, his tough talk instead openly suggested the need for territorial expansion by force, and left few realistic alternatives to non-Serbs. In his speech he stressed that "we must guarantee that we are united within Serbia if we, as the largest and most populous republic, want to dictate the flow of events. The question of borders is a vital issue for a state. As you know, it is always the powerful who dictate what the borders will be, never the weak. Thus, we must be powerful."

Adding that he had ordered a mobilization of Serbia's paramilitary police reserves, he hinted at future actions in support of the allegedly threatened Serbs outside Serbia and revealed that "I have been in touch with our people from Knin [Croatia] and from Bosnia. The pressure [on them] is great." Asked what Serbia's strategy would be, he continued: "Will we announce on the radio all that we are going to do? I do not think we can do so. If we must fight, we will really fight. I hope that there will not be many people who will be willing to fight against us. For if we do not know how to work and how to do well economically, we will at least know how to fight well [applause]."[10]

In March, 1992, Vojislav Šešelj, leader of what was to become the largest opposition party in Serbia, called openly in Parliament for the summary expulsion of minorities from Serbia, with no dissenting voices among the parliamentarians.[11]

The state-run Serbian media also hinted strongly that Belgrade was preparing a political case for its subsequent use of force against its neighbor while Bosnia-Herzegovina was still part of Yugoslavia. Unsubstantiated charges were given wide play, such as those stated in *Politika ekspres* that the Bosnian government intended to set up "an Islamic fortress in the middle of Europe" with the help—however improbable—of a "Catholic and German clique." Their intention was to "wipe out the Serbs." *Narodna armija,* the military weekly, claimed that the Muslims intended to create an Islamic state extending over Bosnia-Herzegovina, southern Serbia [Kosovo], Macedonia, Greece, Bulgaria, and Albania.[12]

Nationalists also helped to prepare a case for action by portraying the Serbs as willing to perform a service to Europe in striking out against the Muslims. One nationalist spokesman asserted that Europe should be grateful, since an Islamic state in Bosnia-Herzegovina would serve as a springboard for mass Muslim migration into Europe. Its objective would be to establish a Muslim majority in the latter, then to Islamize and destroy it. "It is . . . clear," he offered, "that the Serbian people in Bosnia-Herzegovina, by defending its freedom from the Islamic threat, are also defending Europe and the Europeans."[13]

MATCHING WORDS WITH DEEDS. The situation in Bosnia-Herzegovina itself was already being shaped in a way that reflected Serbian intentions toward the Muslims. By the fall of 1990, local Serbs had begun to set up autonomous areas beyond the control of the Bosnian republic's government, as Bosnia-Herzegovina approached its first democratic elections in December of that year. And, it was the Serbian community, not the Bosnian government, which first took concrete steps toward independence. In November, 1991, the Bosnian Serbs' main political party, the SDS, organized a plebiscite on this question, open only to Bosnia-Herzegovina's Serbs. Distributing two million ballots, even though the Serbs numbered only 1.5 million, the ensuing vote was predictably overwhelmingly in favor of independence for the Serb autonomous areas. These areas were formally proclaimed the "Serbian Republic of Bosnia-Herzegovina" on January 9, 1992, well before the Bosnian government had voted in Parliament on January 25, 1992, to hold its own referendum on the issue the following month.

Bosnian Serb leaders were making it clear how they saw the Muslims' future. Truck driver-turned-SDS activist Božidar Vučurević, who eventually became governor of Serbian-controlled Herzegovina, threatened in late 1991: "I would inform the Serbian people that we will correct the injustice with regard to the borders which Josip Broz [Tito] drew with his dirty finger. He gave Serbian lands cheaply to the Croatians and Muslims. The Muslims are only an insignificant minority, and must submit to the Serbian majority. We will not desist, but will pursue them, if necessary, all the way to Zagreb itself."[14]

At the January 25, 1992 session of Parliament, Karadžić had also depicted the Serbs in Bosnia-Herzegovina as enslaved and had claimed that "in Sarajevo all the skyscrapers are built on Serbian land," while other Serbian representatives had added that even the Bosnian Parliament was constructed on a Serbian cemetery. Other Serb representatives chimed in during that session that it "is pure Serbian masochism to keep Broz's [Tito's] borders," that is, the existing borders of Bosnia-Herzegovina. Such sentiments left little doubt that the Serbs were in no mood to compromise and that they were bent on changing the status quo no matter what.[15] It did not help that even Muslim-inhabited areas in Bosnia-Herzegovina had earlier welcomed Serbian and Croatian refugees fleeing from the war zones in neighboring Croatia.[16]

Moreover, the Muslims had already become direct targets of physical attacks by the Serbs by the second half of 1991, well before Bosnia-Herzegovina had made a decision, much less taken any concrete steps, to declare its independence. In one of the earliest such incidents, uniformed police of one of the self-proclaimed Serb autonomous areas killed a Muslim youth in the village of Šipovo, then surrounded and fired into the town's Muslim quarter. This incident reportedly triggered a flood of some three thousand Muslim refugees from the countryside to the relative safety of the city of Jajce.[17] According to a Polish mercenary who served with the Serbian forces, his unit was also pulling Muslims from buses and shooting them near Sarajevo even before the outbreak of fighting.[18]

Reservists in the Yugoslav People's Army deployed from Montenegro went on a shooting and looting spree against Muslims and Croatians in the town of Trebinje in October, 1991. Army units pulled out of Croatia, significantly, were redeployed and massed in Bosnia-Herzegovina, where they took positions to attack and seize territory with greater ease. Arkan's Serbian militia, for their part, were already swaggering menacingly in Bosnia-Herzegovina, singing songs such as "Oh Mostar, my brother, you have always been Serbian," even though Serbs comprised only 19 percent of that city's population.[19] Some members of the Serbian militias, which were also already positioning themselves in the Romanija area around Sarajevo, shared with one reporter their plans to strangle the city: "If . . . we cut off Sarajevo's water and electric power, what will happen to Sarajevo then?"[20]

In all probability, nothing the Muslims could have done—save perhaps arming themselves—would have made a difference to their fate. Ultimately, even those Muslims who, for whatever reason, sought to collaborate with the Belgrade regime were not wanted just because they were Muslim. Thus, by early 1993, despite their loyalty, even those Muslims who had stayed on in the police force in rump Yugoslavia were summarily dismissed because of their origin.[21]

If anything, not recognizing Bosnia-Herzegovina would only have made the situation worse. Had the international community ignored Bosnia-Herzegovina, it would have been that much harder to do anything, however limited, to help the Muslims. In the absence of recognition, Belgrade could have argued that this was a domestic problem and would have felt even less restraint in using whatever means it wanted. It also would been easier in legal terms to deny access to outsiders, including human rights observers and humanitarian relief workers, across an international border. Very likely, Belgrade would even have felt justified in leaving the Yugoslav People's Army in place in Bosnia-Herzegovina, rather than having to resort to a subterfuge with a partial withdrawal.

Lessons Learned from the War against Croatia

In many ways, what had just happened in neighboring Croatia could have been viewed as a dress rehearsal to genocide in Bosnia-Herzegovina. This development may have been crucial for the lessons it provided, particularly about the probable reaction by the international community. There, lightly armed Serbian militias, backed by heavy regular forces of the Serbian-dominated Yugoslav People's Army, alleging a threat to the Serbian minority, effectively occupied as much territory as possible before Croatia's hastily organized armed forces were able to halt them.[22] In the end, the Serbs in the occupied territories—comprising less than 5 percent of Croatia's population—were left in control of well over a quarter of Croatia's area. To achieve ethnic cleansing in an area where half the people were non-Serbs, the Serbs had expelled thousands of Croatians, as well as others (Hungarians, Slovaks, Ukrainians, and Gypsies), while killing many outright.

Serbia's actions, including the leveling of the city of Vukovar in eastern Croatia, however, had led to no appreciable penalties against Belgrade, apart from haphazardly enforced economic sanctions. What is more, it was soon clear that the Serbs could flout with impunity the January, 1992 Vance Plan that had ended the war, including its central provisions that the UN would guarantee Croatia's original international borders, protect all civilians, and ensure the return of refugees to their homes. On the contrary, ethnic cleansing against non-Serbs continued and was made easier by the buffer which the UN peacekeepers unwittingly provided to Serbian militias operating in the occupied territories.

The pattern for Serbia's success and the lack of any effective international reaction could not have gone unnoticed in Belgrade. As Borisav Jović, president of Serbia's ruling Socialist Party, boasted to a convention of Young Socialists, "the war [against Croatia] was conducted far from Serbia's borders," while the Serbian leadership still managed to "liberate" the Serbian population in what "many Serbs until recently did not even know were Serbian territories."[23] In particular, the imposition of a blanket arms embargo, which crippled Croatia's efforts to acquire arms abroad but affected the well-supplied Yugoslav People's Army little, must have been reassuring to Belgrade. This embargo indicated that any future target would likely also have a difficult time obtaining arms with which to defend itself. As an observer wrote in the Yugoslav Army journal, Belgrade subsequently was surprised by the extent of the world's reaction—such as it was—to Serbian policy in Bosnia-Herzegovina. Belgrade based this feeling no doubt on its expectations from the lessons provided by the very weak response earlier to Serbian actions against Croatia.[24]

5. The Implementation Phase

Fortunes of War or Recognizable Pattern?

Overall, ethnic cleansing seems to have followed a premeditated strategy, rather than being an improvisation arising from unfolding events. What has occurred forms a pattern which suggests adherence to general top-down policy guidance and a degree of coordination across the republic and, apparently, with unofficial and government circles in Belgrade.

How Much Control and by Whom?

To expect to uncover a public document detailing how this process was to occur, of course, may be unrealistic. Šešelj noted, even of plans for national expansion: "Plans of that type are not written down for the general public. He who holds power or who has the capability of implementing a plan writes it down [only] for the benefit of his own guidance and that of the necessary circle of people around him who participate in implementing the national plan."[1] There are indications, however, that there was an overarching strategic design to the policy. While on a visit to Serbia, Branimir Savović, mayor of the Bosnian city of Višegrad, hinted at prior coordination with the authorities in Serbia. Criticizing what he saw as Belgrade's recent pressure to halt further advances, he noted with some irritation that the "truth is, we have not carried to its conclusion the struggle that we had planned together. It was not we [Bosnian Serbs] who came up with the slogan 'All Serbs in a single state.'"[2] Before hostilities began, the large-scale evacuation of Serb non-combatants from broad stretches of ethnically mixed areas, which the Serb leadership apparently expected to become battlegrounds, also suggests extensive preplanning and coordination. The common propaganda campaign which the Bosnian Serbs and Belgrade put into motion in tandem throughout much of the war suggests the same type of advance planning. A typical case consisted of measures taken in the town of Zvornik before the Serbs' coordinated assault on April 8, 1992, of the Muslim inhabitants. A young Serbian girl remembered that "two days before those events, nothing was suspected. However, our father sent word to us from Serbia that I must take shelter. . . . I went to the Serb-only village of Ćelopek, near Zvornik, to stay with my sister."[3] Further, the rounding up and expulsion of Muslims from Serbia itself and from Montenegro, along with the Muslims from Bosnia-Herzegovina, is compelling evidence that the authorities in Belgrade and Podgorica at least passively condoned, and more likely promoted, the overall policy of ethnic cleansing. In another case, a Muslim from Foča who was detained in a camp in Bosnia-Herzegovina, met Muslims from Montenegro and Serbia who had been arrested there and expelled.[4]

Indeed, as the UN Secretary General's Commission of Experts found for Prijedor, one of the communities on which they focused their investigations, local Serbs had begun to arm and make plans to take control more than six months before the outbreak of hostilities. It was this preparation that enabled them to seize power in the town in just thirty minutes when the signal was given. The Yugoslav People's Army provided arms to the local Serbs and was in command of the Prijedor area when the initial takeover and subsequent war crimes took place. What is more, the Army itself took a direct part in the atrocities, with its military policemen reportedly serving as guards and interrogators in some of the concentration camps which the Serbs set up.[5]

It is unlikely that Milošević or Karadžić could or need have known about or controlled the details of all operations. Although in some instances direct guidance on what to do was not available, in many cases, "commander's intent" was more likely used, whereby the leadership could set certain policy goals and assume that subordinates would have the latitude to use virtually any means to achieve them. Subsequent claims by the Serbian and the Bosnian Serbian leadership, that they had no control, seem to have been intended primarily to provide convenient plausible denial to the outside world without hampering their policy. Frequently, for example, concessions made at the top on some aspect of policy, such as access to concentration camps, would be nullified by noncompliance at a lower level, seemingly on the latter's own initiative and in contradiction to their superiors.

Numerous individual acts may have been undertaken without the direct approval, or even knowledge, of a central authority, given the fluid situation. During cleansing operations, individual gunmen often had life-or-death power over their targets and could base a decision on whim. In one case, a Chetnik unit attached to the Bosnian Serb Army encountered a Muslim cleric while searching an apartment building in Sarajevo for non-Serbs. The Chetniks intended to kill him since "he was one of their [Muslims'] ideologues, and it was immaterial that he had not done any shooting." However, the Chetnik in charge changed his mind when the cleric's small crying son begged him to spare his father's life.[6]

Nevertheless, Bosnia's and Belgrade's Serbian political and military authorities did not make efforts to delegitimize such local gunmen or to suppress them, until and unless the leadership viewed these groups as a political threat. That the elimination of such irregulars was not possible seems untenable, in retrospect. Even as the party with the least cohesive administrative and coercive machinery, the Bosnians made concerted and successful efforts to shut down rogue elements that had become involved in atrocities and crime.

In the great scheme of things, however, such small Serbian bands helped carry out the overall policy of ethnic cleansing in any case and were viewed with considerable tolerance. What is more, the impact of such freelancers has been small in comparison to the role which the regular Bosnian Serb Army and the mainline Serbian militias have played, since it is these larger forces that have been at the forefront of both large-scale operations and of the political maneuvering that accompanied and supported the process of ethnic cleansing.

Although the procedures may have reflected decentralized execution in many cases, the Belgrade leadership must still bear ultimate responsibility. The conduct of the militias should have come as no surprise to Belgrade, given their proven track record of involvement in war crimes in the just-concluded war in Croatia. Compelling evidence indicates that Milošević armed, financed, and exercised operational control over some of the most ruthless of the Serbia-based militias operating in Bosnia. Disavowing any connection was evidently intended to provide the Belgrade government with a means for ethnic cleansing while preserving some plausible denial.

Notwithstanding its disclaimers, however, Belgrade retained considerable control over the mainline militias, and Milošević could and did act to rein in some militias—such as Jović's White Eagles, Drašković's Serbian Guard, and, later, Šešelj's units—but only when he judged that they had become threats to his regime's own political position.

Milošević's continuing support of the Bosnian Serb government, which included the occasional forays into Bosnia-Herzegovina by the Yugoslav Army (an initially autonomous military organization over which Milošević eventually established direct control) to help out during difficult operations, also contributed to the overall effort. The legitimization and even incitement by Serbia's non-governmental institutions of the process of ethnic cleansing was also a significant factor.

Milošević's own leverage with the Bosnian Serb authorities eroded as the latter built up their own local power base and as their strategies began to diverge. The split started with a disagreement in April, 1993, over whether to accept the Vance-Owen Plan. It was rekindled in 1994 when the Bosnian Serbs proved reluctant to yield land in return for a ceasefire. However, the Bosnian Serbs remained to the end heavily dependent on Belgrade for financing, fuel, and food, as well as for military and diplomatic support. Belgrade controlled all the lines of communication and media links to the outside world. In particular, rounding up draft-age Bosnian Serbs who had fled to Serbia and Montenegro was stepped up noticeably in early 1994, when the Bosnian Serb Army ran into serious manpower problems as Bosnian resistance stiffened. Milošević's support for this effort was key for the Bosnian Serbs' military capability. Overall, without Belgrade's help, however grudging it may have become over time, the Bosnian Serbs would have found it much more costly, and eventually impossible, to continue their policies. Had Milošević seen it in his political interest to do so, he could have exerted significant pressure on the Bosnian Serbs to either have prevented the genocide originally or to have helped stop the fighting at a much earlier stage.

Compelling evidence in Bosnia-Herzegovina, moreover, indicates that the process was organized from the top, with the Bosnian Serbian authorities playing the decisive role in dealing with the Muslim population, as the systematic and thorough way in which the Serbs have gone about carrying out ethnic cleansing suggests. It was the chief of Banja Luka's war crisis committee, for example, who determined the policy that he announced on local television that one thousand Muslims would be allowed to remain in the city (out of over 28,000). All the others would have to go, "one way or another," he decided.[7] In Bijeljina, officials of the Serbian Republic of Bosnia reportedly set the appropriate quota of Muslims who could continue to live in the town—5 percent of the pre-war number.[8]

Similarly, in the town of Kozarac, houses were color-coded according to the owner's ethnicity and then "destroyed systematically." One diplomat concluded from this incident: "It wasn't just some guys running amok. . . . It means responsibility lies with the Serb higher-ups."[9] According to another source, negotiating with armed Serbian elements in the city of Foča was difficult when the latter took over in April, 1992, because the Serbs were continually on the telephone to receive instructions from leaders of the ruling SDS party.[10] In fact, as Roy Gutman reported, members of Karadžić's own inner circle planned and conducted the ethnic cleansing of the city of Foča.[11] Often, eyewitnesses were excluded in a coordinated manner, as when UN ambulances and foreign journalists, significantly, were prevented from crossing from Serbia into Bosnia-Herzegovina by Bosnian Serb border controls, citing orders from the Bosnian Serb Army's commander.[12] An indicator of the significant degree of command and control from the top in attacks against civilians was the micromanagement of General Ratko Mladić, the Bosnian Serb Army commander. In an intercepted telephone conversation, conducted while besieging the town of Zeleni Jadar, near Srebrenica, in 1993, Mladić provided detailed guidance to a subordinate at the scene on how to shell the town. He ordered: "You have my permission [to shell], but do not touch the industrial infrastructure because we need the machinery. Shoot only at human flesh. Shell only human flesh, only human flesh."[13] The fact that, according to a UN report, the Serb-run concentration camps were administered as a part of a network also indicates a significant degree of coordination beyond the purely local level.[14]

In a revealing procedure, Peter van Hugh, head of the UN High Commissioner for the Refugees mission in Banja Luka, reported that Serbian authorities in that city would routinely promise to look into cases of anti-Muslim violence, but such promises never yielded results. In fact, when UN observers would provide names of alleged perpetrators to the police, "those same individuals, the terrorists, then would openly threaten us." Such behavior suggests a substantial degree of collusion between the attackers and the local government.[15]

Testimony—used with caution because of his dependent status as a prisoner—comes from an accused Serb participant in some of the atrocities.

His reports suggest that military and militia personnel were either following orders when carrying out atrocities or at the very least had implied leeway to do so. As he noted, "I could not refuse because the order was that everyone had to do it. And if I refused to carry out the order they would kill me."[16]

Some foreign observers as well as Bosnian Serb officials often argued that Serbian command and control was quite weak. However, the organized withdrawal by the Bosnian Serb regular forces from their positions surrounding Sarajevo, based on their chain of command's orders in August, 1993, and again in February, 1994, suggests that control was considerably more robust than portrayed. Asked why the withdrawal was taking place, one Serb soldier answered, "We have our orders."[17] Strong control was equally evident in 1993 in the abrupt reversal in alliances between the Bosnian Serbs and Croatians. When the Bosnian Croatians turned on their erstwhile Muslim allies and began large-scale overt cooperation with the Serbs, it marked a complete policy turnaround, mandated from above. The Serbian and Croatian communities, which until recently had hurled bitter mutual accusations of being engaged in genocide against each other, virtually overnight not only stopped fighting over a broad area but also actually conducted combined military operations against the Muslims. These actions even included cases of combatants from the two communities deploying together in the same vehicles to the front.[18]

Going well beyond what might be viewed as battlefield expediency, the Serbs reportedly welcomed Croatian civilians and combatants fleeing retaliation by the Muslims, and even treated them cordially, providing good care to their wounded personnel.[19] Croatian children started to give the Serbian three-fingered salute, and Atanasije, the Serbian Orthodox bishop of Herzegovina known for his shrill stance and previously implacable animosity toward the Croatians, now even visited Croatian troops at the front and played soccer with them.[20] Karadžić, too, subsequently expressed uncharacteristic concern for the Croatians with his anxiety to "not allow Islamic domination over the Serbian and Croatian—that is, Christian—majority in Bosnia-Herzegovina."[21]

Such a sudden and complete turnaround indicates, first, that a greater degree of command and control was present than has been often assumed. That is, to order and coordinate such a broad-based reversal of policy, significant command and control and powers of persuasion by the leadership have had to be in place, especially because of emotions probably generated over the preceding months of conflict between the Serbs and

Croatians on the front lines. Second, the abrupt change also suggests that hard-headed interests, which could be furthered by fueling the Croatian-Muslim dispute, were uppermost for the Serbian leadership. The policy revision, apparently, was a reflection of discernible political factors, as interpreted by the leadership, and articulated in a manner to persuade their followers to go along. Still another conclusion is that communal alliances and conflicts have been considerably less inflexible than some observers have posited. Such a reversal in alliances would have been very difficult to explain if one subscribed to the view of the determinism of centuries-old enmities between Serbs and Croatians.

In a parallel move, Serbian support was also forthcoming for the September, 1993 initiative by Muslim leader Fikret Abdić to declare autonomy for the Bihać pocket in northwestern Bosnia-Herzegovina. This ploy made good sense as a way to undermine the Bosnian government. The Belgrade media, which earlier had attacked Abdić as being a fundamentalist and an extremist now portrayed him as a "liberal Muslim politician . . . [who] endeavors for peace to be established with Bosnian Serbs and Croats." At the same time, there were reports of Abdić's receiving military aid from the Serbs to help him to resist pressure from the Bosnian Army.[22] By late 1993, the Bosnian Serb leadership was even pressing the Bosnian Croats on behalf of the Muslims to give the latter access to the sea. No doubt they saw this plan as a way to strengthen Serbian demands for similar access from Croatia and as a way to physically cut up Croatian territory. Again, this position highlighted the inherent importance of political interests in the Serbian leadership's anti-Islamic campaign and its flexibility in adapting to tangible interests.

Patterns of Ethnic Cleansing

Ethnic cleansing has followed a general pattern, with some local and situational variations. Typically, the pattern has consisted of, first, establishing military control over an area, whether from the inside—if the Serbs were already present there in sufficient strength—or by storm or siege from the outside if they were not. According to one Muslim eyewitness from Foča, the pattern at least in his area was phased, with the first priority being to control the cities. This strategy was followed by the imposition of Serbian domination in the countryside.[23] In some areas, as in Trebinje, where the

Serbs were hard-pressed in the confrontation with Croatian forces, Bosnian Serb authorities at first avoided antagonizing local Muslims, and even sought to use them as fillers in the Bosnian Serb ranks.[24] It was only later that anti-Muslim steps were implemented in that city, after the initial need for the Muslims' services had passed. Whenever possible, Serbian officials would try to limit access by international observers, such as relief workers, to areas where ethnic cleansing was suspected of taking place. In one incident, the local Serbian military commander even forced the chief of operations of the UN High Commissioner for Refugees to leave at gunpoint, calling him a "secret Muslim".[25]

Providing the Military Muscle

Serbia-based roving militias—such as the White Eagles and the militia sponsored by Serbia's ruling Socialist Party, as well as forces organized by such Serbian politicians as Šešelj, Arkan and Drašković—were often the key implementers of ethnic cleansing. Reportedly, these groups have also been responsible for some of the worst large-scale killings and atrocities.[26] Milošević supported Arkan's militia, among other groups, and channeled this support through Serbia's Ministry of Defense.[27] The Belgrade government's closest direct cooperation was with Šešelj's militia, at least until the second half of 1993, when competition for political power between Milošević and Šešelj soured the relationship. Up to then, as Šešelj acknowledged after his break with Milošević, Serbia's police and Army had provided Šešelj's Chetniks with arms and training and had mounted joint operations with them in Bosnia-Herzegovina.[28]

More heavily armed conventional forces, however, also played an important role. They often targeted the civilian population directly with their heavier firepower. The Yugoslav Army itself often mounted joint operations with the militias, before its official withdrawal from Bosnia-Herzegovina, although part of the Yugoslav Army was transformed into the Bosnian Serb Army in late May, 1992, and stayed behind. As justification for its operations, Belgrade's pro-government press had suggested, somewhat lamely, that it was the Muslims who had threatened the Yugoslav Army in Bosnia-Herzegovina, rather than the other way around. One official of the SPO, however, recounted how in the city of Zvornik, located in the Drina River border area near Serbia, it was the Yugoslav Army (along with Serbian militias) which mounted an attack, killing between 4,500 and 7,000 Muslims. The victims were "thrown in canyons and buried with bulldozers, the mosques were demolished, and the surviving Muslim population was robbed and then expelled."[29] Even after its announced withdrawal, the Yugoslav Army remained involved in Bosnia-Herzegovina, either through its logistic support or the presence of its personnel serving there. Continued direct cross-border military operations, such as the large-scale attack in January, 1993, against the Muslim enclave of Srebrenica in eastern Bosnia, helped underline their involvement.[30] Again, in April, 1994, the attack against Goražde, another UN-designated safe zone, was also spearheaded by a mechanized infantry brigade, three batteries of artillery, and a battalion of military police deployed from the Užice Corps of the regular Yugoslav Army.[31]

More importantly perhaps, heavy forces took control of most areas, preventing the more lightly armed Bosnian government forces from operating against the militias and local warlords as they normally would have. Heavy Serbian forces thereby created a safe environment in which the more lightly armed Serbian militias and local Serbian activists were able to engage in ethnic cleansing. Often, Serbian militia units were attached directly to regular Army units for this specific purpose. For example, one Chetnik unit had been under the operational command of a battalion of the Bosnian Serb Army since 1992. The militia unit's commander understood his mission thus: "We take care of relations with the Muslims. We only have one Muslim family left which does not want to leave. . . . Of course, we permitted those Muslims who lived in my area of responsibility and who expressed a desire to cross over to Alija [Izetbegović] to do so."[32]

This symbiotic relationship calls to mind the operational procedure the Nazis used in occupied areas of Eastern Europe during World War II. There, light special police, the *Einsatzgruppen*, one of whose principal missions was to target "racially and politically undesirable elements," coordinated closely with the regular army. In a studied division of labor, the *Einsatzgruppen*, along with locally raised and often unruly light auxiliary forces, normally went into action once the more heavily armed *Wehrmacht* combat forces had secured an area, thereby enabling the lighter forces to operate with relative impunity.[33]

Making Life Untenable

ENGINEERING SYSTEMATIC MISERY. The Serbs, one can argue plausibly, identified the Muslims' strategic center of gravity as their population base.

Targeting Muslim civilians—by killing, mistreating, or deporting them—would undermine Muslim resistance, to include hindering the development of an insurgency once the human pool had been removed. It would also advance the central policy goal, that of creating an ethnically pure Serbian state. The Serbs, moreover, probably felt that with the country's dwindling population base, the Muslims were hard pressed to make a convincing case for either a unified Bosnia-Herzegovina or the return of occupied territory. Ultimately, this weakened position would rob them of the requisite base for a viable Bosnian state.

Although the Serbs often appeared to choose targets not having, strictly speaking, any military significance, the targets did make sense in rewriting the demographic balance sheet. Often, such actions caused casualties and damage out of all proportion to any military advantage to be gained. Attacks on cities were marked by drawn-out sieges and used not only conventional means but also starvation and disease among the inhabitants. These weapons could be just as effective as more conventional arms in achieving the intended objective.

Once in charge, the Serbs invariably proceeded to pressure Muslims to leave the area by harassing and terrorizing them. The tempo has differed from one place to another. In some areas, the expulsion was immediate and violent. For example, as soon as the town of Kozarac fell, Serbian vehicles with loudspeakers, accompanied by tanks, roamed the streets, blaring: "Muslims get out! Muslims get out! Surrender and everyone will be safe!" Despite these assurances, according to reports, between 2,500 to 3,000 Muslims were killed.[34] In other cases, the Serbs have offered safe passage out if the Muslims agreed to leave.[35] Coercing Muslims into signing documents relinquishing property to the local authorities before leaving their homes was intended to provide a legal cover for their dispossession and to preempt any later attempt at redress.[36]

However, as time passed, the focus increasingly moved to an indirect approach to ethnic cleansing. The greatest concentration of overt violence seems to have occurred during the early phase of the war. The Serbs probably envisioned a quick campaign initially, hoping to shock the Muslim community into mass flight or surrender by massive use of force. However, if that was the plan, the Serbs miscalculated. They were probably surprised, as were many outside observers, by the Muslims' resilience and their subsequent dogged refusal to give up.

In addition to the Bosnian government's improving but limited capability to resist, the international community's strong disapproval may also have surprised the Serbs and obstructed their strategy. As the widespread publicity of mass killing, rapes, and concentration camps reached the West and put pressure on the international community to take concrete steps to stop it, the Serbs seem to have felt it prudent to shift their focus of effort to measures less likely to generate headlines and to outrage foreign audiences. Simply expelling Muslims from their homes or starving them out by a siege, in the long run, would serve the Serbs' strategic objectives just as well as more violent means and also be less emotive.

Especially in areas where Serbian control has been exercised early from within, Muslims have been pressured to leave less directly and less abruptly, with a less blatant—but no less effective—use of coercion. Restrictive security measures automatically set Muslims, and other non-Serbs, apart and made a normal life virtually impossible. In a village in the Banja Luka area, for example, decrees imposed not only a curfew on non-Serbs but forbade them from meeting in cafes and other public places, traveling by car, gathering in groups of more than three, or contacting relatives outside the town.[37] Muslims were deprived of a livelihood. Their utilities were cut off, their houses often burned down, and individuals beaten, killed, or raped, either selectively or indiscriminately.[38]

As part of this process, officials seem to have established a well-oiled bureaucratic machine to encourage and manage the exodus of non-Serbs. In the city of Banja Luka, for example, Muslims lost their jobs, were harassed and attacked by thugs—including by members of the military police—and then were evicted from their homes, leaving them little choice but to run away. Government posters in Muslim neighborhoods encouraged emigration. "Avoid the hardships of winter. Leave the area now," they proclaimed. The local government even made money by charging "exit taxes" and other fees to those forced out.[39]

By all reports, the strategy of making life untenable in Banja Luka has been effective. According to the official charged with expediting the emigration of non-Serbs from the city and euphemistically called the "Director for Refugees," Muslims were "begging" to leave. He said: "Here what awaits them is a winter without heat, food and, for many, no place to live. The only salvation for these people is if some other country takes care of them now." This same official had turned the departure procedure into a routine, complete with offers of plum brandy and toasts to good health, as the Muslims filled out the necessary forms and paid the obligatory fees before they could leave. By the end of 1993, of the 350,000 Muslims living in the Banja Luka region before the war, only 40,000 remained.[40] If all other methods failed, the Serbian authorities also used deception, such as the promise of non-existent residence permits in Western Europe, to speed up the exodus of the dwindling number of Muslims who remained.[41]

The restriction on food and fuel supplies, in particular, became a key tool to pressure the civilian population, with the reduction of food supplies to near-starvation levels. Although the sieges of Sarajevo and Srebrenica received the most media attention, the pattern was repeated frequently elsewhere, with Serb officials refusing or yielding only reluctantly under international pressure to allow humanitarian aid to pass to besieged cities and regions. The blocking of convoys carrying food or medical supplies destined for the civilian population or the skimming off of a significant percentage of the cargo was a common tactic, intended to degrade the Muslims' living conditions to a level where they would have to leave an area or die. In Prijedor the Serbian-controlled local Red Cross reportedly distributed incoming relief only to Serbs, while a sign at the local mill read: "There is no flour for Muslims!"[42]

Not only local leaders, but Belgrade as well, participated in the strangulation. At border roadblocks within Serbia the police would typically halt trucks carrying aid with the excuse, "We have orders from Belgrade," even though Milošević had made a show of approving such relief convoys.[43] Likewise, although the UN sanctions committee had agreed that 90 percent of gas supplies from Hungary could go to Belgrade if 10 percent went to Sarajevo, as winter neared in 1993, Belgrade stopped the flow to the beleaguered city.[44] While Belgrade could argue plausible denial, UN officials also viewed the latter's introduction of complicated customs regulations in November, 1993, as yet another attempt to obstruct relief convoys.

In some case, only air delivery and air drops were possible to bypass the Serb sieges. However, such expedients too were often uncertain. Up to early 1994, for example, the Bosnian Serb authorities successfully denied access to the airport in Tuzla to the UN for humanitarian relief flights. Karadžić, somewhat lamely, argued that "if this airport is opened, there will be no end to this war, because the Muslims will use the chance to sneak enormous amounts of weapons into the area." In essence, he alleged that the UN would help smuggle in arms to the beleaguered Bosnian government defenders, and that even Serb inspectors checking incoming aircraft "would be blackmailed . . . [and] weapons would get in."[45]

DESTROYING A COMMUNITY'S WILL AND IDENTITY. Destroying the cohesion of the local communities has been central in uprooting the Muslim population and in seeking to break the latter's will to resist. In particular, the elimination of community leaders has been an essential element in the process designed to shatter the Muslims' will. Typically, in the Kozarac area of northwest Bosnia-Herzegovina, prominent local Muslims were identified, separated, arrested, and earmarked for elimination according to prepared lists. A local eyewitness reported, "They were pulling out private entrepreneurs and educated people, anyone who could ever organize any Muslim life in Kozarac again."[46] Religious leaders appeared to be a particular target in the quest to demoralize the Muslim population. Thus, in Bratunac, the local Muslim cleric reportedly was tortured in front of the townfolk, who had been rounded up in the soccer stadium, was ordered to make the sign of the cross, had beer forced down his throat, and then was executed.[47]

Terror against civilians, both random and organized, was a favorite tactic designed to spread panic in order to weaken resistance. Atrocities took place not only in the notorious concentration camps but throughout the country.[48] More often than not, even refugees fleeing an area were the target of gratuitous attacks as they were shelled, sniped at, or stopped and mistreated.[49]

In addition, the use of humiliation was extensive, with a probable goal of highlighting to the Muslims how weak they were and thereby encouraging a mass exodus from occupied areas. In one town, a Muslim described how the Serbs had "destroyed the mosques, then made us clean up the wreckage," while others reportedly were forced to crawl to the local post office to obtain the necessary exit documents.[50] Routinely, Muslims held in concentration camps also told of being forced by their captors to sing Chetnik songs or to make the sign of the cross.[51] Suggestions to Muslims that they convert to Serbian Orthodoxy could be viewed as yet another means to eliminate the Muslim presence, whether by assimilation or as an additional form of extreme pressure to leave.[52] Karadžić himself, in a domestic radio broadcast, openly urged abandonment of Islam as the best solution for the Bosnian Muslims. He claimed cynically that "many Muslims who are well-educated and sensible are being baptized and are becoming Christians in Europe as a way of reacting against fundamentalism and the introduction of militant Islam into Bosnia. . . . it is clear that we must cross the Rubicon [of conversion] since we are dealing with exceptional people in whom the memory of their Serbian origin is alive."[53] The widely reported instances of rape, in particular, would be seen as an especially humiliating gesture in the local culture. Although women who were rape victims had priority in the long lines waiting for documents, an employee at the Bosnian consulate in Zagreb pointed out, "It is rare for any of them to tell you they have been raped, unless she is in desperate straits."[54] The incident, reported by the UN as occurring as late as mid-1994, of the forced use of Muslim women to dig trenches for the Bosnian Serb Army, to cook for the Serbs, and to sweep streets no doubt was a further humiliation intended to induce the remaining Muslims to leave.[55]

The destruction of local mosques by the Serbs has been a particularly direct signal by Muslims that they had better leave.[56] Although Serbian authorities often claimed to foreign observers that "uncontrolled elements" were to blame, in many cases the official cachet was evident. In Banja Luka, the largest city under Bosnian Serb control, the blowing up of two sixteenth century mosques in May, 1993, despite denials, appears to have been a well-planned official job. According to one press report: "Residents of the predominantly Serb district near the mosques were summoned to meetings by ruling party officials on Thursday and ordered to stay indoors after 6 P.M. 'in case of unpleasant events.' Party members were told not to be alarmed if they heard explosions during the night. . . . uniformed security forces blocked off the neighborhood, and two trucks arrived with more than 3,000 pounds of explosives that were detonated at the mosques by remote control."[57]

The elimination of the Muslims has included an attempt to erase any memory of their linkage to the land, not least as a means to help ensure that ethnic cleansing was irreversible. From the account of a Polish mercenary who served with the Bosnian Serb forces, it is clear that this strategy of elimination was a premeditated policy. In the Sarajevo area, for example, he stated: "We began to destroy everything which had any tie to Islam, so that the Muslims would not leave any trace behind them. Mosques were blown up."[58] Mosques, not surprisingly, have been systematically demolished, and, in the town of Prijedor, the land upon which they had stood was leveled and planted over with grass to wipe out all evidence of their existence.[59]

The Bosnian Serb authorities also deleted all Muslim place-names in areas they seized. Justification for these actions, such as changing the name of the city of Foča—which had had a Muslim majority before it was cleansed—was often cast unabashedly in ethnic terms, with perhaps a scholarly veneer. As a member of the Bosnian Serb Parliament, who was at the same time the president of a leading Serbian cultural organization, argued:

"Although the existing name is pretty old, and etymologically contains our roots, in its adapted pronunciation it has acquired the form of a Turkish name, and that with an overtone which was bound to irritate us Serbs, since it continuously reminded us of the centuries of slavery under the foreign Islamic oppressors." Instead, he proposed the new name "Srbinje," based on the root "Serb," since that "contains at its root the word which distinguishes our national name and essence. In this war, the fighters from Foča and from the [surrounding] region were worthy defenders of Serbianness and of Orthodoxy. Therefore, they have merited that their regional capital and the entire region carry a name with an emphatically national hallmark. The name Srbinje is constructed completely in the spirit of the Serbian language. It stands out for its poetry, phonetic ease, and charm."[60] To underline the finality of the process, Serbia's state-run media, significantly, always referred to Sarajevo from the beginning of the crisis as the "former capital of the former Bosnia-Herzegovina."

6. Motivating the Perpetrator

The Serbian Establishment's Calculations

As the sheer magnitude and horror of events became apparent, central questions arose: What would motivate a Serb to take part in or even condone genocide? Why would a Serb act in a way that was out of character with conduct up to that time? For the Serbian political, social, and intellectual leaders in Belgrade and Bosnia-Herzegovina, the motivation to engage in genocide, understandably, was self-generated. In a sense, they themselves were the motivating force for precipitating, implementing, and justifying this process, as the leadership pursued a concrete political agenda outlined in the *Serbian Memorandum.*

It is improbable that the Serbian political elite really believed, or cared, whether the Muslims were "fundamentalist." Few of Bosnia-Herzegovina's Muslims, in any case, seem to have been motivated by political Islam or by movements from other countries. Neither have Muslim clerics played a significant role in politics. On the contrary, it is probable that whatever the level of the Muslims' religiosity or consciousness, Muslims would still have been targeted simply because they stood in the way of Serbian national interests. The propaganda campaign against fundamentalism did provide a convenient basis to the Serbian political elite for a threat portrayal and emotive symbology. Both of these tactics could be used as mobilizing tools and as a hoped-for cover to convince domestic and international audiences of the righteousness of Serbian policy. Serb leaders continued to use the theme of a fundamentalist threat with domestic audiences long after they had abandoned it in dealing with Western representatives. Apparently, their foreign interlocutors did not find such arguments credible.

Although enveloped in the language and symbols of nationalist, and sometimes religious, ideology, political interest was clearly the driving force behind this policy. As Momčilo Krajišnik, speaker of the Bosnian Serb Parliament, later acknowledged, the Serbian objective was fairly straightforward: "Today we have inherited the historical role of fulfilling the incomplete task of preceding generations, that is to grasp [*zaokružiti*] our ethnic space."[1] Given the goal of territorial expansion at the heart of this policy, areas would inevitably be encountered in which Serbs were a minority. This situation would be true, even if the Serbs were willing to settle for partition rather than for the annexation of all of Bosnia-Herzegovina, if this latter goal proved infeasible.

For the Serbian leadership, ethnic cleansing was a rational policy, insofar as such an abhorrent policy can be considered in those terms, with the Serbian decision makers apparently weighing the benefits and costs carefully throughout the process. Within the strategic framework of ensuring an ethnically cohesive national state, having an effective and seemingly irreversible method was a priority in establishing Serbian control over territory, while removing the non-Serbian population. The use of atrocities may have seemed little more than a sensible tactic to support this strategy. That is, the early use of the shock of massive attacks on civilians would have contributed to this population removal, as well as to a quick campaign, which the Serbian leadership no doubt desired. Atrocities may have had the additional benefit of sparking ethnic strife and reprisals so as to leave even reluctant fellow-Serbs little choice but to close ranks behind the nationalist leadership. Using such methods would have so poisoned intercommunal relations as to preclude any accommodation or coexistence in the near-term, thus transforming the leadership's desired strategy of partition into the only remaining political option by default. Subsequently, Karadžić used precisely such circular reasoning to argue against a reunified state, terming it "astonishing" that the "international community should want people who hate each other to the point of extermination to live together again."[2]

Top-Down Guidance and Justification

Apparently, most—but far from all—the Serbs in Bosnia-Herzegovina either joined in or at least acquiesced passively to ethnic cleansing. Although in some instances outside Serbian agitators and gunmen controlled events, in others the locals took the lead and often operated the concentration camps.[3] In virtually all cases, at least some local Serbs provided information and identified Muslims even when they did not lead the campaign. But what would induce ordinary Serbs to turn on those who until recently they had treated as good neighbors? Key factors seem to have been the sanction of authority and the acceptance by society of such extreme actions as legitimate.

Government Legitimation

The attitude of Serbian leaders in Serbia, Montenegro, and Bosnia-Herzegovina undoubtedly played a central role in channeling the behavior of ordinary Serbs against the Muslims. As the legal authority, government figures in particular could command the trust and obedience of their fellow Serbs, while ordinary Serbs in turn could claim to be following official policy.

Even if not explicitly spelled out in any official policy document, the environment created in the preparatory phase and its subsequent reinforcement in the policy's implementation stage could leave little doubt about the leadership's intent from the first. In any conflict, the attitude of the military leadership is crucial in promoting or preventing atrocities. War is a cruel affair, and individual soldiers, even in the British and American armed forces during World War II, for example, although acting contrary to orders, were not immune from such behavior.[4] Most armed forces will contain some atrocity-prone elements, and whether they are discouraged or encouraged in that direction is a responsibility of those in command. In the case of Bosnia-Herzegovina, top military officers, such as Bosnian Serb Army commander Gen. Ratko Mladić and his staff, were outspoken in their denial of any wrongdoing and the justification of all actions by troops under their command. The significance of such attitudes is clear. As one scholar of genocide stresses, "When acts of violence are explicitly ordered, implicitly encouraged, tacitly approved, or at least permitted by legitimate authorities, people's readiness to commit or condone them is considerably enhanced."[5]

Typically, indoctrination in the Serbian militia training camp in Erdut, which was run by Arkan with the support of Serbia's police, emphasized an indiscriminate attitude in preparation for deployment into Bosnia-Herzegovina. According to a Russian mercenary who went through the training program, "The philosophy of brutality drummed into the heads of the fighters—'a Serbian patriot is merciless toward the enemy; he does not have the right to spare the latter's children, women, or the aged'—startled our [Russian] 'gunmen.'"6 In this atmosphere, it is not surprising that when Serbian forces moved against the border town of Višegrad in April, 1992, militia personnel coming from Serbia "made no attempt to minimize what will happen to those Muslims who choose not to flee the town." According to one report, "[A gunman announced,] 'The women and children will be left alone. . . .' As for the Muslim men, he ran his finger across his throat."7

It was not only the militias who had internalized such an agenda, however. The Yugoslav People's Army too saw as its mission a no-holds-barred assault against all that was Muslim. When Army units staging from Montenegro marched off to Bosnia-Herzegovina in early 1992, before the latter's declaration of independence, they sang a popular new song: "Sarajevo and your mosques, the boys from Romanija [a Serbian area near Sarajevo] will destroy all of that." As these same soldiers told an accompanying reporter: "Are you familiar with Genghis Khan, the Mongol who before the common era controlled all of Europe and Asia, and who killed off an entire city of 300,000 people? . . . That's the way we should deal with them [the non-Serbs] too."8

The message from the top did not waver over time. As Karadžić continued to exhort, the fight was against "Asiatic darkness" and reiterated that the "Serb state has no need to incorporate its enemies into its own state. The Serb state should be the home of the Serb nation."9 Living in the same state with the Muslims, in fact, would supposedly mean that even Serb women would have to wear the veil, according to some Serb officials.10 Karadžić could make the average Serb feel that he was struggling not only for his own nation but for the good of the West as a whole. He reassured his domestic audience that "we defended Europe from Islam six hundred years ago. . . . We are defending Europe again from Germany [sic] and from Islamic fundamentalism."11 Even when seeking to benefit from plausible denial, official sources found it expedient to suggest the ultimate justice of acts of ethnic cleansing. Thus, when seventeen Muslims and two Croatians were killed, allegedly by unknown groups or individuals, in the Serbian-controlled town of Prijedor in April, 1994, the government-controlled Belgrade media implied that "there was more than enough motive," namely the death of six Bosnian Serb policemen "who were defending the Serbian border with the [Muslim-controlled] Bihać pocket."12

The Bosnian Serb authorities often used scare tactics, which claimed that Serb forces had to take control because the Muslims were allegedly planning "to circumcise all Serb boys and kill all males over the age of three, and send the women between the ages of fifteen and twenty-five into a harem to produce janissaries [elite Ottoman soldiers]."[13] The official Bosnian Serb media continued to propagate its anti-Islamic message intensively, even resorting to the distortion of texts from the Qur'an as proof that Islam mandated that non-Muslims be killed.[14] Leadership-by-example is an especially strong medium, and the case of a member of the Bosnian Serbian cabinet who reportedly played soccer with members of the Bosnian Serb parliament using a dead Muslim's head as a ball would probably have even more impact in setting the tone than any number of speeches or press articles.[15]

Non-Government Sources of Legitimation

Non-governmental Serbian sources of legitimation in society have also buttressed government policy on ethnic cleansing. Rather than condemning what was happening to the Muslims, non-governmental institutions generally went along with or, in some cases, even were ahead of the government.

Such centers of influence stressed that the Muslims were bent on setting up a Muslim state in Bosnia-Herzegovina, posing a danger both to the Serbs and to Western civilization as a whole. Sometimes, the accusation was that the Muslims wanted to set up an "Islamic *jamahiriyya*," although the latter is a political term invented by Qadhafi for his idiosyncratic political system and is not an Islamic concept at all.[16] In fact, the media and prominent public figures described the situation routinely as nothing short of a "struggle between the Christian and Islamic worlds" and as a "fight for survival." Even self-styled Serbian liberals have taxed Izetbegović as having only a "democratic facade" which concealed a "totalitarian worldview."[17]

THE SERBIAN ORTHODOX CHURCH. The Serbian Orthodox Church, both in Serbia and in Bosnia-Herzegovina, continued to provide its legitimacy to the Bosnian Serb authorities' ethnic policies. It backed the most uncompromising options formulated in Bosnia, which had as their goal to create a Greater Serbia, and did not envisage the continued presence of the Muslims. In April, 1993, Patriarch Pavle and Metropolitan Amfilohije from Montenegro openly came out in support of the Bosnian Serb leadership's rejection of the

Vance-Owen Plan, with Amfilohije also effusively praising one of the most hard-line Bosnian Serb leaders, Vice President Biljana Plavšić.[18] At the same time, the Serbian Orthodox Church's governing Holy Synod revalidated the goal of merging Serbian areas seized in Bosnia with Serbia and reportedly witnessed an oath by Serb leaders from Herzegovina committing themselves not to compromise by accepting the Vance-Owen Plan.[19]

Likewise, in April, 1993, an official high-level delegation from the Serbian Orthodox Church to the Vatican endeavored to assure its hosts that "there is no aggression" in Bosnia-Herzegovina.[20] In late 1993, Patriarch Pavle, in an interview in the Austrian press, addressed a foreign audience, assumed to be familiar with Balkan history only in general terms. Pavle confidently claimed that the Serbs were native to Bosnia-Herzegovina, whereas the Muslims allegedly had only arrived with the Ottoman invasion. Characteristically, Patriarch Pavle had also accused the Muslims of seeking to force Christians into a position "without rights," a position, he alleged, which is outlined in the Qur'an and the Shariah. He further claimed that the Qur'an "preaches holy war as a means to spread the faith. This concept is alien to Christianity."[21] Vasilije, bishop of Zvornik-Tuzla, seemed to sum up the Serbian Orthodox Church's view of the Muslims when he reflected that "we Serbs know very well that for a segment of the Muslims . . . the more 'unbelievers' they kill, the closer they come to heaven."[22]

To be sure, not everyone in the Church structure saw what was going on in Bosnia-Herzegovina as a religious war. When the dean of the Serbian Orthodox Theological Faculty in Belgrade, for example, was asked whether the war was a religious one, he backed the goals of Serbian policy in general terms. Seeking to deemphasize the religious aspect of the fighting, however, he stated: "It is not in any way a religious war. What is the religious issue which is the main motive? There is none. Rather, this is an ethnic and civil war with some elements of religion. . . . Perhaps that sounds paradoxical to you, but that is how it is. How can it be a religious war without religious issues? . . . This is just a case of the religious component pressed into service for either ethnic or secular [interests]."[23]

However, such doubts were overwhelmed by the activist clerics who steered Church policy. Notwithstanding general condemnations of violence by Patriarch Pavle, the Serbian Orthodox Church continued to lend its mantle of respectability to even the most extreme nationalist elements. Arkan provided bodyguards for the Serbian Orthodox metropolitan Amfilohije of Montenegro, who has reportedly used them to intimidate dissidents. In July, 1993, on the occasion of the city of Belgrade's holy day, Arkan marched prominently beside Patriarch Pavle in solemn procession through the city streets. In that same month, Patriarch Pavle himself led an official delegation to Bosnia, where he presided over widely publicized religious ceremonies with the participation of the top Bosnian Serb government and military leaders.

Patriarch Pavle continued to view the Muslims as an enduring threat to the Serbs, which, therefore, justified Serbian policy. He shared these comments to a foreign journalist: "'Daughter,' he says to me shrugging, open-handed, 'if you ask me whether I think the Serbs in Bosnia must now give up *all* that they have worked for all their lives, then what shall I tell you? Do you think that killing is wrong? Of *course!* But do I think an honest man should surrender to thieves? . . . If that is the choice, then I must tell you that, yes—then I will be a politician too, for I believe Serbs must fight, now as never before, to save not only the church but themselves'" [emphasis in the original].[24]

The Serbian Orthodox Church has not only failed to condemn Serbian war crimes, but it has provided chaplains to the Bosnian Serb Army and offered encouragement for operations against the Muslims. Thus, Bosnian Serb recruits recite their induction oaths before Orthodox chaplains, while Orthodox clergymen have blessed Serbian forces, such as the elite Panthers commando unit, which has been accused of committing numerous atrocities, before they set off on operations.[25] During a visit to a Bosnian Serb mechanized infantry unit, Nikola, Serbian Orthodox metropolitan of Bosnia, encouraged personnel there by telling them that "we have always won the wars. . . . God will not abandon us this time either." He bolstered their morale by assuring them that the fight is "in the interest of the Serbian people."[26] On occasion, Serbian Orthodox clergymen themselves reportedly took the lead in cleansing operations. A priest in Trebinje rallied local Serbs by insisting that "this city will be Serbian, since it always was," then himself took over an apartment and several small businesses whose Muslim owners had been forced to leave.[27]

This religious cachet no doubt salved the conscience of and provided guidance to those Serbs who were pious, preventing any dissonance between personal piety and the performance of atrocities. This rationalization may help explain attitudes such as those displayed by a Bosnian Serb policewoman who maintained self-assuredly that "we can live with the Muslims only when we disarm them to the very last one. Victory is surely ours.

God is with the Serbs." This attitude also allows Bosnian Serb fighters to invoke divine help in their actions, or armored vehicles to carry slogans such as "God protect the Serbs."[28] Addressing domestic audiences, Karadžić, understandably, has sought to secure religious sanction for his policy, attributing Serbian success to the fact that "God has helped us. He has turned toward us, just as we have turned toward Him, after many years of errors."[29]

Given its desire to portray the situation in Bosnia-Herzegovina as an assault against Christianity, the Serbian Orthodox Church was uncomfortable that the Catholics were not also hostile to the Muslims and hoped to incite them too against the Muslims. The editor of *Pravoslavlje* railed that the "stand of the Croatians in Bosnia-Herzegovina, by the way, is amazing. Although they are Christians, they have not joined the Serb Christians in defending shared Christian principles. Rather, they have sought to join the unjoinable, the cross—which is the most hated symbol for the Muslims— and the crescent. . . . it is absurd for some Christians to cooperate with the Muslims against the Christians."[30]

THE ORIENTALISTS. As they had done before the breakup of Yugoslavia, Serbian Orientalists lent their expertise in attacking Muslims on an intellectual plane and to defend government policy. Now, however, unlike during the preparatory phase, their arguments appeared against the background of the harsh measures that were actually being inflicted against the Muslims. Beyond simply having an abstract academic flavor, these discourses provided added scholarly explanation and vindication for war crimes. Historian Mile Nedeljković devoted a book to arguing that Bosnia-Herzegovina had always been Serbian and Orthodox, dismissing the Muslims as converted Serbs. Based on this thesis, the book justified the cleansing of Muslims from Serbia in the nineteenth century, portraying this action as getting rid of traitors. The author argued, "As is true of every social group tied to an occupier [the Ottomans], over time, the [Muslim] inhabitants who had based their position and property on the exploitation and plunder of the oppressed population also disappeared."[31] Moreover, for him the process was so successful that it was now forgotten as completely as "snow melted long ago."

Other scholars intensified their warnings on the alleged Islamic peril in conjunction with the propaganda of the Serbian authorities. Darko Tanasković, for example, identified an "economic, diplomatic, and especially a demographic *jihad*" aimed at all of the Balkans and Western Europe.[32] For

Miroljub Jevtić, the threat now allegedly took the form of a "sinister plan" by the Muslims to set up a medieval state.[33] Going further, Jevtić placed Muslims beyond the pale of coexistence, painting Islam as alien to "all mercy and non-violence toward those who have a different way of thinking from the Islamic doctrine in force."[34] In fact, not only did Muslims destroy places of worship belonging to other faiths, but Serb scholars described their actions as "an obligation according to their religion."[35] Jevtić was perhaps at his most uncompromising in his denial of any possibility of coexistence with Muslims simply because of their religion: "It must be clear to all people of good will that there is no peace, and can be no peace, with Islamic fundamentalism. It is a generally known fact that Islam does not recognize the coexistence of Muslims and non-Muslims on an equal plane." In practical terms, his reading of Islam induced him to urge the continuation of violent means to their logical end, for "hope for peace with Alija [Izetbegović] is only an illusion." He added, "All negotiations with him are a waste of time, and only the postponing of the final reckoning, which he is imposing."[36]

Another Serbian academic, Nada Todorov, even purported to see the Muslims in Bosnia-Herzegovina as motivated by their "Islamic way of life, which has nothing in common with European civilization." According to her analysis, carried by the military press, the traditional *Thousand and One Nights* tales, which Muslims are supposed to have read in their childhood, deserves special blame, since these stories have provided "subliminal direction" to the Muslims to torture and kill Christians. As Todorov explains: "Since these stories are full of eroticism, it is certain that they [the Muslims] read them carefully during puberty, so that their effect on the personality of the latter is clearly evident. In committing atrocities in Bosnia-Herzegovina, [their] conscious, sub-conscious, and unconscious levels of personality have been at work."[37]

Dehumanizing by Stereotyping

The negative portrayal, which began in the 1980s, of the Muslims as dangerous and different people was degraded even further once actual violence erupted. Serbian politicians, intellectuals, religious figures, and the media referred to the Muslims almost exclusively as "fanatics," "terrorists," "extremists," and "fundamentalists" and painted them as always "provoking," engaged in aggression, or on the offensive, equating Islam with violence. All of these parties created the impression that violence was inherent to the

Muslims, and the Belgrade media even spoke of the "blood of a subjugator" [*osvajačka krv*] flowing in the Muslims.[38] In fact, the Yugoslav Army journal asked a leading Serbian Orientalist to analyze for its readers the differences between "them and us, the Muslims and the Christians."[39] For the Yugoslav Army press, in fact, the Muslims throughout remained little more than "intoxicated Islamic fundamentalists."[40]

Intellectuals, such as Vojislav Lubarda, a leading Serb literary figure from Montenegro, also perpetuated negative images of the Muslims and justified a harsh policy toward them. He stressed that the Muslims allegedly only understood force. In late 1993, he said: "Let me mention just two personal characteristics that are true of the majority of Muslims: when faced by that which is stronger (such as a stronger man or a stronger force), they become as docile as lambs and submissive beyond words. However, their nature changes as soon as they sense that they are the stronger ones, and that power is in their hands, whereupon they become insatiably ruthless."[41]

The Serbian Orthodox Church also reinforced the perception that the Muslims were defective human beings, specifically Serbs who had betrayed their roots. Claiming that the Muslims were of Serb origin, the Church offered to accept them back only if they abandoned their deviance by changing their current religion. Dragan Protić, an archdeacon and professor at the Serbian Orthodox Church's Belgrade Theological Faculty, clearly believed this conversion was feasible, as the Muslims could be pressured into accepting Orthodoxy. He viewed the Muslims as lapsed Orthodox Serbs and noted with a sense of superiority that the "Serbian Orthodox Church welcomes gladly those who abandoned Orthodoxy, and who repent and return."[42]

Perhaps nowhere was the power of language to categorize and destroy as evident as the choice of the term "cleansing," used freely in unofficial discourse to describe the violent removal of Muslims. Logically, a procedure with such a name—which was a throwback to Chetnik terminology from World War II—could only be viewed as positive and desirable, the implicit antithesis and correction of an assumed impure, unnatural, and demeaning state. When the commander of a Serbian militia unit was able to report that "this region is ethnically clean," for example, he was clearly proud of what he viewed as an achievement.[43]

Also indicative of this approach was Belgrade Television's coverage. Reports such as one from the town of Zvornik that the Muslims had been shelling Serbian homes were often used as justification for subsequent Serbian assaults. However, Western journalists who were in Zvornik at the time of the alleged attack said that no such shelling had occurred and that the Muslims there did not even have any artillery.[44] In contrast, the Serbs were always depicted by the media as liberating an area or referred to by stock phrases, such as being "forced to defend themselves energetically." After his forces had fought their way into the village of Osmarce, General Mladić observed that "it was a large Muslim village in which no Serb had ever set foot until we liberated it."[45]

Even humor, such as the "Mujo and Hasa" and "Mujo and Fata" jokes— so-called because of their use of stereotyped Muslim male and female names—often exploited the Muslims' plight. They reinforced negative images while making light of their victimization. One such joke went: "What is the shortest joke about Mujo and Hasa?" The answer was: "Mujo and Hasa used to exist once." Others revolved around Fata's sale of sexual favors to UNPROFOR (United Nations Protection Force) personnel and her being stripped nude by a sniper's accurate shooting.[46] Such attempts at black humor in the Serb media only reinforced unfavorable images of the Muslims and trivialized the protests of those Serbs who sympathized with the Muslims' plight.

Negative categorizing can have a devastating effect by dehumanizing the target group. It contributes to facilitating their killing as members of an undifferentiated collection of undesirables. As sociologist Kelman notes perceptively: "Sanctioned massacres become possible to the extent that we deprive fellow human beings of identity and community. . . . Thus when a group of people is defined entirely in terms of a category to which they belong, and when this category is excluded from the human family, then the moral restraints against killing them are more readily overcome."[47]

As a result of such campaigns and incidents, it was not surprising that the very possibility of being Muslim, or even of having Muslims in one's family background, eventually came to be considered a blot on one's character among the Serbs, creating a situation that required countervailing proof of one's own "purity." Thus, Dafina Milanović, director of one of the largest private banks in Belgrade, whose first name is not Serbian, felt it necessary to go out of her way to emphatically deny rumors that she was a Muslim. Rumors of her alleged Muslim origins had been circulated ostensibly to discredit her. The rumors, however, may have had political overtones, as the bank was at the center of a scandal which threatened to implicate the Yugoslav government in shady hard currency dealings and financing schemes for the Army. Without a question, she saw such impressions of her origins as especially damaging to her image and credibility. In an interview, she pleaded: "Please write: 'I am not a MUSLIM' [emphasis in the original] as recent rumors have it. My name is of Greek origin. . . . Everyone in my family is a Serb. Anyone who does not believe this should go see my baptism certificate and those of my parents, as well as our family tree."[48]

Self-Image as a Motivator

The Serbs' self-image, as well as their negative perception of the Muslims, provided the all-important context in which government and non-government authorities could exert their influence. The average Serb's acceptance and internalization of this worldview also served as a major facilitator of genocide.

The Serbs' Sense of Superiority

As nationalist elites in Serbia became active in the 1980s, they devoted considerable effort to redefining their fellow-Serbs' self-image and their relationship with other ethnic and religious communities. Their goal was to mobilize for action in pursuit of nationalist ends. In general terms, the result was to draw a Manichaean contrast between the Serbs and others—a lopsided philosophy of dualism in which the Serbs monopolized all such positive virtues as bravery, tolerance, long-suffering patience, superior morality, culture, and even intelligence. Milošević provided major impetus to this trend in his 1989 keynote address at the celebration of the Battle of Kosovo. In this speech, he treated his fellow-Serbs as a special people and reassured them that the "fact that the Serbs are a great people in this region is not a Serbian sin or anything of which to be ashamed. It is, rather, a privilege. . . . the Serbs have never used this privilege even on their own behalf." At the same time, he faulted the "inferiority" of past Serbian leaders for the "humiliation" of Serbia.[49]

Intellectuals and political leaders reinforced this perspective. Prominent nationalist leader Drašković, in a speech in December, 1991, claimed that "within this Yugoslav area, biologically we [the Serbs] are the strongest nation and have the strongest historic roots; we have the breadbasket [Vojvodina], we have the most intelligent people, the best writers, the best theater, and the best soldiers."[50] According to another Serbian opposition political figure, in fact, of all the peoples of Yugoslavia, the "Serbs are the only people who have the talent, energy, experience, and tradition to form a state."[51] For yet another nationalist leader, Šešelj, the Serbs are "a historical people in the true sense of the word, unlike the Slovenes and the Croatians. When I say that, I am following good old Hegel, to the effect that a people is historical if it knows how to build its own state, and how to defend it."[52]

A spate of books and articles, propagating a patriotic view of the superiority of the Serbs, appeared in Serbia during this period. One such book, by Olga Luković–Pejanović, was suggestively entitled *The Serbs: The Oldest Nation*. Such writings claimed, among other things, that the biblical Garden of Eden was located in present-day Serbia, that the Serbs invented writing, that the poet Ovid composed his works originally in Serbian, and that Serbian books had been among those destroyed when the conquering Arabs allegedly burned the library of Alexandria, Egypt, in the seventh century.

The concepts of Serbia as the "new Byzantium" and of the Serbs as a "heavenly people" [*nebeski narod*] were to become increasingly frequent motifs in both popular and intellectual circles in Serbia. Although some individual clerics seem to have become uncomfortable with the implications, the Serbian Orthodox Church has reinforced this self-image of uniqueness, bestowing an almost messianic quality to the nation. Speaking of his fellow-Serbs, Metropolitan Amfilohije of Montenegro preached: "Our destiny is to carry the cross on this blazing divide between [different] worlds. Therefore, it [the Serbian people] is also divine. . . . Our people . . . preserves in its bosom, in its collective memory, Jerusalem's holiness."[53] Serbia's Minister of Culture, focusing on the Serbs' uniqueness, concluded that the "Serbs are one of the five imperial peoples. It is an ancient people and one of the most Christian ones."[54] In fact, according to another minister in the Serbian government, "Today, many around the world dream about being Serbs: the individual on Fifth Avenue eating a hamburger, the Eskimo breaking the ice and fishing, the Frenchman strolling along the Champs Élysées. . . . Be happy that you are Serbs. . . . Be happy that you belong to this people. . . . You are eternal."[55] Likewise, in Bosnia-Herzegovina itself, Velibor Ostojić, president of the Executive Council of the dominant Serbian party, the SDS, announced that "every nook of Serbian land and the Serbs themselves are a heavenly wonder, and an inspiration and example to all other peoples and countries."[56]

Russian extremist Vladimir Zhirinovskiy's triumphant visit to Yugoslavia and the Serbian-controlled portions of Bosnia-Herzegovina and Croatia in February, 1994, only reinforced such self-perceptions. He gave his unqualified support and praise to his hosts by expressing these public comments: "The Russians and Serbs are the best people on this planet. But, we are too good. For a while, we should be tougher in order to show Catholicism from the West and Islam from the East how strong we are. . . . Brother Serbs and Montenegrins, be proud that you are Orthodox. We are spiritually and economically richer [than others]."[57]

Under the circumstances, average Serbs may have been logically tempted to see themselves as superior beings with a natural mandate to rule. Others, as they had been told by sources of authority, represented all that is base, undesirable, and naturally subordinate.

The Serbs as a Threatened Nation

At the same time, however, Serb opinion makers have portrayed their people as maligned, cheated, and threatened. They have reproached others as ungrateful for Serbian efforts in establishing Yugoslavia and for being unwilling to recognize the Serbs' uniqueness and rightful position. In Belgrade in January, 1989, at a meeting of Serbia's leading intellectuals, one speaker allowed with some condescension that "it is not easy [for others] to live alongside a people which liberated itself [the Serbs], [a people] which has a history of its own. Envy of this is very much a human emotion. There is also something called a lack of gratitude which exists between peoples . . . a debt is both psychologically and morally burdensome. . . . What Serbia did for others, which she is forced to talk about herself [because no one else will], did not arouse gratitude, but stimulated other types of feelings instead."[58]

Moreover, Serbian spokesmen painted their people not only as non-threatening to anyone else but, on the contrary, as the target of threats emanating from all of Yugoslavia's other communities. In one case, the pro-government weekly *Ilustrovana Politika* had recourse to a leading Belgrade psychiatrist to provide an explanation for what was called Serbia's surprise at finding itself "surrounded by hatred" when it "awakened three years ago" [in 1987, when Milošević consolidated his power]. The doctor agreed that "Serbia has always been the object and the sweet prize for those who surround it, and I believe that will always be the case whatever trends civilization takes." Asked for an analysis of this "pathological hatred for the Serbian people, the Serbian leadership, and Serbia," he placed the blame on non-Serbs, concluding that the "pathological hatred for all that is Serbian stems from a guilt complex [on the part of non-Serbs], which is anesthetized precisely by hating."[59]

Even the Slovenes, in their turn, came to be portrayed as a threat to the Serbs when they refused permission to pro-Milošević Serb nationalists to hold street rallies in Slovenia, similar to the ones which had helped overthrow the leadership in Vojvodina and Montenegro. Danger—as the meek, just, and non-threatening Serbian couple faced by a menacing Slovene dragon, a cartoon that appeared in *Ilustrovana Politika* on December 12, 1989—always came from other quarters. In this case, it was from the unlikely source of the Slovenes. The dimension of a foreign threat was interjected frequently in order to enhance its magnitude, although this portrayal was routinely stretched beyond plausibility. Such campaigns included the theme that the United States was engaged in an anti-Serb policy through its support for pro-independence movements, such as those of the Albanians and Croatians, whereas the truth was quite the opposite.

Going well beyond this, Serbian leaders depicted their people as oppressed and even literally menaced with extinction. As the *Serbian Memorandum* stressed, both the Serbian people and their very culture have allegedly been under a merciless assault since 1945. The "cultural currents of the Serbian people are alienated, encroached upon, or are declared valueless, neglected or crumbling, its language is repressed, and the Cyrillic script gradually is disappearing."[60] In particular, the Serbian minorities living outside of the Serbian republic's boundaries allegedly were targets of discrimination and attacks by other communities. They were being prevented from uniting with the motherland, while Serbia was unable to help them because it was restrained by the Communist yoke. Well before the breakup of Yugoslavia, prominent Serbs were promoting in the mass media the likelihood of a doomsday scenario for the Serbs. Drašković even equated the Serbs' situation with that of Israel: "Israel and the Serbs live in a hellish siege where the sworn goal is to seize, and then cover with mosques [*podžamijati*] or Vaticanize, the lands of Moses and of the people of Saint Sava [Serbia's patron saint]."[61]

The government-controlled press suggested, without any basis, that the upcoming November, 1990 democratic elections in Bosnia-Herzegovina would resurrect the wartime Fascist government, thus threatening the Serbs. Scare tactics, just before the outbreak of conflict, heightened the fears that were already being stirred up within the Serbian community. For example, a Serbian representative to the Bosnia-Herzegovina Parliament warned in January, 1992, that "I have learned from my sources that Izetbegović has reached an agreement with [German Chancellor Helmut] Kohl that, since the Germans do not love the Turks [working in Germany], they are to transfer them to Bosnia-Herzegovina, with the German government paying the costs."[62] Another nationalist writer informed his audience that Turkey, with the encouragement of the United States, planned to send four million Turks into Bosnia-Herzegovina as settlers in order to set up the "first *jamahiriyya* in Europe."[63]

As Yugoslavia began to disintegrate, the Serbian government and the nationalists stepped up their emphasis on the threat even more, including their allegations of a menace from abroad. The reason for foreign hostility toward the Serbs was attributed to the Serbs' supposed blocking of the aggressive plans of outside interests. Serbian sources have claimed to see conspiracies by various combinations of Germany, NATO, the Masons, the Vatican, the CIA, "American generals," Saudi Arabia, and even by a "Bonn-Vienna-Zagreb-Sofia-Tirana-Rome axis," among others. One political observer assured his readers that what he claimed was an assault against the Serbs was part of the "Freemasons' anti-European strategy. . . . [designed] to establish an 'Islamic corridor' as a pathway for the breakthrough of Turkish hegemony and of the Islamic masses into Europe."[64]

The specific motives for this alleged hostility toward the Serbs purportedly have variously included: the Vatican's wish to undermine Eastern Orthodoxy; schemes to reconstitute the Hapsburg and Ottoman Empires; Germany's drive toward "warm waters," the oil of the Balkans, and trade routes to the East; Germany's desire to find a dump for nuclear waste materials; and Germany's desire for revenge for its defeat in World War II. The obsession with raising the specter of the German threat extended even to allegations by the Yugoslav Army journal that Americans of German origin, including Gen. H. Norman Schwarzkopf and the United States ambassadors to Belgrade and Moscow, were actually manipulating American foreign policy to Germany's benefit.[65]

Although the threat could take on any form, the goal was usually portrayed as a full-scale assault against the Serbs. For example, for historian Radovan Samardžić, one of the architects of the *Serbian Memorandum*, the Vatican was motivated by what it saw as an opportunity "to push the Orthodox Church and the Orthodox people out of the neighboring Balkan Peninsula once and for all."[66] For Orientalist Miroljub Jevtić, the threat was that "international Islamic planners, aided by domestic fellow-thinkers, have as their objective to Islamize all of Serbia, but only as the first step of a breakthrough into Europe."[67]

General Mladić, especially, continued to present the purported threat to the Serbs as a stark one, describing the goal of the Germans, Croatians, and Muslims as nothing short of the "complete annihilation of the Serbian people."[68] So did the Serbian Orthodox bishops, who at their synod in January, 1992, warned that the Serbs in Bosnia-Herzegovina were living "under the threat that genocide will again be visited upon them."[69] Metropolitan Amfilohije described the danger to the Serbs in virtually cosmic proportions. He saw the objective as the destruction of Orthodoxy in the Balkans, which is "the last island on which holiness is preserved. . . . Therefore, all the demonic forces are directed against the last redoubt of unsullied holiness, of untroubled and unpolluted truth."[70]

Through all this, the idea of the Serbs' being misunderstood and treated unfairly has run as a plaintive unifying thread. Dobrica Ćosić, for example, equated the Serbs' ostracism with that of the Jews in an earlier period: "We Serbs feel today as the Jews did in Hitler's day. We are a people who are [considered] guilty. . . . Today, Serbophobia in Europe is a concept and an attitude with the same ideological motivation and fury which anti-Semitism had during the Nazi era. That, of course, is not by chance, since Germany and its allies from the First and Second World Wars are the deciding force against both the Jews and Serbia."[71] The Serbian Orthodox Church contributed to this atmosphere, lamenting Europe's indifference both to the genocide which was allegedly being carried out against the Serbs in Bosnia-Herzegovina and to their very survival.[72] General Mladić, too, saw the Serbs as veritable martyrs and victims of betrayal across the ages. He said: "It seems that we Serbs always wait until it [the threat] reaches our throats. Only then do we retaliate. . . . In the thirteenth century, we were more numerous than the Germans. Now, there are just over twelve million of us, while they have grown to one hundred fifty million. It is not that their women are any better at giving birth than ours. It is because [our] dead have given their contribution to freedom."[73]

The Precarious Image Balance

This dualistic self-view of superiority and accompanying vulnerability bordering on paranoia can be a particularly explosive mix. This perception is further exacerbated when others, such as the Muslims, whether as individuals or as a community, are portrayed as antithetical, negative, and threatening, and as the cause of the Serbs' deprivation. As sociologist Ervin Staub notes, "The cultural self-concept of a people greatly influences the need to protect the collective psychological self. A sense of superiority, of being better than others and having the right to rule over them, intensifies this need" and predisposes a group to violence. The obverse, which can coexist with a sense of superiority, is a collective self-doubt—"another motive for self-defense. When a sense of superiority combines with an underlying . . . self-doubt, their contribution to the potential for genocide and mass killing can be especially high."[74]

Often, according to Straub, this self-view "includes a belief, realistic or paranoid, that other countries or internal enemies are inhibiting the group from getting its due in material possessions, prestige, or honor." This view can lead to justification for demanding and taking more, as expressed in the need for greater *lebensraum* for one's group.[75] The Yugoslav Army's then-chief of staff, Gen. Života Panić, in fact, interpreted foreign condemnation of Serbian policy in Bosnia-Herzegovina as just such an attempt to cheat the Serbs out of the special position due to them. He warned: "The Serbs are the largest nation in the Balkans. There are many people who do not like that and want to take away our *lebensraum* in Bosnia."[76]

Zhirinovskiy, again, seemed to validate such fears and sense of unjustified deprivation on behalf of the Belgrade government when he suggested during his 1994 visit to Bosnia that "Catholics from the West, Muslims from the East, some enemy forces from the North—they all want to take a chunk of Greater Serbia for themselves." He reassured the Serbs of the legitimacy and ultimate success of their goals, for in the Balkans of the twenty-first century, two languages would be dominant: Serbian and Russian.[77]

The dual influence of perceived Serbian superiority and the alleged threat of biological Serbian extinction was now in place. Using any means possible, therefore, to manipulate the population balance by ethnic category would now appear normal and desirable, since it would increase the number of Serbs in relation to that of other communities. Thus, a Serbian academic proposed the following plan: "In order for the [Serbian] people to survive, every woman must give birth to at least three children. . . . Let those cliques who take pride in liberty, planned parenthood, and the unquestionable right of women to abortion remember that in a law-abiding state no one is master of his own body, whether male or female. Women must give birth to replacements, while men must go to war when the state calls them."[78]

To that end, one of the most strident Serbian supremacists, artist Milić od Mačve, even proposed setting up a special government ministry whose mission would be to increase the Serbian population. He also suggested that a "gynecological bus" be made available in every population center and that "any woman who is physically able to do so must give birth every nine months." If she was unwilling, he threatened, "we will hand her over to the *mujahedin* from the [United Arab] Emirates. Let her have them inseminate her [instead] if she does not want to do so here."[79] In 1993 Belgrade University's Obstetrics Hospital, shifting from words to actions, instituted a fund to encourage Serbian mothers to bear more children, while that same year the Serbian Orthodox Church in the mostly Muslim areas of the Sandžak and Kosovo began to offer medals to Serbian mothers according to how many children they bore.[80]

When the Serbian Orthodox Church sought in 1993 to have the state declare abortions illegal, the argument was cast in ethnic rather than in moral terms. The Church's spokesman on the issue, Vasilije, a bishop from Bosnia-Herzegovina, noted, "I had in mind, above all, Orthodox Serb women." He stressed that even now Serbs made up less than two-thirds of Serbia's population and that this proportion would shrink there and in Bosnia in the future. "This," he warned, "will continue until the Serbs in Serbia end up as a minority, no longer living in their national state. The state will belong to those who have the [greatest number of] people."[81]

Conversely, the Muslims' higher birth rate has been a frequent target in Serbian nationalist discourse. The increase has been portrayed as a conscious, coordinated strategy by the Muslims to spread Islam and to menace the Serbs. Even scholars, such as Miroljub Jevtić, suggested that other countries, and especially Saudi Arabia, were orchestrating this plan as a calculated policy. In the course of political negotiations, the Bosnian Serb leader Karadžić reportedly focused specifically on the Muslim birth rate as supporting proof for his concern about the Muslim threat.[82] In the short term, however, the Serbs were likely to see ethnic cleansing as a more effective and quicker population rectifier than other means.

Conviction as Motivation

Justifying the measures taken against the Muslims proved less of a dilemma than one might have expected, thanks in no small part to the conditioning of

80

views by the government's intensive information campaign. This rationalization has often been used to counter the threat to the very basis of Serb values and survival. Almost any action, however, would appear reasonable in response to a threat of this magnitude, particularly given the concept of innate Serbian superiority. In such an atmosphere, and with the Muslims portrayed in such negative and dehumanizing terms, it is perhaps not surprising that there were so many Serbs ready to carry out atrocities without qualms. The use of stereotypes not only served to mobilize the Serbs but helped to lump Muslims into a common category as dangerous, alien, and implacable enemies against whom it was legally and morally acceptable, and even mandatory, to use any means available.

The official Serbian interpretation was that their own people were defending and liberating only what was historically and legally theirs, while the Muslims were interlopers who had usurped Serbian lands. If anything, from the Serb leadership's perspective, the Serbs were being modest in their demands. General Mladić explained to a group of journalists from Belgrade: "As far as terminology, you reporters from the Federal Republic of Yugoslavia have not yet learned the basic terms: I have not conquered anything in this war. I only liberated that which was always Serbian, although I am far from liberating all that is really Serbian. . . . Even Trieste [Italy] is an old Serbian city."[83]

Serb leaders also emphasized that their actions were only legitimate self-defense and assumed that anyone else in their place would do the same. When Lord David Owen commented in an interview that he had promised not to allow General Mladić to create a Greater Serbia, Mladić responded: "Come on, who is this Owen who is so concerned about the fate of the Serbs in the former republic of Bosnia-Herzegovina? General Mladić is not creating any Greater Serbia; he is only defending his country, just as Lord Owen would do."[84]

Belgrade's official reply to reports of Yugoslav Army forces deploying into Bosnia-Herzegovina in early 1994 was also cast in terms of a warranted defense against a worldwide Islamic threat. According to a spokesman for the Yugoslav Army, such "volunteers" from Serbia could not be stopped from their understandable desire to cross the border in order to help their neighbors stem what had become part of a global plot against the Serbs. As he put it, "Volunteers from the FRY [Federal Republic of Yugoslavia], as free people, cannot be denied the right to decide on their own fate and fight for the survival of their people, especially since Islamic fanaticism has acquired planetary proportions in its struggle against the Serbs."[85]

Such strong official conviction no doubt provided compelling positive justification and rationale for the physical elimination of the Muslims and other non-Serbs. With the overwhelming impact of such unchallenged normative guidance, internal moral qualms could evaporate easily, especially in the rush of apparent political and military success to which the leadership could point. Many Serbs, no doubt, were convinced by the official campaigns and assurances from authority figures that the Muslims were a genuine threat. They felt in fact that they were doing their patriotic, and even religious, duty by engaging in or supporting anti-Muslim actions. The commander of one Serbian militia from the nearby Krajina region, operating in Bosnia, believed that his men were there to "protect Serbian children from the [Islamic] crescent."[86] A Bosnian Serb soldier also claimed, apparently in good faith, that he was fighting because the "Muslims want our houses, [and] our women."[87]

Such an atmosphere could have a numbing effect on an individual Serb's sense of morality and basic perception of right and wrong. In a revealing insight, one young Bosnian Serb soldier admitted that "when I was on duty and had to evict women and the old from Muslim villages, I turned my head away and tried to avoid that task." However, time and repetition apparently took their toll, for "later on, I understood that we Serbs have a noble soul, [since] we could have killed them all instead of only evicting them."[88]

Under the circumstances, the elimination of the Muslim population even came to be viewed as cause for celebration. Such was the case in Trebinje, where the Muslims' expulsion and the destruction of the city's mosques were followed by a night of revelry by the local Serbs with champagne and dancing in the streets.[89] In many instances, this process of genocide could degenerate into a macabre tragicomedy, with Serbs treating cleansing operations in a lighthearted manner. In one case, a Serb combatant, asked by a reporter about a destroyed Muslim village, replied: "'Who said we mine mosques? These are failed rocket launches,' referring to the mosque's destroyed minarets. His joke brought an explosion of laughter from fellow fighters. . . . 'We are actually helping their [Muslims'] future business by opening shop windows in their homes.'"[90]

Yet, for some Serbs involved in the ethnic cleansing, paradoxically, no personal animosity was apparent as they went about their methodical routine of harassing and rounding up Muslims. In one incident gunmen from one of the most ruthless militias—the White Eagles—passed out candy and chocolate to quiet frightened Muslim children when they invaded and searched their parents' apartment.[91] Even some of the top Serbian leaders were anxious to show that they too, as individuals, had no personal dislike for non-Serbs. Thus, to illustrate his lack of bias, Karadžić argued that he counted friends among all the ethnic groups and that his wife's best friend had been an Albanian woman before the latter had moved away.[92]

The Lure of Material Gain

The prospect of easy booty from the hapless Muslims—in the form of land, livestock, houses or apartments, cars, cash, farm machinery, or appliances, or women to be raped—apparently was also a powerful inducement for many Serbs.[93] That criminal activities were officially condoned is suggested by the fact that, at times, the Bosnian Serbian police officers themselves were participants in the looting.[94] Sometimes, the Muslims were allowed to sell their possessions, as in Trebinje, where they received an order to leave within forty-eight hours. One refugee described the situation: "We sold whatever we could in that rush. It was a question of life and death. We were unable to defend our houses and property, and people were selling the most luxurious cars, cows, horses, television sets, and VCRs for fifty or at most one hundred marks! We had to do that in order to pay for our transportation."[95]

Swimming against the Tide: The "Disloyal" Serbs

Finally, coercion was also a factor in inducing Serbs to cooperate in the process of ethnic cleansing. However, not all Serbs in Bosnia-Herzegovina or Serbia participated in or condoned ethnic cleansing. Some, although apparently only a minority, were appalled and tried to help individual Muslims. One Muslim refugee observed that under the circumstances he considered as "good Serbs" even those Serbs who "did not help me, but did not harm me and sometimes even spoke to me."[96] Other Serbs, especially in the early phases, defended Sarajevo along with their Muslim and Croatian neighbors. According to one report, in fact, "in a recent 'cleansing' action [carried out by Serbian forces], out of a hundred or so personnel from the

[Bosnian government] 'home defense units' which [the Serbian forces] captured, about forty of them were Serbs."[97]

Those Serbs who were in favor of the anti-Muslim strategy were not only a majority, at least eventually, but also controlled the guns, the government apparatus, and the sources of legitimacy, and had the support of Belgrade. However, those Serbs who were unwilling to go along with the Serb leadership's ethnic policies were viewed as a special threat, as they embodied an embarrassing challenge to the basic legitimacy of the nationalist ideology. Overt resistance to ethnic cleansing, therefore, could be dangerous. At the onset of the crisis in the city of Foča, pressure on Serb policemen to join the nationalist cause had ranged from cajoling by their already coopted peers from other towns to naked threats to them and their families from Bosnian Serbian politicians if they did not join.[98]

Any Serb who nevertheless continued to be recalcitrant ran a considerable risk of being labeled a traitor to the Serb cause and of suffering the same fate as his non-Serb neighbors. According to Serbian dissidents in Prijedor, for example, the "'true' Serbs punished the Serbs caught helping the Muslims and Croats in the same manner, imprisoning them in the same camps. . . . The Serbian authorities were brutal in their treatment of disloyal Serbs."[99] One Muslim detainee released from a Serbian-run camp reported the following incident that occurred after he and other Muslims had been rounded up: "Some [Serb] individuals wanted to kill us on the spot. Žika Marković [a Serb] at that moment placed himself between us and the Chetniks and told them not to harm us. He had often gone hunting with us. However, the son of Neda Petković, our neighbor, struck him on the head with the butt of his rifle. They killed two of my companions then and there."[100]

In Trebinje another Serb reportedly was killed after he questioned fellow-Serbs as to why they were beating Muslims who had served in the Bosnian Serb Army.[101] Dissident intellectuals were especially troublesome from the Serb authorities' perspective. Characteristically, a Serb gynecologist, Miro Kundurović, known for his opposition to ethnic cleansing, was taken from his home in a Sarajevo suburb by Bosnian Serb security forces and was not seen again, whereupon his family fled abroad.[102] In the charged atmosphere, it did not take much to arouse suspicions. In one Serb-run detention camp, an American journalist ran into a prisoner who told him: "I'm a Serb! . . . Baptized in the Orthodox Church. But the day the Serbs rounded up the Muslims in Prijedor I was taking a walk with four Muslim friends, all girls. When I explained I was a Serb, they [Serb militiamen] beat me up."[103] To prove their patriotism and to avoid such accusations, some Serbs apparently were willing to do whatever the leadership requested. One Serb accused of war crimes claimed the reason for some of the killings he had committed was that "my commander said that because I came from Sarajevo and lived with the Muslims, I could be suspected as a spy, so I had to prove myself."[104]

The difficult choice that Serb representatives made to remain in a multi-confessional Bosnian government was a particular source of recriminations for the Bosnian Serb hard-liners. Those politicians who had tried to reject ethnic cleansing became the target of threats by extremists, such as Biljana Plavšić, a leading SDS figure, who warned that the "Serbs know what they will do to them [those Serbs remaining in the Sarajevo government] if they ever get their hands on them."[105]

7. The Denial Syndrome

The Serbian Perspective

As the Serbian leadership in both Serbia and Bosnia-Herzegovina came to see their actions as counter to international norms, or at least as having potentially negative consequences for their relations with the international community, they sought to deny all accountability and even the very existence of genocide. Denial was also important for the general domestic audience in order to make any further action more palatable and to avoid a questioning of the leadership's morality. This deceptive strategy could take the form of outright denial by the leadership that anything had occurred at all, or it could entail repackaging an act as something noble, often under a euphemism. In many cases among average Serbs, genuine self-denial was no doubt at work, stemming from an internalized belief that their actions were in no way wrong. This perception was bolstered by domestic propaganda from multiple sources.

Many in the leadership may have actually rationalized their denial by legitimizing anything that would assure the greater good for their nation, given the polarized analytical context they had created for themselves. Power and decision making within the Bosnian Serb leadership seemed to be exercised in a collegial manner. Varying approaches on strategies and methods reflected personality differences and factional loyalties. However, on the ultimate goals there was substantial consensus.

In general, and particularly when dealing with foreign audiences, the Serbian leadership usually displayed an acute awareness that their actions lacked moral approval. As such, it is no surprise that they made a conscious effort to deny their actions. If genocide is viewed as a deliberate Serbian strategy intended to achieve certain political objectives, deliberate denial was necessary. This approach would not only thwart obstruction by negative foreign opinion but would also avoid triggering concrete measures by the international community.

Official Denial and Damage Control

The Serbian power structure, as a matter of course, baldly and cynically dismissed any report of atrocities or genocide against the Muslims and actively and systematically sought to conceal such acts at almost every step. In April, 1993, the Serbian Academy of Arts and Sciences, representing the country's intellectual community, organized a conference entitled "The System of Lies about the Crimes of Genocide, 1991–93." Its specific objective was to counter what the participants saw as foreign "disinformation" about alleged Serb involvement in war crimes.

To be sure, most Serbian leaders—including Milošević, Milan Panić, Karadžić, Ćosić, and Patriarch Pavle—at one time or another all declared their opposition to ethnic cleansing in statements directed to foreign audiences. Patriarch Pavle on several occasions even went on record as saying he preferred there not be a Greater Serbia if its establishment were a result of war crimes. However, the intent of such declarations appears to have been more to assuage world opinion than to reflect true policy goals or practice. Such condemnations were more than countered by repeated accompanying denials that ethnic cleansing was occurring at all or that the Serbs were responsible for the violence.

Perhaps more insidiously, Serbian spokesmen also sought to trivialize the term genocide to void it of its meaning and impact and to confuse the issue. Serbian representatives applied the term even to diplomatic measures taken by the international community against Serbia. Yugoslavia's minister of sports even claimed that "banning our athletes from taking part in international competition is genocide committed against the young."[1]

At the same time, any impact at home was diluted by the Belgrade government's continued and all but open backing for the Serbian war effort in Bosnia-Herzegovina. Serbia's leadership still tolerated the state-controlled media's favorable coverage, support for the militias operating from

Serbia, and provided extensive material help and direct military involvement. In Bosnia-Herzegovina itself, Karadžić maintained to the end that the "Serbian people have nothing to be ashamed of," admitting at most that, in the period before the Yugoslav People's Army had withdrawn in May, 1992, some Serbian individuals, bearing only "personal responsibility," may have committed some crimes. "We can affirm with certainty that our [Bosnian Serb] army defended our people and their borders in a model manner," he explained, "and that it did not commit a single crime, rape, or attack against civilians."[2]

Karadžić maintained that ethnic cleansing "has never been part of our policy." "The Serbian authorities have never forced any Muslim or Croat to leave his home," he continued. "I believe it is obvious that the Muslims feel uncomfortable in Serbian territory and are leaving, but no one is forcing them to do so." In his view: "What is happening in the Serbian part of former Bosnia-Herzegovina is that the Muslim population, considering that it was in Serbian regions, demanded the right to leave. We allowed them to do so. . . . They are demanding to leave, and they are leaving." He also used euphemisms to describe ethnic cleansing by calling what was occurring just "ethnic transfer," and noting that it was "not deliberate" in any event.[3] Even Serb officials involved directly in the process sought to continue the denial. In the town of Višegrad, where foreign journalists saw burned-down Muslim homes and mosques, the Serbian mayor told them, "I don't know what you mean by 'ethnic cleansing'! The Muslims left voluntarily. We even supplied the buses. We didn't force them to leave, I swear."[4]

Whenever possible, the perpetrators were anxious to cast the expulsions in a positive light. Thus, a major in Arkan's notorious Tiger militia insisted that the Muslims had left the town of Bijeljina voluntarily, as part of a swap of houses with Serbs transferring from Muslim-held areas. Reacting to suggestions that, on the contrary, he had acted criminally, the major countered indignantly: "Me, a criminal? . . . Me, a criminal? I, who am a greater humanitarian than anyone else! Why, fellow, the Muslims even kiss my hand. I will show you videos from these [house] swaps, [in which the Muslims] bow to me [in gratitude]. . . . Ask any of them about [me]."[5]

Likewise, in Banja Luka, the Serbian official in charge of organizing the expulsion of non-Serbs tried to justify the process to a foreign reporter by portraying it as a favor done to the local Muslims: "'People can look at this any way they want. Look, [the Muslims] give us a list and say, "Get us out of here." They want to go. There is no business here, no medicine, no food.

They can't even get the absolute necessities of life.' Mr. Bojić [the official] feels that he should be thanked, not condemned. . . . 'I can't understand why the world treats us this way. We're not so terrible as people say.'"6

The very existence of concentration camps was denied forcefully at all levels by Serbian authorities, at least at first. Milošević himself evinced surprise when asked about the existence of concentration camps in Bosnia-Herzegovina. He claimed, "I was astonished when I heard information that such camps existed there," but at the same time sought to cast doubt on the validity of such reports by placing conditions on the sources. "I cannot be sure. . . . I cannot even be sure that those who inform me about it have the right information."7

Even Milan Panić, the California-based businessman-turned-politician who served as Yugoslavia's prime minister for a time and who was widely considered in the West as a liberal alternative to Milošević, shared in denying war crimes. Despite compelling evidence by international organizations to the contrary, he disingenuously requested journalists "to help him in his search for concentration camps," offering a five-thousand-dollar reward "to the person who succeeds in finding such a camp."8 Denial was also present at lower levels of authority. Thus, the local militia commander in Bijeljina could tell a visiting reporter, "We don't have prisons. . . . I have no reason to lie to you."9 In September, 1992, Belgrade television announced that the Yugoslav government was considering bringing to trial anyone spreading "disinformation" about such camps.

The Serbian Orthodox Church convened an extraordinary session of its governing Holy Episcopal Synod specifically to refute such accusations. The resulting communique stated unequivocally that reports of camps had been based on false information and concocted with the intention of "blackening" the Serbs. It went on to state: "In the name of God's truth and on the basis of testimony from our brother bishops from Bosnia-Herzegovina and from other trustworthy witnesses, we declare, taking full moral responsibility, that such camps neither have existed nor exist in the Serbian Republic of Bosnia-Herzegovina, nor in the Serbian Krajina."10

Some Church leaders, such as Patriarch Pavle, in fact, never came to terms fully with this issue, for he continued to cast doubt on the existence of the camps long after such a tack had been abandoned by other Serb spokesmen. In an interview with an Italian journalist in early 1994, when asked about the camps, he still replied: "I believe that investigations should be undertaken, and visits carried out on the ground. If it turns out that the camps do exist, then we are guilty and should be punished. I do not believe that this is organized, but rather that what may be happening are actions by individuals."[11]

Eventually, as outright denial became unrealistic, the thrust of most rebuttals switched to one of damage control. Karadžić, reversing his earlier blanket denials, eventually sought to justify the camps' existence by casting them in a positive light. He claimed they were a result of the Serbs' unwillingness to kill prisoners: "We, unlike the Muslims, do not kill prisoners; that is why we had camps, not extermination camps as has been claimed, but prison camps." Forgetting earlier denials of their existence, Karadžić went on to reassure foreign audiences that "today we have dismantled them completely, and have freed everyone. The Muslims, however, still maintain theirs. Europe is being deceived by the media and by their governments."[12] On occasion, extreme cynicism accompanied Serb explanations of the concentration camps, as when local Serb officials insisted that the Trnopolje camp was not what it appeared to be; on the contrary, it was only an "Open Reception Center." They went on further to claim that the camp "is an El Dorado for them [the Muslims]. They think this is a guaranteed way to go abroad. Many people have closed their houses and apartments in order to come here."[13]

At the same time, whenever possible, Serbian authorities sought to refuse or hinder access to camps, or to deceive inspectors if access could not be prevented. On occasions, even firefights would be staged nearby to discourage the media from proceeding. When official visits by foreigners could not be avoided, camps would be cleaned or closed. All buildings were not shown, and occasionally the inmates were transferred.[14] If that plan failed to deny access, Serb spokesmen sought to minimize the dreadful living conditions. One camp commandant was proud of how well he treated his prisoners, although a visitor could see clear signs of starvation.[15] Belgrade's media also played a role in helping to dispel such negative images. As a former inmate of one camp recounted: "One day, a Serbian television crew came by. The guards ordered the women and children to go outside and then distributed apples and cakes among a small group. The TV crew then filmed these people eating the apples and cakes."[16]

The Serbian Orthodox Church, moving beyond earlier denials of the existence of such camps, later shifted to denying reports of mistreatment in the camps. They rejected Western accounts as lies motivated by hate towards the Serbs and Orthodoxy. An editorial in *Pravoslavlje,* for example, assured its readers that not a single woman or child had been interned in the camps. It also claimed that detainees ate the same food as Serbian soldiers, that there was neither harassment nor torture, and that "some prisoners stated that they are better off in prison than at the front, because they at least have guaranteed food and lodging."[17]

In practical terms, public denial also served to neutralize Muslim resistance by downplaying to the intended victims the real nature of the concentration camps. According to an inmate of the Trnopolje camp for women and children, Serbian guards had told Muslims that they were being placed in the camp for their own protection from the Green Berets (that is, the Muslim militia), even though in that area all the Muslim combatants had already surrendered.[18]

Significantly, the Serbian media later viewed with some pride that allegedly lethal "reprisals" were not conducted against the Muslims being expelled. Reports noted that, instead, "everyone knows that approximately four thousand Muslims, mostly young men and women, were sent away on buses from the collection center [sabirni centar] at Trnopolje alone."[19]

The occurrence of rapes was also rejected out of hand, often with considerable cynicism. Karadžić claimed that "there is no evidence to prove women were raped," and labeled the accusations of rape "a horrible lie." "Our generals are extremely sensitive about moral behavior," he added.[20] The Serbian Orthodox Church, in official statements called such reports "monstrous" and interpreted accusations as the conscious building of justification by foreign countries in order to embark on the "annihilation" of the Serbs.[21] Milošević sought to dismiss the entire rape issue by appealing to the average person's incapacity to imagine such crimes. He argued with an interviewer, "Please don't repeat that story! . . . It is not true at all. . . . You really believe that? [Are the Serbs] wild tribes, monsters, killers?"[22]

In denying such cases, some officials even sought to shift the blame to the Muslim women for enticing Serbian soldiers, who were placed in a position of having to resist temptation. The newsletter of a Bosnian Serb military unit reported that "there have been many opportunities for Serbs to abuse Muslim women sexually. We thus had an entire convoy of about two thousand Muslim women. . . . Those women stayed for days on Banj Hill near the Serbian positions, drying their intimate apparel, exposed to the view of Serbian fighters. No one raped them."[23] According to the same source, however, when incidents did happen, Muslim women were as much at fault as their Serb rapists: "On the entire territory of Semberija and Majevica, I am aware of literally only one rape of a Muslim woman committed by a Serbian soldier, and it happened with several extenuating circumstances. . . . one of Blagojević's Chetniks (now dead) grabbed one pretty captured Muslim woman by the hand, telling her to come with him because he had not slept with a woman for a long time; she went along, saying that she had not slept with a man for a long time either."[24]

On other occasions the rape stories were attributed to the desire of Muslim women to hide the result of their alleged relations with UNPROFOR peacekeepers. One Serbian woman claimed: "Just let us get our hands on them [the Muslims]. We'll show them what rape really is, their damn Turkmen mothers. They lie to the world about how our modest young men raped so many Muslim women, while the latter give birth to little black girls in European hospitals, having become pregnant by UNPROFOR personnel. Everyone is lying in order to denigrate our men, our Serbs."[25] Other nationalist spokesmen sought to dismiss charges of rape with dubious logical arguments. Radomir Smiljanić, president of the Serb nationalist White Rose, which had blockaded foreign ships on the Danube in the summer of 1993 in protest against the UN sanctions placed on Yugoslavia, reasoned that if the "Serbs had raped so many Muslim women, when would they have had time to win the war in Bosnia-Herzegovina?"[26] Perversely, still other Serbs took pride in the reports of rapes, with one woman concluding: "Since the world glorified our menfolk for raping 120,000 Muslim women, why should we Serbian women not give birth to even more such heroes for the future? Real supermen."[27]

For some Chetniks, the rape issue became not only a source of pride but also a symbol of their power, at least when out of sight of foreign observers. At an SRS rally in Montenegro, for example, party stalwarts chanted in unison, "In the glade in the little forest, a Serb is f——ing a Muslim woman; the Muslim woman is covered with blood, the Serb was her first [man] ever." Šešelj and the other party leaders present reportedly found the ditty amusing.[28]

Blaming Others

Serbian representatives also accused the Muslims preemptively of committing the same atrocities which ironically the Serbs were committing. For example, in Banja Luka, the site of extensive ethnic cleansing against non-

Serbs, Roy Gutman saw local authorities churning out reports for foreign journalists of grisly crimes allegedly being committed instead against the Serbs.[29] Alternatively, a Serbian public relations campaign sought to promote the idea that what was happening was the unavoidable result of warfare or that all sides were equally guilty. Whatever themes were highlighted at any one time, the apparent intent was to discredit reports of atrocities being committed against the Muslims. These actions were meant to confuse the issue, dilute international criticism, and reduce the potential for outside support for the Bosnian government on moral grounds.

The Bosnian Serb authorities typically promoted accounts such as one that the Muslims were allegedly feeding Christian children to the lions in the Sarajevo zoo. This claim was eventually dropped in the face of international skepticism and official UN proof to the contrary. Likewise, in rebutting charges of rape, Bosnian Serb spokesmen charged that it was instead Serbian women who were being sold "as white slaves in the Arab world."[30] When asked about Serbian concentration camps for the Muslims, Karadžić parried the question with a counatercharge that "there are six brothels in Sarajevo where Serbian women are confined."[31] Patriarch Pavle, somewhat more discreetly, assured an Italian journalist that "it was not the Serbs who fomented hate. Instead, it is the Muslims who bear that grave responsibility."[32] He too blamed all atrocities on the Muslims, while rejecting that the Serbs were the aggressors as the western media depicted them. As he saw it, the interpretation of blame differed based on which side one was on. He said defensively that the "Serbs cannot be portrayed as devils. People, admittedly, by their nature look at everything from a specific vantage point and through specific eyeglasses, and from a specific direction."[33] Likewise, the director of a psychiatric clinic in Belgrade, interviewed in the Yugoslav Army's journal Vojska, tried to shift responsibility to the non-Serbs for what he called the phenomenon of "great hate" present in the former Yugoslavia. He attributed this hate to the "inferiority complex" from which Muslims and Croatians allegedly suffered.[34]

Serbian officials routinely also accused the Muslims of committing atrocities against their own people in order to have the blame fall on the Serbs. In Banja Luka, for example, the largest Serb-controlled city, local authorities leveled charges against the Muslims of blowing up the city's mosques themselves in order to attract international sympathy, although UN officials reported that it was the Serbs who were responsible.[35] Such claims were common even at the highest levels of the Bosnian Serb hierarchy. Contradicting UN observers, Maj. Gen. Milan Gvero, deputy commander of the Bosnian Serb Army, on one occasion blandly denied that Serb forces had shelled the besieged city of Srebrenica in contravention of a just-concluded agreement. Instead he blamed the city's Muslim population with having "faked the explosions in the street to make UN officials believe it had come under Serb attack."[36]

Karadžić also disputed foreign media and UN reports of intensified Serb shelling of Sarajevo in late 1993, attributing that instead to attacks staged by the Bosnian government to gain sympathy. This process was highlighted particularly in the case of the February 5, 1994 attack against Sarajevo's marketplace, by mortar fire, which left more than sixty dead and almost two hundred wounded. Initially, Karadžić accused the Bosnian government of masterminding the entire incident in order to convince NATO to launch air strikes against Serb artillery positions surrounding the city. He argued that the Muslims had used mannequins, actors, and cadavers supplied by the Croatians to mount an elaborate hoax.[37] The government and, with few exceptions, the media in Belgrade followed suit with the denial. Their arguments, however, centered more frequently around the Yugoslav Army's claim that it had proof that the explosion had not been caused by a mortar shell at all. Instead, a mine had been set off by the Muslims themselves. In addition, according to U.S. military sources, information indicated that the Serbs had considered deflecting attention from the incident. They had also considered staging a recovery of air-dropped weapons packaged to look like the food normally delivered by parachute, then blaming the United States of violating its humanitarian mission.[38] When their official accounts were not taken seriously abroad, Serbian representatives adopted a more sophisticated approach based on plausible denial. They stated that it could not actually be proved who had fired that specific mortar round. Although similar rounds had been fired from Serb positions on preceding days, identifying the source of the round which fell on February 5 was a difficult task without the presence of eyewitnesses and the appropriate tracking technology.[39]

In numerous other instances, Serbian officials also sought improbable culprits to deflect blame from themselves for attacks on Muslims. For example, the shelling of UN helicopters evacuating the wounded from Srebrenica in April, 1993, had caused casualties among both Muslims and UN personnel. The Bosnian Serb military command lodged an official protest with the UN, accusing them of being guilty. The protest claimed that UN troops had "fired explosives themselves in an attempt to discredit the Serbs."[40]

As a way of diverting attention from the situation in Bosnia-Herzegovina in general, Serbian representatives often also countered that other countries had even worse human rights records. Thus, in May, 1992, Serbia's Parliament voted to dispatch its own fact-finding mission to the United States to investigate what Belgrade claimed were human rights violations during the Los Angeles riots earlier that month. Yugoslavia's representative at the UN demanded at an August, 1992 session dealing with the Serb-run detention camps that the United States' role in Vietnam be examined instead. To deflect criticism of the Serbs' actions against the Muslims, Orientalist Miroljub Jevtić countered with a non sequitur that it is the Islamic countries who are themselves the biggest offenders against human rights.[41]

Indeed, for General Mladić, the Serbs could not be criticized, since, as he claimed, other nations had done as much during their own history. Reportedly, during a chat in Geneva with an American general who had asked him by what right the Serbs were acting as they were, General Mladić had countered: "I told him by that same right by which you Americans admit to having carried out chemical cleansing of the Indian tribes. . . . yes, chemical, exactly, since you did not leave any of them alive."[42] Likewise, in rejecting any international tribunal to try war criminals, Nikola Koljević, vice president of the Bosnian Serb Republic, used as his basic argument that other countries allegedly had also committed similar crimes in wartime. He claimed, "As far as a tribunal for war crimes is concerned, I believe there are no legal grounds for its ad hoc establishment, especially in Yugoslavia, because since World War II so many wars have been waged, including ethnic ones, without setting up such moralistically condemnatory institutions."[43]

At best, some Serbian spokesmen sought to present all sides as equally guilty, especially to foreign audiences, when this clearly was not the case. Milošević insisted that "we are witnessing, in effect, an inconceivable explosion of hate and cruelty by all three parties involved in the struggle, not only by the Serb side as the western press wants us to believe."[44] Although implicitly acknowledging wrongdoing, such unwarranted equal distribution of guilt was intended to divert attention from Serbian actions and had the impact of diluting the accountability of the Serbs.

Even Milan Panić did little more than facilitate a version of "ethnic cleansing with a human face," rather than representing a realistic appreciation of the situation or offering a reasonable solution. He characteristically castigated western reports of massacres by the Serbs as a "very organized public relations program which succeeded in misleading the American public."[45] He also promoted an assessment of the situation as an unfortunate civil war in which everyone was equally to blame. This position served as the basic premise for his repeated push for a return of the almost exclusively Serbian Yugoslav Army to Bosnia-Herzegovina as a peacekeeping force, although the army itself had been involved both directly and indirectly in much of the ethnic cleansing. Panić argued: "As soon as the U.S. recognizes [rump] Yugoslavia and lifts the sanctions, I will cooperate on its side with my army. It would be best, overall, if the United Nations permitted the [Yugoslav] Army to return to Bosnia-Herzegovina. Within three days, there would be peace. We have a large, well-armed, highly motivated army."[46]

Often, as a way of denying responsibility, Serbian representatives accused foreign observers and the international media of fabricating stories of atrocities, or at least of grossly exaggerating them, or of acting out of crass material interest when expressing concern. For example, a weekly, apparently published with the help of Serbia's Ministry of Information for the Serbian diaspora in North America (with the probable intent of helping sympathizers make a case for Serbian goals to foreign audiences), tried to explain the reason for the "phenomenon of the Jews' uncritical support for the Muslim side in Bosnia and for the demonization of their allies and friends—the Serbs—who proved themselves faithfully in the last war." Ignoring questions of morality, the author of the article reached the unlikely conclusion that American Jews were distressed about the fate of the Bosnian Muslims because of the American Jewish community's economic interests related to the Muslim Middle East. As he put it, American Jews were concerned because of the "barrels of oil which have an Arab and Islamic origin."[47]

Routinely, the state-run Serbian media also repeated whatever foreign commentaries cast doubt on reports of war crimes. No doubt, the Serbian authorities hoped that such ostensibly independent accounts would diminish their own responsibility for any denials and would also have greater credibility with the domestic Serbian audience than did official government reports. However, it appears that most of these reports were themselves based on information provided by Serbian government sources.

Typical of this effort was the multi-part series, "The Jews, the Serbs, and the Yugoslav Conflict," published in 1994 in the state-controlled Belgrade daily *Politika* by an obscure Indian professor. He denied the Serbs were responsible for any war crimes and dismissed out of hand the existence of concentration camps. He claimed, "Up to now. . . . only two underweight individuals have been shown. . . . All [the rest of the detainees shown] were in perfectly acceptable [condition]; all were smiling, even those two under-weight men. One of those, it turned out later, had been suffering from tuberculosis for ten years."[48] One of the main themes in his series was that the reporting of war crimes was unwarranted in any event and that much of it was the result of "a campaign by American Jews" and "Jewish interference in the Yugoslav conflict."[49]

Ethnic Cleansing as "Combat"

Another means of denial was the Serbs' portrayal of the situation in Bosnia-Herzegovina as one exclusively of "combat," an argument that lent legit-imacy to virtually any target attacked, including civilian ones. Typically, Karadžić denied that Serb forces were guilty of mounting sieges against towns: "We do not conduct sieges. . . . We defend our territory."[50] According to Karadžić, even the siege of Sarajevo was not really a siege: "It seems we are besieging the city, but in fact that is not true. There is no siege on our part, we have no aggressive intentions; we are only protecting our people who live in the outlying districts around the city."[51]

This argument was used whenever convenient, including during the Ser-bian effort in March and April, 1994, to eliminate the eastern Bosnian enclave of Goražde—a UN-declared safe zone. Seeking to turn the tables between victim and perpetrator, and contrary to all other reports, the Bos-nian Serb authorities portrayed their attack as combat imposed on them. They claimed that it was actually the Muslims in the enclave who were on the offensive, with the Serbs forced to fight a defensive action for survival. According to the commander of the Bosnian Serb police field force engaged in the area, the Muslims in Goražde were supposedly even firing chemical shells from their "large-caliber artillery pieces and [detonating] monstrous explosive devices with which they are targeting civilian objectives with the intent of obliterating all that is Serbian, cultured, and civilized." Terming this incident "just another episode in the full-scale attempt by Izetbegović's followers to annihilate the Serbs," the official concluded that this action even constituted a "direct attack against all the democratic forces of Europe."

The commander of the Bosnian Serbs' Herzegovina Corps responsible for the Goražde operation claimed that the Muslims had begun their alleged assault "with the UN's blessing." One of his staff officers accused the UN of actually supplying arms and ammunition to Goražde's Muslims, even through its established relief air drops.[52]

What is more, the intensity of combat did not necessarily correlate with the number of victims and the level of brutality. In the opening days of the fighting, the border city of Višegrad was reported to have fallen with little resistance, while the surrender of the city of Brčko, in northern Bosnia, also took place "without much opposition." Both events, though, were still accompanied by the deaths of numerous civilians because of the widespread killings which followed at the hands of the conquering Serb forces.[53]

The Serbs also abused the category of "combat" and "combatant" on a significant scale by extending those terms to virtually everything and everyone. Although even the Serbs' treatment of genuine prisoners of war routinely violated international law, most of those whom the Serbs classified as such were actually unarmed civilians. In one concentration camp, according to a visiting reporter, "I ask the Serb authorities about weapons captured from those 'prisoners of war,' they say there are none." Later the police chief of the city of Banja Luka confided to the same journalist: "In ethnic warfare the enemy doesn't wear a uniform or carry a gun. Everyone is the enemy."[54] The police chief of another city, Prijedor, likewise justified the destruction of the Muslims' houses in military terms:

"They all had bunkers."
"So the fact the Muslim houses had basements meant they had to be dynamited?"
"Yes. . . . You are beginning to understand!"[55]

Preemptive arrests of Muslims also found justification because of the "threat." Security forces in Zvornik told reporters that forty-nine local "Islamic terrorists" had been rounded up because they "wanted to stir up trouble and even to carry out crimes against the Serbs and against loyal Muslims in the city."[56]

The lopsided ratio of casualties reported, such as 403 Muslims killed in one encounter and only eight Serbs slightly wounded, is significant in highlighting the type of action which the term "combat" often masked.[57] By insisting that what was happening was really "combat," the Serbs could also claim that whatever harm befell the civilians was because they were really combatants and fair game, or, at best, an indirect and unintended consequence of a situation for which all parties were allegedly more or less equally guilty.

Justification to Foreigners as Denial

Ultimately, in order to avoid, or at least mitigate, criticism from abroad for their behavior toward the Muslims, the Serbs attempted to seek justification. They tried to convince the West that the Muslims "deserved" their treatment, that there was, in fact, an Islamic "threat," and that the Serbs were performing a service to the West by their policy, however severe it may have appeared.

The theme of justification was clearly present in January, 1993, when Serbia's Ministry of Information published a pamphlet intended for English-speaking audiences abroad. One of the contributors, an Orthodox priest and member of the Bosnian Serb Parliament, stressed the immorality and per-fidy of the Muslims and of their religion, maintaining that:

They [the Muslims] want, for the second time, to create a Turkish Bosnia or a Bosnia in Turkey . . . with the Shariatic law and other life norms unacceptable in the twenty-first century. Behind all this is a century-old [sic] dream of a primitive man to live off the backs of the subjugated people, to have his own harem, dreaming of Istanbul, where, according to him, there is a paradise on earth, "where fairies are bathing in sherbet." . . . they [the Muslims] . . . invited to this bloody feast all other worldly bums, murderers and dogs of war. Mujahedins [sic] and Jihad fanatics from the Islamic countries [came] to fulfill their "sacred duty" and to exterminate us. This unscrupulousness completely fits their religion and tradition and culture.[58]

On the diplomatic front, Serbian Orthodox Bishop Atanasije of Her-zegovina, while visiting the United States and Canada in 1992, warned that "militant Islam has used the conflict to establish a foothold in the Balkans" and that "the West is not aware of the penetration of Islam" in the Balkans, where "mosques are rising where there were none before."[59] Karadžić similarly claimed that Izetbegović "wants to found the first Islamic state in modern Europe in order to allow Islam to enter the West. If he succeeds, this will be a big problem for civilized Europe."[60] Trying to link the issue of militancy to worldwide currents, to which he believed foreign audiences might be more sensitive, he claimed that the "fact is that coexistence with the Muslims is impossible [in Bosnia-Herzegovina], as is the case elsewhere in the world."[61]

When he was president of Yugoslavia, Dobrica Ćosić, too, warned that a "pan-Islamic internationalization of the war in Bosnia is the greatest danger looming over both the Balkans and southeast Europe."[62] Other Serbian politicians, including Milošević, also continued to hammer this justification to foreign audiences.[63] In fact, Karadžić was to go further, describing the

"Muslim threat" using a metaphor of disease. The only reason, he claimed, that the Serbs were willing to accept a notional transitional confederation in Bosnia-Herzegovina with a Muslim state was "so we can control it. . . . We are doing that for Europe—to make sure Islamic fundamentalism doesn't *infect* Europe from the south" [emphasis added].[64]

Karadžić's message to the outside world that the Serbs, by their policy toward the Muslims, were willing to perform a valuable service on behalf of an unwary West remained unchanged: "They [Saudi Arabia, Iran, and Turkey] have dark schemes, wishing to make Bosnia a springboard for Islamic penetration of Europe. This is as plain as a pikestaff. It is amazing that the U.S. is aiding and abetting militant Islam through its uncritical backing of the Muslims in Bosnia. . . . They [the Serbs] are the most powerful nation in the Balkans. . . . The Serbs can restore stability in the Balkans and here the U.S. can absolutely rely on the Serbs.[65]

Serbian Orientalists also lent their academic authority to buttress such anti-Islamic arguments abroad. Professor Darko Tanasković, an Islamic studies expert at Belgrade University, warned a prime-time American news audience that the Muslim countries helping Bosnia "have long-term aims . . . not so much to help the Moslems from Bosnia, but to organize their own stronghold in Europe for their future activity."[66] He was to claim subsequently that the West Europeans at least were coming to appreciate the alleged monolithic "continental phenomenon" of a political and cultural Islamic threat to all of them, of which Bosnia-Herzegovina was but a link.[67]

At times, Serbian spokesmen sought to create and exploit differences of opinion between the United States and Europe by playing to what they perceived as European sensitivities. For example, Dragoš Kalajić was a member of a team of Serbian intellectuals who toured Italy in December, 1993, to publicize the Serbian cause. This initiative was known as the "Truth Caravan." His role in this effort was to tell his Italian audiences that the "goal of the United States is to foist Islam on Europe; that is why Washington supports the Muslims in Bosnia so wholeheartedly."[68]

Serbian nationalists were confident that others would eventually also realize the danger that Islam allegedly posed. To bolster this effort, Karadžić noted self-assuredly that "we are going to have volunteers from Christian countries, particularly from Orthodox and Protestant countries, volunteers who are going to fight on [the] Serbian side." Meanwhile the Bosnian Serb defense minister added: "I believe that it is not in the interest of the American people that we have a Muslim republic here in the heart of

Europe. Surely the Serbian people and Western Europe will not allow the construction of a Muslim country in the heart of Europe."[69] The Yugoslav Army journal even concluded that the Vatican "certainly will not look on indifferently to the spread of Islam on the old continent."[70] General Mladić, who had offered Serbia's services to Europe as a bulwark against an alleged Islamic—and German—threat remained puzzled when his views were not shared by other Europeans. He blamed this response on political myopia: "Unfortunately, I must conclude that Christian Europe does not see the danger of either Germanization or Islamization."[71] However, he too remained optimistic that Europe would finally come to its senses, as he continued to press the argument. Ultimately, as Karadžić also assessed, even though the Serbs might be criticized for their actions, this reaction would be temporary. He contended that the "West will be grateful to us one day because we decided to defend Christian values and culture."[72]

The democratic opposition in Serbia followed the hard-liners closely on this issue. A representative of one of the more moderate political parties claimed that the "West is much more concerned about preventing the creation of a Muslim state in Bosnia than in preventing the creation even of a Greater Serbia. . . . A Muslim state in the Balkans could become the springboard for the most extreme Islamic fundamentalism . . . and such a state could wreak havoc in Europe."[73] In fact, one Serbian activist based his optimism on his reading of the West's mild reaction to the Algerian government's crackdown on domestic Islamic activists. He concluded that Westerners would be so worried about the appearance of an Islamic state in Europe that they would be willing to overlook the violation of democratic principles by the Serbs in Bosnia in order to avoid it.[74]

The Silence of Serbia's Conscience

Did the Serbs Know?

To what extent did the Serbs know about the war crimes being committed in their name? Clearly, those in the government and intellectual elite not only were well aware of what was occurring but approved of it, as indicated by their participation in or spirited defense of Serbian actions. The hierarchy of the Serbian Orthodox Church must also have been well informed through its network of clergymen and church members. Thus, although Patriarch Pavle maintained that he did not pay attention to politics and that he neither read the press nor followed the electronic media, the frequent references to this problem by him and by the Church as an organization suggest a substantial degree of awareness at the highest levels.

In Bosnia-Herzegovina, even average Serbs would have been hard put to overlook what was going on around them. A young Serbian girl from Zvornik later remembered the Serbs in charge made no effort to hide the measures they were taking against the Muslims: "Last summer [1992], I watched with my own eyes as they took Muslims by truck to the schoolyard which had been turned into a camp."[75] In Serbia itself, those with access to the foreign electronic media would have also had ample information available. Even the general population, however, was painfully aware at least of foreign allegations. If nothing else, they heard the repeated and vehement denials by their own government, media, or the Orthodox Church, although many may not have believed such foreign reports. Nevertheless, the local media from time to time would also allude to specific incidents.

Moreover, thanks to contacts with relatives in Bosnia-Herzegovina, with refugees, and with the thousands of militia and regular Yugoslav Army personnel who operated in Bosnia-Herzegovina and who would have witnessed or participated in war crimes there, news would no doubt have filtered back and circulated in all social milieux in Serbia. In particular, many militiamen back in Belgrade for rest and relaxation, seem to have had few qualms about relating their experiences to foreign journalists. On the contrary, they were often more than eager to boast about their exploits.

Significantly, however, there have been no real institutional voices in the Serbian community critical of the genocide. Serbian politicians and parties representing virtually the entire ideological spectrum have differed only in degree on how to handle the Muslims. The Chetnik parties, predictably, have promoted the harshest solutions. These groups include not only the hard-line Chetnik parties, such as the Srpska Radikalna Stranka (the Serbian Radical Party—SRP) headed by Šešelj and the SNO led by Jović, but also the more flexible Chetnik party, the Srpski Pokret Obnove (the Serbian Renewal Movement—SPO) led by Drašković. Smaller, more liberal, Serbian parties by and large have remained quiet on this issue. They have done so not only to avoid being labeled unpatriotic but probably also because they are in agreement, in most cases, with the general goals being accomplished by ethnic cleansing, if not necessarily with all the measures that involved.

Dissident Criticism

A small number of Serbian dissidents, many of whom have clustered around the liberal Belgrade weekly *Vreme* and the reformist ex-Communist daily *Borba,* to their credit, have borne the burden of criticism in Serbia of the anti-Muslim measures, often at considerable risk of ostracism and retaliation. Several individuals have been especially outspoken in their condemnation, including Bosnian Serb writer Vladimir Srebrov. Although he had been a founding figure of the Bosnian Serb SDS political party led by Karadžić and a strong supporter initially of the Yugoslav People's Army, Srebrov had become disillusioned by the war crimes. Subsequently, however, blaming Serbia and Bosnia's Serbs for the war and calling the attacks a case of "classic aggression" against Bosnia-Herzegovina, he invited the Serbs to lay down their arms and to rally to the Bosnian Army. Arrested in September, 1992, he was tried for treason in April of the following year and sentenced by a Bosnian Serb military court to five years in prison.[76] Likewise, the Montenegrin poet Jevrem Brković has lived in self-exile in protest after he said of the Montenegrin reservists who had rampaged through the town of Trebinje in October, 1991, "these are not [true] Montenegrins."[77]

In April, 1994, a small group of Belgrade intellectuals calling themselves the "Free Intellectuals" protested what they taxed as Serbian persecution of the Muslims in Bosnia-Herzegovina and in the Sandžak region of Serbia. One of them, film director Lazar Stojanović, predicted that Serbia's Muslims and other non-Serbs would continue to be threatened, "since the Serbian regime is consciously opening the gates to Fascism and Nazism in this part of Europe." The pro-government Belgrade press, predictably, reacted harshly and accused them of "hatred against their own people and their legally elected leaders."[78]

Such individuals have been ostracized and hounded not only by the state but also by their fellow intellectuals. Well-known literary figure Momo Kapor has insisted that accounts of concentration camps, rapes, and the siege of Sarajevo have all been "invented" by the West. He and others have lashed out at such domestic dissidents and suggested that they were inspired by Islam in their concern.[79] Despite their personal courage, the impact on events by such critics has been very limited in the absence of mainstream support in Serbian society and among the institutional elites.

Genocide and Party Politics

To be sure, general allegations of war crimes did surface periodically in Serbia, with political rivals often seeking to blame each other for such acts. These claims took on special vehemence in late 1993 as part of the electoral campaign in Serbia, with candidates trying to incriminate their political opponents in the jockeying for position before the impending December vote. The Milošević government, Arkan, and Drašković, tried to pin all blame for atrocities on Šešelj and his militia. Šešelj countered that others were involved instead. He additionally claimed that the ultimate responsibility lay with the Milošević government, since Serbia's Army and police had armed, supported, and operated alongside the militias. Moreover, according to Šešelj, Arkan's militia has been responsible for the murder and rape even of Serbs.[80]

In one of the rare instances where specific criticism reached the political arena and was openly discussed, Danica Drašković, wife of SPO President Vuk Drašković, publicly condemned on television a recent massacre carried out by the SPO's own militia, the Serbian Guard, against Muslims in her husband's home village of Gacko, in Herzegovina. Although Mrs. Drašković's criticism was limited, it set off a firestorm within her own party and led to a special plenum to condemn her. At the party session, she amplified her charges: "There are no Ustaše knives there [in Gacko]. There was no battle there, no Serbs had been massacred. . . . You have not presented a single comparable example of a similar massacre of the Serbs as has occurred [to the Muslims] in Nevesinje, Trebinje, or Foča." She recounted: "I listened to members of the Serbian Guard . . . as they told how they had raped a thirteen-year-old Muslim girl, all twenty of them, and how they had then placed her on a tank and drove her around, and laughed about how all that was left of her was a skeleton." Had Vuk Drašković been there at the time, she affirmed, he would have defended the Muslims in his hometown. Concluding her argument, she lamented: "I think we have said this too late. I think that we should have spoken out earlier at least about what we knew. We did not have the right to keep silent about anything."[81] Many of the delegates were openly hostile and refused to countenance admitting any wrongdoing. One party leader exclaimed indignantly that "I have never been a witness to such crimes, and I never will be."[82] In the end, although Mrs. Drašković weathered the session, as it degenerated into a power struggle over the leadership and direction of the party, those present officially sidestepped the genocide issue. There was no known follow-up by the authorities.

Yet at the same time, Mrs. Drašković, seemingly unaware of the inherent contradiction, continued to praise her husband's original views, which had been seminal in creating the anti-Muslim atmosphere. She even defended her party's continued allegiance to the World War II Chetnik program. The official SPO magazine, *Srpska reč*, of which Mrs. Drašković is the director, continued to promote the sale—at eight million dinars—of her husband's recently reprinted works, including the novel *Nož* and some other of his most virulently anti-Muslim writings from the 1980s. In an interview at about the same time, Mrs. Drašković herself strongly defended her husband's writings and dismissed any role that he might have had in creating the current hostile environment.

What is more, in the same interview, she was full of praise for the World War II Chetnik movement and its leader Draža Mihailović and appeared baffled by the interviewer's question about whether Mihailović had differed from present-day Serbian extremists. She responded:

I do not understand what is not clear to you here. Draža Mihailović is different from Milošević's policy and from Šešelj's fascism. . . . We want to rehabilitate General Mihailović in the name of historical truth and human justice. It is our national duty to rehabilitate many Serbs, and above all General Mihailović, and through him to rehabilitate the historical role of the Serbian people in World War II. We Serbs should be ashamed of the historical role and actions of the Serbian Communists in the last war, not about those of General Mihailović. He did not commit any of the crimes which are attributed to him.[83]

What Mrs. Drašković had also failed to note was that it was her husband who in the first place had set up the Serbian Guard, which had engaged in numerous atrocities throughout Croatia and Bosnia-Herzegovina long before the Gacko massacre. Furthermore, Mrs. Drašković herself had also personally played a large role in running the Guard.[84] Apparently the Gacko operation had taken place without the Draškovićs' knowledge and permission, suggesting an erosion of their control and one of the possible reasons for their annoyance.

Although her husband had supported her in the party plenum and had also spoken out against genocide in general, he still nevertheless stuck to his original agenda for a Greater Serbia, which had been a prime mover for genocide against the Muslims. On May 13, 1993, at an event that was symbolically held at Mihailović's wartime headquarters of Ravna Gora, Drašković delivered a keynote address at the celebration of the one hundredth anniversary of Mihailović's birth. On that occasion, he exhorted:

"Our ideal, brothers, which we will attain, is to lead our motherland of Serbia, Montenegro, Macedonia, all of Bosnia-Herzegovina . . . and all of the Serbian Krajina under the roof of a single state."[85]

Indeed, Drašković opposed all subsequent partition plans for Bosnia-Herzegovina on the grounds that they would split the latter into three. Taking a harder line than even Milošević or Karadžić, Drašković countenanced only a binary division, as he continued to propose that while Western Herzegovina could join Croatia, the rest of the territory had to be Serbian-controlled, with no separate Muslim entity to be envisaged at all.[86]

As he stressed in a campaign speech in November, 1993, "On whose land is Sarajevo? On whose land is Mostar? And Kupres? And Ozren? And all, all [of Bosnia-Herzegovina] except for western Herzegovina? That is historically, linguistically, culturally, and by nationality the Serbian people's [national] space. . . . If Tudjman wants to create an Islamic state, let him do so in Zagorje [an area near Zagreb]; but on Serbian land there will be no Islamic state.[87] The SPO's Secretary-General, Vladimir Gajić, also argued against an Islamic state on behalf of Drašković's party: "The SPO has been opposed to the creation of a Muslim state having even a single kilometer of land."[88] He also remained extremely sensitive to any suggestion that he might have hinted that the Serbs had committed genocide in Bosnia. In an election campaign speech in Loznica, Serbia, in December, 1993, he went out of his way to deny that he had ever made such a claim.[89] What was more, in the same anniversary speech, Drašković had also denied outright the Chetniks' responsibility for any wrongdoing during World War II. According to Drašković, war crimes attributed to the Chetniks during that period had been only a result of Communist fabrication, for "it was the Communists who in 1945 staged that and dreamed up that Draža and his Ravnogorci [the Chetniks] had done it."[90] Moreover, rather than seeking to stem passions, in January, 1994, Drašković announced that his inflammatory best-seller Nož would be turned into a movie—a move that could be expected to fuel stronger anti-Muslim feelings among even broader segments of the general Serbian public than the book had already done.

8. The Denial Syndrome

The Victims and Bystanders

Genocide, by its very nature, is a relationship between at least two actors—perpetrator and victim—however unwelcome it may be on the part of the victim. The victim's perspective, however, may have an impact on the outcome of events. To a great extent, the Muslims were unprepared for what happened to them. For a long time, many in the Muslim community were prone to deny even to themselves that something like ethnic cleansing could occur, and, specifically, that any harm would befall them as individuals.

Muslim Self-Denial

The revival of the Chetnik movement in the mid-1980s in Serbia, and later in Bosnia-Herzegovina itself, reintroduced the old uniforms, flags, songs, and slogans as part of its rehabilitation as the mainstream of the Serbian nationalist movement. Such overt signals should have set off alarm bells throughout the Muslim community, but relatively few individuals heeded them. Since Bosnia-Herzegovina had been governed by a hard-line Communist system, until the 1990 multiparty elections brought Izetbegović to the presidency, attempts to make the Muslims aware of their defense needs were hampered.

Serbian nationalism became an increasing cause of concern in Bosnia-Herzegovina, only once Milošević had consolidated his power base and had begun to provide official support for the Chetniks' agenda beyond Serbia's borders. Despite those concerns, Muslim leaders were so anxious to avoid a confrontation—and so unsuspecting that anything like ethnic cleansing could occur—that they remained surprisingly passive. They were unwilling to condemn the early Serbian verbal attacks, prepare for a defense of their community, or mobilize domestic and international support. Muslim political and religious figures by and large either did not believe their community would become victims or were confident that the international community would put a stop to such a situation in the unlikely case that it did occur. Asked subsequently whether he had been naive in believing that massacres would not occur, Haris Silajdžić, later Bosnia-Herzegovina's foreign minister and prime minister, acknowledged: "Yes, that is our own fault, and a big one. We believed in an international order which would not accept that genocide could occur in Europe."[1]

To be sure, Serbian leaders had begun to mix their threats with blandishments. Apparently, they intended to lull the Muslims, or at least complicate their political mobilization, in the crucial period while the crisis in Bosnia-Herzegovina gathered momentum. As Karadžić reassured his audience in January, 1992, before large-scale fighting had begun: "We [Serbs] are truly a good and powerful people, who have never done any harm whatsoever to anyone. The Serbs in Bosnia have never threatened anyone, and they will not do so now. All they are doing is organizing themselves."[2]

Because they hoped to avoid doing anything which the Serbs could construe as provocation and justification for action, Muslim leaders usually tried to downplay to domestic and outside audiences any sign of trouble. Thus, when the lone mosque in Belgrade was firebombed in December, 1988, officials at the mosque tried to stifle news of the attack. They hoped to avoid inflaming intercommunal relations by withholding information about the incident even from the Muslim clerical hierarchy in Sarajevo for almost a year.[3] Likewise, when speaking abroad, Muslim clerics minimized any likely threat, as was the case when the *mufti* of the Belgrade mosque visited Egypt in late 1989. During the visit he informed his hosts that the "Muslims' situation in Yugoslavia is good and differs markedly from the situation in the neighboring European countries."[4]

Characteristically, the recently elected Bosnian government cooperated in turning over the arsenals of Bosnia-Herzegovina's Territorial Defense reserve forces to the Army in 1991, as the latter had demanded. When the Yugoslav People's Army attacked Croatia, the Izetbegović government sought to avoid provoking Belgrade. Izetbegović not only remained neutral but even bent over backwards to avoid obstructing the operations against Croatia which the Army launched from and supplied across Bosnian territory. While this passive policy prevented a confrontation at the time with Belgrade and the Yugoslav People's Army, in retrospect, it was also an error, as it left the Bosnian government virtually unarmed and isolated when the conflict spread subsequently to Bosnia-Herzegovina.

To a great extent, the Bosnian government's policy was premised on what can be termed a crucial strategic blunder, namely the assessment that Bosnia-Herzegovina would not be attacked. Even just before the outbreak of open warfare, Bosnia's president Izetbegović still expected that "there will be no war in Bosnia, neither a domestic one nor one caused from outside." He also assured readers in Saudi Arabia that "peaceful coexistence between the Muslims, Croats, and Serbs in the independent republic of Bosnia-Herzegovina will be possible. . . . the republic is considered a model of peaceful coexistence."[5] Such expectations appear to have been shared by the majority of the Muslim community, who also displayed a lack of aggressive intentions toward their Serbian neighbors and Belgrade. The reaction expressed in retrospect by a Muslim in Banja Luka appears typical: "I was an idiot. . . . I thought ethnic cleansing would never happen here."[6]

Even as the situation in Bosnia deteriorated, many Muslims still hoped to avoid all trouble. They refused to buy weapons in order to set up local defense forces and instead sometimes even informed the police against those who did so. A common attitude, analyzed later by one Muslim, seems to have been: "We did not know what ethnic cleansing meant. We thought they would leave us alone if we did not have rifles."[7] Despite the outbreak of fighting, some Muslims even relinquished their weapons. They took the Serbs at their word that nothing would happen to them if they remained unarmed, much to their subsequent chagrin, since this approach did not prevent victimization. As one Muslim woman remembered: "The Serbs came a few months ago and said there would be peace if we gave them our weapons," she sighed, "And so we did."[8]

Even as events unfolded, many Muslims still found it difficult to come to terms with what was actually happening to them. One Muslim artist in Banja Luka, for example, expressed his disbelief thus: "I have some Serbs I thought of as close friends, and not even one has called me to say 'I'm sorry—I do not agree with what is happening to you.'"[9] Self-denial as a desperate hope perhaps reflected many Muslims' unshakable expectations of coexistence. A Muslim scholar who had been saved from intended execution on the spot by his small son's intercession did not even realize the danger he had run. Instead, as he was being bundled off—probably to a concentration camp—the scholar asked his tormentors to take care of his books. His request caused one of the Chetnik gunmen to remark, "In his confusion, the man was not even aware that his child had saved his life."[10] This attitude was illustrated even as Muslim detainees were being pulled off a bus by Bosnian Serb policemen prior to their execution. One Muslim, who survived the massacre by chance, alerted his cousin as they dismounted the bus, "It is our last day." His disbelieving cousin would not hear of it, admonishing, "You shut up, it won't be like this."[11]

Rationalizing and Cooperating to Survive

Another reaction among the Muslim population was to rationalize that as bad as things were, they could always get worse. Individuals tried desperately to just hang on and to avoid doing anything that could provoke even more violent reactions. For example, although Serbian forces had seized Banja Luka early in the conflict, non-Serbs were forced out gradually. According to one observer there, despite the rising tide of harassment and intimidation by Serbian thugs, many local Muslims were likely to say: "What is key is that there are no shells falling on our heads. Everything else is easier to bear."[12] In desperation, some Muslims hoped that they could escape a worse fate by bribing Serbian security personnel. A family from Foča paid hard currency to members of a special unit of the Bosnian Serb Army in return for being taken across the border into Montenegro. Once across the border, they were killed.[13]

Even Muslim individuals who tried to collaborate with the Serbs in an attempt to save themselves fared badly. A number of Muslims were forcibly drafted into the Bosnian Serb Army, which was continually plagued by draft-dodging and a manpower shortage among the Serbs. Muslims received promises of safety in return for their service in the front lines. "They promised us we would live like Serbs if we were loyal," remembered one disabled Muslim veteran of the Bosnian Serb Army. However, in the end, even they and their families met the same fate of ethnic cleansing as the other Muslims. One Muslim veteran from Trebinje lamented, "We fought with them [the Serbs] in the trenches, but now I know that all they wanted us for was cannon fodder." Another summed up his feelings by saying, "I feel rejected and cheated."[14]

Despite their expectations, even those Muslims who had identified closely with the Communist Party and the Yugoslav regime and who had opposed Izetbegović and independence, were not spared. Perhaps they were the most surprised by their mistreatment, which was based not on any disloyal political act on their part but simply because they were Muslim. This attitude was illustrated in the diary of one of the relatively few Muslims who had considered himself a "Yugoslav" for statistical purposes until the end. This designation indicated his conscious effort to identify with the earlier Communist state as opposed to the Muslim community. As late as April, 1992, he had even taken part in demonstrations against the new Izetbegović government. While being harassed by Serb gunmen who had entered his apartment, the victim sought to explain to them that he was really a "Yugoslav," as if that declaration would make any difference. Instead they insisted on calling him a "Turk" and in treating him as they did all the other Muslims.[15]

In an attempt to avoid deportation or worse, some Muslims converted to Serbian Orthodoxy and Serbianized their names. In the city of Bijeljina, group baptisms reportedly were carried out by Serbian Orthodox clergymen. According to the rationale of one of the recent converts, who had had his named changed from Ferhat to Filip, "If you choose to live in the Serbian Republic [of Bosnia], then you have to do something in return."[16] In some cases, Orthodox clergymen reportedly sold baptism certificates to Muslims seeking to avoid persecution or expulsion. Allegedly this service cost fifty Deutsch marks in the town of Brčko.[17] To escape the fate of their fellow Muslims, some prominent personalities in Serbia tried to either "pass" as Serbs or went to extremes to prove their loyalty to Serbia irrespective of events around them. Pop singer Lepa Brena (a Muslim originally named Fahreta Jahić) changed her name yet again to make it sound even more Serbian and went to Serbian-controlled Bosnia to perform in person for the Serbian troops. She and another prominent Muslim musician, Džej Ramadanovski, also became members of the Serbian Unity Party—one of the most extreme of all Serbian parties, headed by Arkan—and performed on behalf of Arkan during his 1993 electoral campaign.[18]

Some Serbian clergymen seemed to view the abandonment of Islam as an encouraging sign. Archdeacon Protić cited with approval the precedent of conversions from Islam in the wake of the Balkan Wars of 1912–13, although this option had been the only one aside from death or flight. He claimed that those converting to Orthodoxy represented what for him were the

better sort of Muslims, those who are "moderate . . . intelligent and educated." At the time of conversion, the Serbian Orthodox Church made sure
that Muslims signed a document stating that they were converting to
Orthodoxy of their own free will. As Archdeacon Protić explained, this
procedure precluded that "someone some day might claim that our Church
forced people to join Orthodoxy. . . . This is really security against potential
embarrassment, since one does not know what the future will bring."[19]
Despite desperate measures, however, acceptance of the Muslims remains
elusive, and their treatment is likely to continue to be harsh. The Serbian
director of the local committee responsible for what is euphemistically
termed "population exchanges" noted, "Even when they [the Muslims] are
baptized and officially go to church, they will always be suspect. . . . How can
they be trusted when they change their affiliation as easily as the wind
changes [direction]?"[20]

Yet another facet of Muslim denial was the belief that a fair deal could be
struck with the Serbs. When Muslim leader Fikret Abdić broke with the
Bosnian government, he declared autonomy for his native Bihać pocket in
Western Bosnia-Herzegovina. Quite apart from any personal ambitions he
may have nurtured, he no doubt hoped to spare the population, at least of
his enclave, the fate suffered by the Muslims elsewhere. His calculations for
success probably hinged on the benefit his action would represent for the
Serbian authorities. His breaking ranks with the Bosnian government would
put pressure on the latter to capitulate and accede to the plans under
consideration in Geneva, while Bihać would provide a trade corridor with
the outside world for Serbian-held territories. Despite Serbian encouragement, in the long run Abdić's expectations may be in vain. Similarly, during
World War II, the *Judenrat,* Jewish councils which administered the ghettos
under Nazi occupation, also hoped that by collaborating the Jewish population could be saved.

Although in the short term the Bosnian Serbs welcomed such splits in the
Bosnian ranks, in the long term the Serbs are likely to seek to eliminate
Bihać as well as the other enclaves. They may do so abruptly or by squeezing
out Bihać's beleaguered population over time, once they consolidate their
position and the utility in weakening the Bosnian government has been
achieved. In particular, Bihać, which is totally surrounded by Serbian-held
territory, would have been hard put to avoid an eventual Serbian takeover
because of its importance for communications between the Serbian-held
Krajina and Serbian-held territories in Bosnia, its railroad network, and its

significant underground airfield, even if Abdić could have avoided the apparently impending collapse of his rule as a result of increasing pressure from the Bosnian government in the summer of 1994.

Western Denial—Establishing the Analytical Premises

The role of foreign observers in evaluation the situation in Bosnia-Herzegovina has also been important in influencing policy responses. At times, their reaction was not only outright denial that the Muslims were being victimized but even, on occasion, implicit justification for that policy.

In Russia, public opinion was solidly in the pro-Serbian camp, with the military and nationalist media from the first reflecting Serbian views on Bosnia-Herzegovina. All blame was placed on the Muslims, who allegedly represented a threat to the Serbs' existence. The Russian Orthodox Church, out of religious solidarity with the Serbs, for example, declared that it was the Serbs who were the victims of genocide, not the Muslims. The Church condemned the "annihilation of the peaceful Serbian population" at the Muslims' hands. Increasingly, the mainstream Russian press, as well as the Yeltsin government, also began to tilt toward the Serbs, under pressure from the strengthened Red-Brown coalition, which was composed of die-hard Communists and new extreme nationalists.

Predictably, Russian ultranationalist Zhirinovskiy, known for his deeply ingrained anti-Islamic outlook, approved unreservedly Serbian policy with regard to the Muslims. He equated the policy with a defense of Europe from "Islamic fundamentalism." "We in Russia have the same problem with the Muslims. . . . The Muslims want to conquer Europe," he argued, adding that "I don't have anything against the Muslims. Let them live according to their tradition and the Shariah. . . . However, I don't think they can live that way in the middle of Europe." Comparing the Muslims in Bosnia-Herzegovina are [thereby] preventing AIDS in Europe. It is better to have an influenza in Bosnia-Herzegovina than AIDS in Europe." Asked what he thought should happen to Bosnia's Muslims, Zhirinovskiy replied: "What Muslims? They do not exist as a nation. They are an artificial creation. What do I know what will happen to them? Let them emigrate to Iran!"[21]

More perplexing was the stance taken by some public figures, including UN officials, in the West. Their reactions contributed to the victimization of the Muslims as they shaped or delayed government and public reactions abroad. For example, many observers' opinions, which reflected a minority view, were assigned unwarranted credibility simply because they were featured so prominently at such public forums as official venues or in the mass media. As a result, Western reaction was often based on an inaccurate context, which provided, although unintentionally, justification or extenuating circumstances for war crimes. Likewise, the impact of those views in framing the issues was out of proportion to their accuracy. Unfortunately, Western policy makers anxious to find a rationale to avoid involvement in Bosnia-Herzegovina could seize upon any of these flawed interpretations.

Initially, some observers, though apparently acting in good faith, downplayed the magnitude of what was occurring through their erroneous initial appreciations of the situation. Just after leaving as Chief of Staff of UNPROFOR in Sarajevo, Canadian Maj. Gen. Lewis MacKenzie clearly placed much of the blame on the media for concern about war crimes committed against the Muslims. He testified before the United States Senate: "I think what has happened is that there have been atrocities, and those atrocities have been sophisticatedly exaggerated. Do not forget, the international media is there in big numbers in Sarajevo, and the propaganda that has been perpetuated has now entered into the minds of the people and they do not trust, and will never trust, in my estimation, the other side."[22]

In fact, MacKenzie contended that the Muslims often attacked their own people in order to win international sympathy, although State Department sources—and others—found little factual basis for his claims.[23] One prominent incident was the blast early in the crisis that had killed a number of Sarajevo civilians waiting in a bread line. Major General MacKenzie rejected the explanation that the cause had been a mortar shell fired by the Serbs. Instead he blamed unequivocally the Bosnian government, which allegedly had set off a mine to kill its own people in order to generate international sympathy for the Muslims and to have blame fall on the Serbs encircling the city. Subsequent investigative work by journalist Tom Gjelten revealed that not only did other UN personnel on the scene contradict MacKenzie's version, but so did all the available physical evidence.[24] Although MacKenzie's account of the incident mirrored the official version which the Yugoslav government had announced to deflect world criticism, he would continue to repeat it constantly in his public appearances. He used his version as his proof that all the parties were equally guilty and that the Muslims, in particular, could not be trusted. Likewise, his frequently repeated conclusion that it was the Muslims who often broke truces was also misleading. In truth, according to other UN officials there, it was the Serbs' attempting to secure tactical advantage by redeploying their forces that had led to the Muslims' violations of the truces.[25]

In his memoirs, Major General MacKenzie portrayed the Yugoslav People's Army as having been a victim of events in Bosnia-Herzegovina. His opinion of the situation, which was presumably reported at the time to his superiors, clearly reflected an inaccurate understanding of the situation. According to MacKenzie, the Yugoslav People's Army was an organization surprised by what was happening and a force that was "stuck" there. Their only objective was to get away as quickly as possible.[26] Ignored in this interpretation was the key role the Army had played in creating this situation. Not only had the Army organized, armed, and supported the Serbian militias, it had also spearheaded the seizure of territory, then later set up and supported the Bosnian Serb Army as a task force drawn from the main body of the Yugoslav People's Army.

Other UN officials at times presented equally eccentric estimates of the situation, thus tending to diminish the sense of urgency. They often resorted to euphemisms as in December, 1992, when Lt. Gen. Satish Nambiar, commander of UNPROFOR in the former Yugoslavia, gave an unwarrantedly optimistic assessment of his forces' ability to protect the Muslims. He claimed that "our presence is having a calming effect," and that he now had enough men and armor to "move into towns that are threatened by Serb attack and [to] thereby deter further shelling."[27] British Brig. Vere Hayes, chief of staff of the UN force in Bosnia-Herzegovina, insisted in mid-1993 that there was no siege around Sarajevo and contended that the 1,400 Serbian pieces of artillery ringing the city had never engaged in "humanitarian strangulation." Canadian Com. Barry Frewer, spokesman for the UN forces in Sarajevo, likewise, insisted in mid-August, 1993, that the siege had already ended and that the Serbian artillery and armor surrounding the city were instead only an "encirclement" and a "tactically advantageous position." This view echoed exactly what the Serbs had been trying to convince the West of all along.[28]

At first, most western governments hoped to play down the situation in Bosnia-Herzegovina in order to avoid having to take difficult concrete steps. The United States was initially hesitant in confirming the existence of concentration camps.[29] In general, according to a former State Department Yugoslavia desk officer, senior policy makers in both the Bush and Clinton administrations sought to soften judgments. They were reluctant to call the process in Bosnia-Herzegovina "genocide" and feared that a more direct approach might create calls for a stronger response by the United States.[30] Some officials dealing with the problem never seem to have grasped the magnitude of the victimization that was occurring. Maj. Gen. MacKenzie, for example, euphemistically spoke not of ethnic cleansing, but of a more benign "population redistribution."[31] One senior-level American military officer, intimately involved with the issue, could still assert in a briefing, which the author attended, in November, 1993, that "there has been *no* genocide in ex-Yugoslavia" [emphasis in the original]. He stressed inexplicably that only "more than one hundred thousand [have been] murdered."

Some governments also visibly dragged their feet on the process of setting up and supporting a war crimes tribunal for Bosnia. The delay may have resulted in an unintended signal to the Serbs that the international community was not that perturbed by their actions and that legal retribution would be slow in coming, if at all. According to former U.S. Assistant Secretary of State Lawrence S. Eagleburger and the former U.S. State Department Adviser for UN Affairs, Michael Scherf, Great Britain, in particular, was unenthusiastic in principle about establishing a war crimes tribunal and sought to obstruct the process in practice by withholding its cooperation.[32]

A number of observers in the media and academia in the West, too, insisted specifically that what was occurring, although perhaps deplorable, was certainly not genocide. Their argument ranged over a wide area, with their evidence often stacked for cumulative effect and redolent with euphemisms as they sought to downplay the severity of the situation. Among the key points made by one *Washington Post* columnist, for example, was that calling what was happening in Bosnia genocide would somehow cheapen or distract from the Holocaust. To that end, he held that: "Indeed, to my mind, the comparison [of the Bosnian Muslims to the Nazi-era Jews] exaggerates the crimes of the Serbs and diminishes those of the Nazis. . . . Such references not only exaggerate the problem and inject emotional terms into the debate, they also hold the Serbs to a standard of evil that they may be unwilling or unable to meet."[33] In fact, he commented that "ethnic cleansing, while indefensible, is not genocide, the attempt to eradicate a people. It is something else—an effort to rid certain Bosnian areas of Muslims. . . . The eradication of the Muslims as a people does not appear to be a goal of the Serbian Bosnians."[34] Moreover, for that writer, a decisive difference which failed his genocide test was that the Muslims were not totally defenseless, for the Jews had had neither an army nor a state, whereas the Muslims did, although, in terms of logic, that argument is a non sequitur.

Another American observer, who also denied that genocide had occurred, argued that the number of victims seemed low, which he attributed to the fact that "instead of exterminating members of other ethnic groups, the Serbs have generally expelled them from specific territories." In fact, the same analyst felt safe in concluding that, rather than dealing with a victim and a victimizer, what was occurring was only "a mundane struggle over the territorial spoils resulting from the breakup of the Yugoslav federation." If anything, both sides were morally equivalent for him, for "although it may be an especially acrimonious political divorce, it need not and should not have wider strategic or moral significance."[35] Moreover, apparently linking arbitrarily the right of other countries to condemn genocide in Bosnia-Herzegovina to their stand on all other such situations, he held that since the U.S. had failed at times to condemn similar crimes elsewhere, the "Serbs have a point when they contend that the United States and its allies employ a blatant double standard."[36]

On the contrary, one could argue that an assessment of genocide in this case is based on objective standards, not on subjective notions dependent on whether outside observers have themselves been sufficiently consistent and responsive in dealing with every such other case in recent history. Barring a revision of the standing definition of "genocide" and of "crimes against humanity" in international law, the Bosnian case fits the criteria only too well. Moreover, it is hard to argue for moral equivalency between the Bosnian and Serbian policies, which have been in no way the mirror-image of each other—either in concept or methods.

To be sure, while the numbers of those killed may well be lower than those in some other cases of genocide, there is no precise numerical threshold that has to be crossed before one can speak of "genocide." As noted earlier, genocide need not entail a group's total destruction. Rather, killing is a matter of degree, and the thoroughness displayed can vary from case to case. In fact, one sociologist cautioned, "making the definition of [genocide] a matter of percentages [of the population killed] risks creating a morality based solely on bookkeeping."[37] What is key is the willful destruction or attempted destruction of large numbers of people innocent of any specific crime other than belonging to a certain group. There is compelling evidence that the Serb authorities did indeed desire and plan for the elimination by various methods of the Bosnian Muslims' presence in its entirety and openly argued in support of that policy.

On the issue of the ratio of those actually killed to those expelled, Hitler, too, had planned "merely" to clear out large areas of Eastern Europe of its population to pave the way for German settlement as part of the New Order. As it was, in Bosnia many thousands more of those cleared out of their homes at gunpoint would probably have perished from hunger and the elements had it not been for the crucial relief and safe haven provided by foreign benefactors. That even greater numbers of Muslims were not killed can also be attributed not to the Serbs' forbearance but to the stiffening resistance by the Bosnian government and by the Serbs' growing awareness that it was best not to exceed certain parameters which could trigger a more decisive outside reaction. Serbian forces did indeed attempt to seize considerably more, if not all, of Bosnia-Herzegovina, where one can assume they would have attempted to implement the same policies as in the areas which fell under their control.

Often, those unwilling to term such behavior genocide seemed to be concerned, in particular, that U.S. intervention could follow if genocide were established. Extending their argument, they emphasized that, on the contrary, any intervention could only be based on a strategic threat, which the Serbs could not possibly pose. To clinch their argument, the point was often made that according to this criterion the Serbs could not be compared to the Nazis at all because, unlike the latter, the Serbs were not a threat to the rest of Europe. According to one analyst, the difference was that "we are not going to see Serb Panzer divisions advancing on Paris or Serb invaders conquering Ukraine as part of a quest for Lebensraum."[38]

Perhaps most inexcusable of all was the reported frequenting by UNPROFOR personnel of at least one Serb-run brothel, where non-Serb women prisoners were interned and abused.[39] While this incident involved a local, tactical-level, unofficial action, the Serbs nevertheless could have interpreted this behavior as an implicit approbation of, or indifference to, their plight, thus undermining the credibility of western protests about Serbian war crimes.

A surprising number of well-placed foreign observers also seemed to justify the Serbs' control over most of the territory of Bosnia-Herzegovina and, therefore, their policy objectives. For example, Major General Mac-Kenzie, displaying a distinct innocence of historical awareness in his attempt to inform policy, pontificated in front of a U.S. Senate committee: "Just a little bit of history—the Serbs and the Croats were peasants and farmers. That gives you a lot of territory. The Muslims were business people concentrated in four or five of the towns and villages. . . . business people do not have a lot of territory."[40]

Similarly, buying into a canard which the Serbian information program had promoted, Lord Owen and others implied that the Bosnian Serbs had a right to the territory they had seized. According to Lord Owen: "They've [the Serbs] always had 60 percent [of the territory in Bosnia] before the war. They were the rural people. . . . The Serbs are actually occupying less land than they were before the war."[41] Cyrus Vance used his claim that the "Serbs had settled on and owned 60 percent of Bosnia's territory before the fighting began" as a clinching argument to counter criticism about the large amount of territory allotted to the Serbs under the Vance-Owen Plan.[42]

Actually, what the Bosnian Serbs may have owned was a high proportion of the private property, thanks to preferential land regulations dating from the interwar period, when many Muslim landowners were dispossessed. However, private property accounts for about 2.375 million hectares of Bosnia-Herzegovina's total area of 5.113 million hectares, or some 46 percent. Even if the Serbs did own 60 percent of this private property, that would account for less than 28 percent of the country's area.[43] No ethnic group owns the roads, mountains, lakes, or public lands, which constitute the majority of Bosnia-Herzegovina's territory. In no way could land ownership (even of 28 percent of the country's area) have been construed as a rationale for expansion by force of arms and the accompanying depopulation of the areas seized.

Often, a vague familiarity with history and a misreading of the Serb leadership's objectives combined to provide the basis for rationalizing, if not justifying, the Serbs' overall policy and the specific acts of genocide being used to achieve it. Thus, negotiator Lord Owen seemed to explain Serb actions on their behalf, noting that the Serbs had been the victims of genocide during World War II. Furthermore, he claimed: "It is a basic fear that they will be forced to live under a Muslim domination and that they will be deprived of their basic nationalism, if you like. I mean the Serbs are a great nation, despite all these horrible things that have been done. This is not typical of these people."[44]

Lord Owen further claimed that the Serbs were the sole victims of genocide in Yugoslavia during World War II at the hands of both Croatians and Muslims. This unfounded argument remained an enduring element in his understanding of more recent events and was repeated time and again in his assessments.

At the same time, some foreign observers also downplayed the role of specific Serbian institutions, such as the Orthodox Church, on the unfolding of events in Bosnia-Herzegovina. Speaking of war crimes, Lord Owen seemed to exclude the Orthodox Church from any responsibility. He noted that what had happened in Bosnia-Herzegovina was an aberration, something that may have happened despite the Orthodox Church. After all, "Serbia is a religious country," and such acts went "against all the tenets of the Serbian Church."[45] Even as late as February, 1994, he continued to balance his commentary on the advisability of war crime trials of alleged Serb perpetrators by noting that "Serbia is, again, a great country. And we must recognize that the Serbs have got genuine grievances."[46]

Again, in late March, 1994, when the Bosnian Serb Army renewed its assault on the eastern Bosnian enclave of Goražde, with the intent of eliminating it, some UNPROFOR officials went out of their way to downplay the gravity of the situation at first. One unspecified senior UN official attributed the Serb action to the fact that the Serbs "feel threatened and excluded by the [newly established Croatian-Muslim Bosnian] federation."[47] In fact, the Serbs' exclusion had been by their own choice, and the removal of such enclaves had already been a declared Serbian goal long before the federation had even been discussed. UNPROFOR commander Lieutenant General Rose called what were already all-out Serb attacks "limited military moves." He stressed that, in any event, his first priority was to ensure that relief aid got through and that this mission was not being threatened. A few days later, despite the Serbs' seizure of a dominant position which gave them direct line of sight into the town, Rose's spokesman, Maj. Bob Amnink, shared with foreign journalists his superior's somewhat reassuring but, as it turned out, naive assessment. He stated that "we do not think Goražde is under imminent threat of being taken because it is strongly defended, and we do not believe the Serbs actually want to take the town."[48]

More fundamentally, the common portrayal of the situation in Bosnia-Herzegovina was usually as a civil war, and often as a substitute for analysis. As Lord Owen concluded with some finality: "I mean, the fact is there is a civil war. It's become more apparent that there's civil war."[49] Whatever the accuracy of his appraisal, Lord Owen was certainly confident when he elaborated: "One side in the civil war was aided and abetted, if you like, by Serbia from outside. But you are essentially dealing with a conflict between people who live in Bosnia-Herzegovina. . . . The next most extraordinary thing is they're all from the same ethnic group. . . . They are the same ethnic people."[50] Drawing a questionable dichotomy between "aggression" and "civil war," he concluded that "I'm also careful not to use the simplistic classification of 'aggression' because this is both a civil war and a war of aggression. The Bosnian Serbs are fighting for territory in which they have lived for centuries."[51] Frequently expressing his "indignation [with] the horror of it," he nevertheless accepted the incidents as par for the course: "Civil war's a horrible business."[52] If anything, for Lord Owen, that was the direction which the situation had increasingly taken. Speaking in 1994, he said: "There's no doubt that there was aggression at the early stages of the war. . . . as the war went on, it became more of a civil war, more of a history, more of a village on village war."[53]

This attitude implied that the basic flow of events was more and more of a substantially spontaneous or haphazard nature occurring at a local level. Thus, the events were not part of a grander strategy and neither controlled nor controllable by higher authorities. A logical corollary for those who focused on such arguments was that resolute action would be tantamount to taking sides and should therefore be avoided. As Lord Owen and others stressed repeatedly, intervention by the international community would be considerably less appropriate if the conflict were simply a domestic one. As such, Owen opposed lifting the arms embargo and air strikes, which the United States favored, since, by doing so, "he [President Clinton] will put the United States on the side of the Muslims."[54]

Another implicit, but key, corollary of this questionable assumption was that all sides had the same basic goals, methods, and responsibility. In fact, for Major General MacKenzie, there was little difference between the Muslims and the Serbs, commonly viewed as, respectively, the victims and aggressors. As he left Sarajevo in August, 1992, MacKenzie responded thus to a question on where the blame lay: "On a particular day of a particular month, you'd better ask who the bad boy is in this particular operation, and depending on what day of what month, you might well have a different answer."[55] Testifying before Congress in May, 1993, he pushed this view further by using an analogy: "Dealing with Bosnia is a little like dealing with three serial killers—one has killed fifteen, one has killed ten, one has killed five. Do we help the one that's only killed five?"[56] Writing in the *Army Times*, a weekly publication that is widely read by U.S. Army personnel, an American analyst claimed in the same vein, "There are no good guys."

Perhaps expressing an extreme, but not isolated, viewpoint based on this premise, the same analyst concluded, "If you want a permanent solution to ethnic hatred and violence in what was Yugoslavia, you would have to kill every living thing in the region."[57]

The readiness to assign equal blame soon became almost an automatic reaction for some officials. Commander Frewer, on one occasion, blamed the blocking of relief supplies to Sarajevo on both the Serbs and the Muslims. Eventually, he was obliged to back off this accusation when he was unable to cite any cases of the Muslims having done so.[58] The attitude of assigning equal blame easily led to treating all the parties as equally legitimate players with similar goals. It also led, as a corollary, to the perceived need on the part of foreign mediators to ensure equally the interests of all the parties in formulating solutions. The usual justification for ensuring everyone's position equally was that of merely recognizing reality.

This approach ignored the identity of the vast majority of the victims. Equally significantly, the actual situation was distorted when the goals of the Muslim and Serb leadership were equated. Whereas the Bosnian Serb movement entailed a revival of the wartime Chetnik movement and its destructive racist goals, the Bosnian government had no link to the wartime Ustaše movement. This difference was reflected in the Muslim leadership's stated and operative goal of a multiconfessional, secular state, with no intention of eliminating any community, violently or otherwise. For the Bosnian Serbs, the avowed objective was partition along ethnic lines and the physical elimination of other ethnic groups.

Perhaps nowhere were the two diametrically different perspectives captured so succinctly as in the question presented to the voters in Bosnia-Herzegovina's two referendums. In the Serb-only referendum of November, 1991, voters were asked to cast ballots for or against the ethnically exclusive proposal of whether to "remain in Yugoslavia together with the Serbs of Serbia, Montenegro, Krajina, Vojvodina, and Kosovo." In the referendum, which the Bosnian government held in February, 1992, on the contrary, the question was far less exclusionary: "Are you in favor of a sovereign and independent Bosnia-Herzegovina, a state of equal citizens, constituted by the peoples of Bosnia-Herzegovina: the Muslims, Serbs, Croatians, and members of the other peoples who live there?"

9. Spin-Off War Crimes in Bosnia-Herzegovina

The Victimization Process

Enough evidence already exists to predict the potential for "spin-off geno-cide" in the former Yugoslavia, illustrated by the breakdown that occurred in Croatian-Muslim relations. Perhaps what encouraged the Croatian HVO organization to undertake its own ethnic cleansing against the Muslims in 1993 was its cost-benefit assessment in the wake of the successful and relatively low-cost Serbian experience. Similarly, in the increasingly intol-erant environment which resulted, even some Muslims themselves started to retaliate against others, though in the latter case it seems to have often been a new and unsanctioned policy born of desperation rather than from a desire for expansion.

The Croatians as Perpetrators

Although much less extensive than the Serbian actions, serious war crimes against the Muslims were also committed by Bosnia-Herzegovina's local Croatian authorities. Indeed, tensions in the original Croatian-Muslim alli-ance had developed as soon as the pro-partition faction, headed by Mate Boban, had become dominant. This faction achieved its position over the Bosnian Croatian community's branch of the ruling party of Croatia, the Croatian Democratic Union (Hrvatska Demokratska Zajednica—HDZ), and its local military arm, the HVO. The Tudjman government, with a probable eye toward partitioning Bosnia-Herzegovina, had helped engineer Boban's takeover. It was able to establish a controlling capability over the HVO through its economic subsidies, security assistance, and direct military support by regular forces from the Croatian Army operating in Bosnia-Herzegovina. The very consolidation of this militant faction within the HVO was facilitated by the inability of the woefully underarmed Bosnian government to establish its authority throughout the country. Also helping the situation along was the Zagreb government's eventual assessment that more could be gained by partition or by cooperating with the Serbs than by cooperating with a weak Bosnian government. Both strategically and morally cooperating with the Serbs made little sense in the long run.

PREPARING THE GROUND. The government-controlled portion of the media in Croatia had already set anti-Muslim rhetoric into motion by late 1992. By early 1993 slanted media coverage had escalated, although it was not always based on religious themes. Initially, accusations most often centered on charges against officials in the Bosnian government by alleging their cooperation with KOS, the Yugoslav military intelligence. However, the focus increasingly shifted to Islam, with news reports about "fundamentalist extremism" and an alleged threat to Western civilization.

By early November, 1992, Croatia's hard-line Defense Minister, Gojko Šušak (originally from Bosnia-Herzegovina) sought to use a threat of "Islamic fundamentalism" to court Israeli support, believing the argument would find resonance there. He alleged that there were 110,000 Bosnian Muslims studying in Cairo alone and appealed to his Israeli audience by asking, "Can you imagine a fundamentalist state in the heart of Europe?"[1] Tudjman, likewise, referred often to a threat of "Islamic fundamentalism," and to an "Islamic holy war." He justified Croatia's policy by maintaining that the goal of the Bosnian government was allegedly to set up "an Islamic state in Europe," which was part of a "conflict between the Islamic and Catholic worlds," and of "a confrontation between the Islamic world and the West."[2]

The portion of Croatia's media which is government-controlled also routinely presented exaggerated accounts of Muslim attacks against Croatians, often by means of HVO representatives and reporters from Bosnia-Herzegovina, who seemed to enjoy privileged access to television newscasts. One of them in particular, Smiljko Šagolj, became associated in the public eye with such shrill tirades. Although opinion polls in Croatia indicated strong doubts about the reliability of such reporting, this steady irresponsible campaign contributed to an increasingly hostile attitude toward Muslim refugees among many ordinary citizens in Croatia. However, despite complaints about an upsurge in officially instigated harassment by the police and thinly veiled threats by Tudjman himself, such as one in a July 5, 1993 press conference threatening to expel the Muslim refugees, over a quarter million Muslims nevertheless found refuge in Croatia.

Instances of localized fighting between HVO forces and Bosnian government forces had already occurred on a number of occasions in late 1992 and early 1993. However, the line into genocide was not really crossed until the spring of 1993. It was then that officially sanctioned HVO forces began to attack and expel the Muslim population from their homes, preparing for what they thought would be the ultimate partition mandated by the Vance-Owen Plan. In essence, they were following a strategy driven by concrete political interests as interpreted by Tudjman and his fellow thinkers in the HVO.

An argument can be made that the Vance-Owen Plan perhaps consciously sought to split the rickety Muslim-Croatian alliance in order to facilitate movement on talks, since international mediators had viewed the alliance as a factor encouraging the Muslims to reject agreements tabled up to that point. The plan, which allocated to the Croatian community far more land than either its population or existing control warranted, apparently enticed Boban and the HVO to adopt the same strategy as had been pioneered by the Serbs with success. In February, 1993, according to Jadranko Prlić, the prime minister of the emerging Croatian HVO-run zone, the Vance-Owen Plan gave the "Croats, like the Serbs, carte blanche to divide the country along ethnic lines." He scornfully dismissed the Muslims as not constituting a nation.[3] Having interpreted the plan as a green light, the HVO proceeded to try to seize additional areas from the hard-pressed Bosnian government, especially in central Bosnia and around the city of Mostar, and including areas where Croatians were in a distinct minority. In part, the HVO's adoption of this policy may also have stemmed from a miscalculation that the Muslims would be easy prey. This conclusion had been based on the success the Serbian forces had had against them and on the Bosnian Army's limited military equipment. HVO commanders had reportedly boasted that the Muslims were poor fighters and that the HVO could deal with them in a single day, a misperception apparently shared by Boban himself.[4]

IMPLEMENTATION AND DENIAL. As part of its strategy to control territory and to sharpen ethnic tensions meant to hasten partition, the HVO had recourse to harsh measures. This approach included setting up its own concentration camps for Muslim civilians in the Mostar area and elsewhere, where thousands were held in dreadful conditions and abused, despite cynical claims that they were being held prisoner only "for their own safety."[5] In order to compel people to leave, the HVO also attempted to cut off UN relief convoys to Muslim settlements by blocking them and by attacking the civilian drivers.[6]

In the process of expelling Muslim residents from a wide area, HVO forces were guilty of massacres, most notably the brutal killings in the village of Ahmići. At first, the HVO tried to deny responsibility for Ahmići, blaming instead the Bosnian Serbs, Bosnian Croatian irregulars, and even the Muslims themselves.[7] The Tudjman government in Zagreb came to Boban's defense, in part by laying all the blame on the Muslims for the situation.[8] The pro-government weekly *Danas* even attributed Croatian atrocities to British intelligence operatives, who allegedly had acted as *agents provocateurs*.[9]

While the HVO later suggested that it was rogue HVO elements who were responsible for the atrocities, it was clear that the HVO leadership continued to promote the same overall policy that made such atrocities likely. Furthermore, although Boban himself promised to investigate and punish all such crimes, nothing resulted from such pronouncements. Boban, on the contrary, sought to deflect criticism with the dubious logic that all these incidents were in the nature of war. Besides, he claimed, other countries had engaged in similar activities in the past. He continued: "Every war is horrible, and I would note that those who lecture us today on morals are themselves stained in this regard. Name for me just one great world power that would not wage an immoral war."[10] While HVO representatives, responding to international pressure and counsel from Zagreb, subsequently committed themselves to end such practices, HVO forces nevertheless reportedly continued their involvement in atrocities, including the destruction of mosques.

The HVO worked for complete ethnic separation even to the extent of urging Croatians to abandon areas under HVO control but outside the Herceg-Bosna entity that the HVO had set up. Boban himself went on the radio with inducements of resettlement to Croatia's coastal regions of Dalmatia and Istra for those Croatians who agreed to leave their homes in central Bosnia.[11]

To be sure, there were Croatians, as there had been Serbs, clergy included, in Bosnia-Herzegovina who sought to help Muslims in distress.[12] Individual members of the HVO were often disgusted themselves by what they were ordered to do. One militiaman told a Muslim refugee and former friend, whom he met subsequently in Croatia, that he had been ordered to take Muslim women and children by bus and deposit them outside the city. He confessed: "That was my most awful day. All those women and children knew me and were calling me by name, asking for water. The children were crying because they were thirsty. But our commander refused to let us give them water, saying 'We do not provide water to Muslims. Let God give them water.'"[13]

Opposition could be dangerous, as Bosnian Croatians who disagreed with the HVO's anti-Muslim policies were brushed aside or even liquidated physically. At times, Croatians unwilling to go along with HVO policy were imprisoned alongside their Muslim neighbors.[14] In order to clear the way for the attack and massacre on the Muslim village of Stupni Do in October, 1993, HVO forces from outside the area had reportedly engineered the removal and arrest of local HVO officials and had undertaken the intimidation of ordinary Croatians who were opposed to the ethnic cleansing plan.[15] Whatever dismay others may have felt toward Boban's views, it was Boban and his entourage who controlled the coercive power over most of the Croatian community in southern Bosnia-Herzegovina. The continued backing of the Tudjman government was crucial in allowing him to determine policy locally.

Croatian Opposition to Ethnic Cleansing

Both in Croatia and in the Croatian community in Bosnia-Herzegovina this strategy did not go unchallenged. Croatia lacks a genuine anti-Islamic tradition in modern times. Notwithstanding well-documented atrocities against the Muslims (and equally violent retaliation by them) in Bosnia-Herzegovina, the anti-Muslim media campaign in Croatia did not develop the broad scope, racist tinge, or legitimacy that its Serbian equivalent did.

Nor was an anti-Islamic policy implemented everywhere. In areas beyond Boban's direct control in Bosnia-Herzegovina itself, as in the north, in the Tuzla area, and in Sarajevo, Muslim-Croatian cooperation continued, despite often considerably more tense relations. The Croatian deputy mayor of Sarajevo, for example, condemned the HVO's atrocities, while the HVO commander in Sarajevo confirmed that the local HVO and the Bosnian Army were still united in defending the city.[16] Although, by November, 1993 the Bosnian government had carried out the incorporation of the HVO structure in Sarajevo into the Bosnian Army, the plan was carried out without any loss of life, and Croatians continued to defend the city. In northern Bosnia, in the area of the Posavina corridor abutting Croatia, the local HVO also emphasized cooperation with the Muslims, including operations by mixed units. The local HVO explicitly distanced itself from Boban's approach.

At least until the large-scale clashes of 1993, public opinion in Croatia was also favorably inclined toward the Muslims. Initially, there had been overwhelming popular support for an alliance with Bosnia-Herzegovina (by a two-to-one margin) and for providing security assistance to them (by a four-to-one margin). Even after the spring, 1993 fighting, only 46 percent of those polled in Croatia declared themselves in favor of partitioning Bosnia-Herzegovina along ethnic lines. However, after continued Croatian-Muslim fighting and the intensive one-sided government-sponsored information campaign, opinion seemed to become increasingly less favorable toward Muslims. By August, 1993, over 71 percent of those polled in Croatia opposed a united Croatian-Muslim state in Bosnia-Herzegovina. However, in early 1994, following the HVO's embarrassing reverses on the ground and of increasing questions about the Zagreb government's inept handling of the situation, fewer than 15 percent of those polled in Croatia were in favor of partitioning Bosnia-Herzegovina along ethnic lines. Most of the rest of those polled supported some form of unified Bosnian state. Following the February, 1994 agreement for a federated Croatian-Muslim state, fewer than 30 percent of those polled in Croatia viewed the result negatively, although a large plurality of those responding also viewed negatively the prospects of Croatia's confederation with Bosnia-Herzegovina.[17] In the latter case, however, the results may reflect the Croatian public's reluctance to be tied not only to the Muslims but also to the Croatians of Herzegovina, who have attracted growing resentment, based in part on the perception that they had dragged Croatia into a needless war.

In fact, there was considerable dismay in Croatia with the HVO and with Tudjman's policy, and Tudjman lashed out at his domestic critics on this issue. Even Croatia's ruling HDZ itself was split, with a more liberal wing opposing Tudjman's anti-Muslim tilt. Tudjman subsequently removed or shunted aside a succession of officials from his government for disagreeing with him on this question. Disagreement within the HDZ's policy came into the open in January, 1994. Father Tomislav Duka, the only cleric in Croatia's Parliament, clashed with another representative, Antun Vrdoljak, who was then also the director of Croatia's state radio and TV as well as a close associate of Tudjman's. In a heated exchange, Father Duka challenged Vrdoljak's exaggerated reports of Muslim oppression of Catholics and his tendentious reading of Izetbegović's philosophical work *The Islamic Declaration.* Basing his argument on that booklet, Vrdoljak—a political figure known equally for his uncompromising stands on Bosnia and for his pompous attitude—sought to prove that the war in Bosnia-Herzegovina was the inevitable result of "a Muslim fundamentalist policy." Father Duka argued, instead, for renewed Croatian-Muslim cooperation and for a unified Bosnia-Herzegovina. This plea, in turn, was to spark an accusation by Vrdoljak that Father Duka was "an enemy of official Croatian policy."[18] In a subsequent roundtable, Father Duka, undeterred, reiterated his belief in coexistence and in a unified Bosnia-Herzegovina. He stressed: "Neither Milošević nor Owen nor Tudjman nor Alija Izetbegović, nor the devil himself, and much less Mate Boban has the right to divide up Bosnia! Bosnia and Herzegovina is indivisible! . . . Bosnia and Herzegovina is a single unit in which diverse ethnic, religious, and cultural communities live, communities which for almost one thousand years have shown that they can live together, despite internal conflicts."[19] Disagreement with Tudjman's policy toward Bosnia-Herzegovina led to the abandonment of the HDZ by some of its officials in March, 1994.

Institutional Opposition to Anti-Islamic Policies

Significantly, moreover, whatever the similarities between the conduct of Croatia and Serbia vis-à-vis Bosnia-Herzegovina, a fundamental characteristic differentiated the two: not only individuals but influential institutions in Croatia and in the Croatian community in Bosnia itself came out against any persecution of the Muslims and against the ethnic partition of the country. Such institutional critics included the Catholic Church, virtually all the opposition parties, and many cultural bodies, such as the Matica Hrvatska, Croatia's leading intellectual organization, as well as an emerging political body of Croatians in Bosnia-Herzegovina itself. Ultimately, such organized opposition deprived Tudjman's and Boban's policy of the legitimacy and consensus needed to weather setbacks on the ground and may have been one of the deciding factors which led to the reversal in policy in early 1994.

THE CATHOLIC CHURCH'S OPPOSITION TO GENOCIDE. The Catholic Church in Croatia was one of the earliest and most resolute critics against the anti-Islamic policy. In the late 1980s, the Catholic Church in Croatia was then perhaps the only voice independent of Zagreb's Communist government. As the anti-Muslim campaign was gathering force in Serbia, however, the Catholic Church in Croatia, had publicly protested against anti-Muslim attacks despite the threat of official retaliation.[20] In an appeal for peace in May, 1993, following the first major Croatian-Muslim clashes and HVO atrocities, Cardinal Franjo Kuharić, Metropolitan of Zagreb, expressed his consternation. He blamed the conflict in Bosnia-Herzegovina squarely on the local Croatian authorities as he spoke of "war crimes" by the HVO against the Muslims. His statements triggered Boban to issue an unusually insulting public reply, in which he rejected any coexistence with the Muslims and castigated the Cardinal in harsh terms for his stand. The Croatian government joined Boban in rebuking the Cardinal, with Defense Minister Šušak (whom Tudjman had delegated to manage Croatia's policy in Bosnia-Herzegovina) cynically inviting Cardinal Kuharić to go to Herzegovina to become "better informed."[21]

While a few in the local Catholic hierarchy in Herzegovina seems to have supported Boban and the HVO's actions and helped to spread an anti-Islamic message (fig. 1), Croatia's clergy and most of Bosnia's Catholic hierarchy backed Cardinal Kuharić solidly.[22] The editor of the Catholic Church's official publication, *Glas Koncila*, for example, reiterated the Church's continued stand, noting that the "Church is resolutely against ethnic cleansing. . . . If Croatia's government leadership is obliged to accept some less humane solution, the Church will not bless it."[23]

Likewise, Brother Petar Andjelović, provincial, or superior, of the Franciscan order in Bosnia, excoriated Boban's actions as "bordering on scandal." The Provincial, who had accompanied Izetbegović on a diplomatic mission to the Vatican to seek support for Bosnia-Herzegovina, also spoke out against the Croatian-run concentration camps. Asked if he had visited any, he replied sarcastically: "Visiting the camps is a privilege of the 'favored.' I wanted to do so, but was unable to. According to the account of eyewitnesses, such camps exist and ugly things go on in them."[24] At the same time, Brother Andjelović criticized Croatia's media for spreading exaggerated accounts of Muslim atrocities for political purposes. He noted: "False information is of little help in a propaganda war. The truth eventually triumphs, while the harm from false information becomes even greater. In truth, one

The cartoon depicts the United Nations shielding a Muslim fez and bloodied dagger, implying that the UN approves of and is implicated in Muslim atrocities. Published in *Crkva na kamenu* (the official organ of the Catholic Church in Herzegovina), in Mostar, Bosnia-Herzegovina, August–September, 1993, by Ante Markovic.

must say that Muslim units have not mistreated either priests or nuns. They have not destroyed religious buildings, unlike what Serbian, and Croatian, units have done."[25]

Similarly, at the height of the HVO-Muslim fighting, the Catholic bishop of Banja Luka met publicly with representatives of the city's Muslim community to express his solidarity with them after two of the city's mosques had been blown up by the Serbs.[26] Sarajevo's Catholic archbishop, Vinko Puljić, also resisted pressure by the HVO leadership for him to move to HVO-controlled territory as a sign of protest against the Bosnian government and the Muslims and preferred instead to stay on in Sarajevo to show his support for communal cooperation. In August, 1993, he attended the Bosnian government's official independence celebration in Sarajevo rather than the simultaneous ceremony held by the HVO proclaiming Herceg-Bosna's independence in the town of Grude, to which he had been invited.

In a clear move also to distance itself from actions by the Boban circle, an editorial in *Glas Koncila* commented on the presence of local clerics at the proclamation of Herceg-Bosna's independence under the auspices of the HVO: "This cannot in any way be understood as a blessing [by the Church] of all that has happened so far, of what is happening, or what may happen on the territory of the Croatian Republic of Herceg-Bosna."[27]

Even the faculty and students of the Franciscan seminary in Sarajevo,, who had found refuge from the war in Samobor, Croatia, and who therefore might have been expected to be under pressure from the Zagreb government to go along with its policies, came out instead strongly in June, 1993 in support of a unified Bosnia and interreligious cooperation and tolerance. In a later interview, their rector condemned the premise that intercommunal life was not possible in Bosnia-Herzegovina, as the HVO preached. He declaring instead: "As a human being and a believer, I find the position that coexistence among people of different nations, cultures, and religions is impossible to be totally incomprehensible and unacceptable. Only people with a racist, nihilistic, and atheist view of life can promote that. To conduct a war in the name of such a goal and to ask that blood and lives be given for something like that is completely inhuman."[28] Their stance earned the Franciscans Boban's undisguised ire. Boban replied, "The only ones who can philosophize are those friars and priests who idle away their time in the salons of Zagreb and who meet with the president of their state of Bosnia [Izetbegović]."[29]

POLITICAL OPPOSITION TO GENOCIDE. In the political arena, influential portions of the Croatian political elite also expressed their strong condemnation of the HVO's actions and of the Croatian government's basic policy of support for the HVO and the partition of Bosnia-Herzegovina. Virtually all of Croatia's opposition parties, including the largest one, the Croatian Social Liberal Union (HSLS), expressed their disagreement with the anti-Islamic stance. The head of the HSLS, Dražen Budiša, for example, had stinging criticism for the Tudjman-Boban policy, claiming that the "Muslims could indeed become our greatest enemies, but only through our own fault."

Instead he proposed "offering a hand of conciliation to the Muslims."[30] This statement led an angry Boban to strike out against "those gentlemen who, from their party meetings and from Parliament in Zagreb, give us lessons without knowing anything about what is happening here and without showing the least willingness to understand and to help us." Responding to the demand by Croatia's opposition parties that the HVO and the HVO-controlled Herceg-Bosna entity be disbanded, Boban dismissed them indignantly, contending that "Alija [Izetbegović] could cooperate with them on that basis."[31]

Although even the independent press in Croatia at times got caught up in the government-promoted anti-Islamic campaign, for the most part its treatment of the Muslims was considerably more sympathetic and balanced than that in the pro-government print and electronic media.[32] The independent Croatian media's approach included critical reporting about Croatian-run concentration camps where Muslims were being held and the lampooning of Boban himself for his inhumane actions (fig. 2).

The independent Zagreb mass-circulation weekly *Globus,* for example, deconstructed the HVO's propaganda case which claimed that the Bosnian government had formulated plans to massacre Croatian civilians. *Globus,* however, showed that the documents which the HVO had adduced as proof were actually HVO forgeries. In the process, *Globus* undertook a critical review of the HVO's lack of overall credibility, its anti-Muslim policy, and its negative influence on Croatia's policy toward Bosnia-Herzegovina.[33] Another independent publication, *Magazin Glas Slavonije,* noting that in Croatia the term "fundamentalism" was often abused for political ends, took to task Croatia's defense minister for his anti-Islamic tirades to foreign audiences by pointedly asking, "Who, in the end, runs this country's foreign policy?"[34]

With time, those Croatians in Bosnia-Herzegovina opposed to the HVO policies also became organized. In January, 1994 Croatian representatives opposed to the HVO policy attended the Geneva conference as part of the Bosnia-Herzegovina government delegation, much to the HVO's dismay. They also formed the Croatian National Council (Hrvatsko Narodno Vijeće— HNV) and in February, 1994, held their congress in Sarajevo. Enjoying the official backing of the Catholic Church, the HNV's platform called for a united Bosnia-Herzegovina organized in cantons and rejected the HVO's goal of ethnic partition and its methods. To meet this direct challenge to its legitimacy, the HVO organized a counter-congress in Herceg-Bosna. Predic-

The cartoon depicts Mate Boban as the owner of a tavern, serving emaciated customers, representing prisoners. The black humor highlights the miserable treatment in the HVO-operated detention camps. The sign reads: "Herceg-Bosna Croatian Union [i.e., the name of the political entity of Herceg-Bosna, led by Boban], Mate's: The Ideal Place to Lose Excess Weight." Published in *Nedjeljna Dalmacija,* Split, Croatia, September 15, 1993, by Nikola Listes.

tably, the HVO congress accused the Croatian body meeting in Sarajevo of "flirting dangerously with high treason," and the HVO's defense minister labeled the Sarajevo gathering "Alija Izetbegović's Trojan horse" and its participants "a suborned and manipulated crowd."[35]

The Possibilities of Change

By late summer 1993, Tudjman—followed by the pro-government media—had begun to discard most references to a "fundamentalist" threat. His actions may have been in response to the criticism at home for what many were now calling a disastrous policy coupled with the realization that foreign audiences did not find the message credible. While continuing to lay all blame for the Croatian-Muslim fighting on the Muslims, the focus, however negative, was now placed on the Muslims as a political community rather than as a cultural and religious menace. Tudjman, nevertheless, revived such rhetoric on occasion. In a press conference in November, 1993, Tudjman offered an unsolicited defense of the "western world," while dwelling on "a certain kind of Islamic irrational attitude" in explaining why the Bosnian government continued to fight on.[36]

Izetbegović had offered a union between Croatia and Bosnia-Herzegovina in August, 1993, reportedly proposing to Tudjman: "Let us no longer have borders. Let Croatia extend to the Drina [River], if you want, and us to the [Adriatic] sea. . . . As for the Croatians, I believe, that the majority of them—apart from Boban—want [a unified Bosnia]."[37] At the time, Tudjman had rejected the possibility, and fighting had continued. By early 1994, though, the Tudjman government had decided that concrete interests dictated yet another change in Croatia's policy toward the Bosnian government, necessitating an abandonment of earlier efforts to split up the country. The goal of a separate Herceg-Bosna entity was dropped quietly in favor of a federated state, based on mutual benefit for both communities. Tudjman and Izetbegović now appeared to seriously consider negotiations toward renewed cooperation, including the possibility of setting up a confederation between Croatia and a federated Muslim-Croatian Bosnian state. As part of this policy shift, Boban was obliged to leave the political scene in February, although he and other hard-liners from his circle remained in the background. In Croatia, the state-controlled media discarded its anti-Muslim rhetoric. Tudjman did also, although he revealed a disturbing propensity to adhere to old analytical paradigms. In April, 1994 he concluded that the West had favored the Croatian-Muslim deal because the West wanted to prevent an "extremist fundamentalist mujahedin Islamic state" from being formed in Bosnia-Herzegovina, a comment all the more tactless as it was made in an interview meant for Bosnian television.[38] Moreover, the official Croatian media continued to treat the Croatian-run Herceg-Bosna entity as a legitimate body, contrary to the spirit of the Washington Agreement. Extremist elements within the Herceg-Bosna power structure, with or without Tudjman's approval, still sought to undermine a lasting accommodation, using such means as blowing up the mosque in Livno in April, 1994.[39] Moreover, in July, 1994, an inveterate anti-Muslim, Dario Kordić, was chosen leader of the HDZ in Bosnia-Herzegovina, despite strong indications that he had been responsible for war crimes in central Bosnia. His selection supposedly came about thanks to the decisive backing by Tudjman, who reportedly sent a senior official, Ivić Pašalić, to the local HDZ conference in Mostar with instructions to select Kordić over more conciliatory candidates. This development seemed to raise doubts about the sincerity of some key officials in Zagreb toward long-term cooperation with the Muslims and their acceptance of a unified Bosnia-Herzegovina.[40]

International pressure, including the threat of economic sanctions and accompanying economic and political incentives, no doubt played an important role in Zagreb's policy reversal. Washington's active mediating role in the process, too, can be viewed as a notable diplomatic achievement. Perhaps more important, however, as some observers have suggested, was the opposition to Tudjman's policy on Bosnia by domestic institutions and the push for change by officials within Tudjman's own government, such as by Foreign Minister Mate Granić.[41] Arguably, though, the catalyst was the Croatian forces' difficult position in central Bosnia in the wake of continuing military setbacks to the HVO. After all, even after the threat of sanctions was delivered by the United States in the first week of January, 1994, Tudjman had continued to escalate Croatia's military presence in Bosnia-Herzegovina. This action resulted in the deployment of at least several thousand troops by the end of January, 1994 to deal with the improving Bosnian Army, which had become better organized in the last half of 1993 and had acquired more—mostly light—weapons.[42] Despite the reinforcements, however, Bosnian victories in the field and the Sarajevo government's strengthened military position against the HVO now threatened Tudjman with a potential policy disaster. He now faced the prospect of having to mobilize and dispatch even more regular forces from Croatia. This unpopular move in itself had already triggered domestic discontent and could have undercut his position at home.

Whether the Sarajevo-Zagreb rapprochement proved to be a definitive turning point or a future failure, it nevertheless underlined the importance of changing the military balance as a prelude to negotiations. Had the Bosnian government forces been unable to check the HVO on the ground and had HVO forces taken additional territory at low cost, even if needing regular Croatian reinforcements, it is unlikely that Tudjman would have acquiesced to negotiations, despite the pressure of potential sanctions. Tudjman may have assented then only if such talks had been based on stopping operations in exchange for a recognition of a new status quo confirming HVO gains. In addition, this sequence of events once again illustrated the centrality of political interests in determining policy and the relative fluidity of alliances. The pattern, however, is at variance with foreign paradigms that are based on the implacability and irrationality of "centuries of hatred" as an analytical tool.

Retaliation by the Victims

After prolonged brutalization, accompanied by a sense of hopelessness and a feeling of abandonment by the international community, some elements among the Muslims were tempted to turn increasingly on members of other communities. Even average Muslims at times themselves became more accepting of indiscriminate violence as the normal way of doing business.[43]

In some parts of Bosnia-Herzegovina by mid-1933, forcing out non-Muslims was eventually considered a means of survival, as the Muslims tried to salvage territory following Serbian and Croatian drives to deprive them of as much land as possible prior to partition. Muslim retaliation against the Croatian community began to occur on a regular basis and, by the end of the summer of 1993, the Bosnian Army had eliminated thirty-three Catholic parishes in central Bosnia. In the process, Muslim forces had also committed atrocities, such as the September, 1993 massacre of the Croatian population of the village of Uzdol and similar attacks elsewhere in the Vareš area. These actions included the killing of civilians, deportations, rape, attacks on churches, and the burning and looting of villages.[44] With the Croatian-Muslim agreement in 1994, the Bosnian government was able to bring such elements under control and to stop the attacks by arresting and bringing to trial some perpetrators, such as the murderers of two Franciscan monks in the Fojnica monastery.

In a way, this turn of events may have been the consequence of the Muslims' own tragedy, and a lesson of the radicalization which victimization can engender. Although Izetbegović had continued to call for coexistence and Serbs and Croatians continued to live together in many areas under the control of the Bosnian government, such as Sarajevo and Tuzla, radical elements in the Muslim community ignored these efforts toward cooperation. They concluded, instead, that ethnic cleansing may indeed be a rational alternative, since the international community was not likely to act effectively to save the Muslims. Furthermore, this policy would provide the Muslim community more territory without fear of international reprisal.

The ultimate irony may be that in cases of genocide, if stable and just solutions are absent, some in the victimized group may themselves develop a strategy of despair and a process of brutalization, based on their own feelings that they have been abandoned with no redress. They may subsequently come to believe that they have nothing to lose by adopting the methods of their tormentors in order to survive. Or, they may simply decide that they have a right to retaliate. Of course, revenge may often not be desired, much less carried out, by the victims themselves but by others from their community. Others may exploit the situation for their own ends by attacking individuals who may themselves be completely innocent. Such a process appears to have occurred as a result of World War II, as former inmates of Nazi death camps used similar methods when they were themselves permitted to set up camps for German civilians in Eastern Europe in 1945.[45]

If and when final partition is implemented, unless the reconfigured Bosnian state includes adequate territory, the cramming of hundreds of thousands of uprooted Muslims—including potential refugees from the Sandžak—into a small area could in itself lead to the radicalization of part of the traumatized population inhabiting the new state. The area could become by default an increasingly Muslim-majority entity. The pressures might then lead to retaliation—even if not sanctioned officially—against the remaining Serbs there, who might now be seen as part of the enemy camp responsible for the Muslims' plight.

10. Stopping Genocide

Could More Have Been Done?

Whatever the international community's policy toward Bosnia-Herzegovina and whatever measures of success it used, it failed to prevent genocide. More decisive action may have been taken earlier by the international community to prevent or halt this tragedy. Working-level officials in many countries were disappointed with their government's inaction. In the United States, for example, an unprecedented five Department of State officers resigned over this issue, citing their frustration with the reluctance to formulate an effective American response in a timely manner.[1]

Making the Worst of a Bad Situation

Part of the delay in intervening may have been because international policy makers also sought to achieve two other objectives aside from stopping genocide, namely, the implementation of humanitarian relief and containment of the conflict to prevent its spread to the rest of the Balkans.

Although the three objectives were parallel and perhaps mutually supporting, they sometimes came into competition. Policy makers did not always assign the prevention or halt of genocide as their first priority. In a March 10, 1994 speech, for example, U.S. Secretary of Defense William Perry noted that "our first emphasis is on actions that can prevent the war from spreading, since this is where our most profound national security interests lie."[2] Often policy makers simply blurred their priorities. As Major General MacKenzie asked perceptively at a Senate hearing: "Is the aim to feed people while the war is going on? Or is the aim to stop the war?" Pressed as to whether he was saying that military measures would "worsen the problem," he replied: "Did I? . . . ask me the question again. Will it worsen their problem? Yes, it will if you are going to take the next step and deal with your personnel who will be killed while you are delivering this humanitarian aid. Yeah, I guess that makes the problem worse. But what is the objective? Are you going in there to feed or are you going there to stop the fighting?"[3]

Often, policy makers were most concerned with avoiding any step that might interfere with or threaten the other two objectives, even if at times the cost, however much regretted, was continued ethnic cleansing. Thus, military intervention or lifting the arms embargo was often viewed as an impediment to relief operations, since such actions might increase the threat to foreign personnel and stop all aid deliveries. Lieutenant General Nambiar articulated this same concern in December, 1992, when he argued against any form of military intervention. He asked rhetorically, "Do we want all the things that we have accomplished [in the humanitarian field] to be set back?"[4]

Beyond doubt, there were remarkable, though always tenuous, achievements in the area of humanitarian relief. Certainly, aid was very important and thousands of military and civilian personnel selflessly risked their lives to ensure its continuation under very difficult circumstances. If given a choice, however, most Muslims would clearly have preferred to be able to defend themselves rather than become "well-fed victims," as both the Bosnian government and average Muslims frequently told foreign audiences.

Yet, by late 1993, some foreign advisers had come to consider seriously whether ending food deliveries could be used as a way to make the Bosnian government more pliant. Lord Owen, for example, threatened in no uncertain terms in November, 1993, that unless the Bosnian government signed the peace plan then on the table, humanitarian aid might end and the sanctions against Serbia be lifted:

We must also face up to the reality that food aid is feeding the armies of all sides. The arms embargo is being evaded by all sides. Economic sanctions are hitting not just the Serbian and Montenegrin people but dragging down the neighboring countries, Macedonia, Bulgaria, and Rumania. There must be limits to this intervention and it could become even harder to justify. Governments are right to start, therefore, as an incentive for peace to define the conditions for suspending sanctions and the exact shape of the settlements on which they expect all the parties to compromise.[5]

Asked in a subsequent interview to clarify whether he thought the delivery of such items as food and blankets was prolonging the war by freeing the combatants from such responsibilities, he replied: "Yes, of course. For how long can one justify that?"[6]

Although ending both humanitarian relief and the UN's presence might indeed have made an end of the war more probable, these actions would likely have only eroded those obstacles remaining to a more complete and speedier achievement of the ethnic cleansing sought by the Serbs. Only the peace of a graveyard would have resulted.

Although humanitarian aid represents understandable human response to seeing the plight of fellow human beings, it addressed only short-term needs without solving the more basic, long-term problem of ethnic cleansing. If the Bosnian government had acquired an ability to provide for its own defense, the need for the relief effort would have been unnecessary in the long run. As for the objective of containing the crisis, it is too early to tell, pending the outcome of the political process in other potential hot spots in the former Yugoslavia.

What Can Have an Impact on Genocide?

Could the international community have done more to prevent genocide in Bosnia-Herzegovina? There is no simple solution or guaranteed way to prevent or stop genocide in every situation, although there may be some basic principles and strategies that appear to be more effective than others. In particular, in Bosnia-Herzegovina, if genocide were a conscious, cost-efficient way for the Serb leadership to achieve concrete political objectives, then raising the cost of implementing its strategy would have been more effective in countering genocide.

The Importance of Publicity and Condemnation

THE LIGHT OF PUBLICITY. Early and widespread publicizing of genocide is key in combatting it, especially at the hands of a relatively weak power like the Serbs. Perpetrators are likely to interpret passivity or a low-key approach by foreign bystanders as indifference, tacit approval, or proof of their own imperviousness. At the same time, the non-recognition of genocide abroad is likely to delay or undermine attempts at prevention.[7] Quiet, behind-the-scenes diplomacy in most instances does not seem to be effective except, perhaps, as a supporting strategy. In the case of Bosnia-Herzegovina, extensive media coverage, in particular, may have been instrumental in at least mitigating some of the worst excesses of ethnic cleansing, if not in stopping it. Even such a simple step as documenting detainees can provide some insurance against their killing, as detainees released from Serb-run concentration camps were to attest. Media publicity, in fact, may have been what eventually led rival Serb leaders to accuse each other of the atrocities committed, realizing that their acts could not be hidden.

Intensive media coverage (such as the type CNN is noted for) and the ensuing mobilization of public opinion made it harder for governments to ignore the situation. In most instances, public opinion was considerably out in front of official policy in both the West and the Islamic world, which usually was in a reactive mode. Pressure from the public actually goaded policy makers to do more. For example, in August, 1993, media reports highlighted the plight of a wounded little girl named Irma who had been refused entry to Britain for medical treatment. Because of the extensive media coverage, some European governments were probably shamed into agreeing to provide medical care for evacuated Bosnian victims. Until then, UN requests for evacuee care had been adamantly ignored. Even the initiatives for a ceasefire following the February, 1994 mortar attack against Sarajevo can be attributed to some extent to the intense media publicity which the mortar attack elicited.

In the United States, media attention flowed in cycles. After the flurry of interest surrounding the initial reports of genocide in 1992, coverage waxed and waned depending on the likelihood of American military involvement. Interest would dramatically drop whenever the United States appeared to not take significant steps, then surge, as in early 1994, when the possibility of intervention increased. In Islamic countries continuous media coverage maintained interest at a high level and gave vent to the considerable popular frustration and feeling that their governments could have done more (fig. 3).

By and large, the international media was critical of the Serb policy. This attitude can be attributed to the media's assessment of the situation on the ground, however, and not, as Major General MacKenzie speculated, because the reporters allegedly were "all stuck" away from the Serb camp by

The Arab world is shown trying to extinguish the fire in Bosnia with just a stream of words. Published in *Al-Ittihad,* Abu Dhabi, United Arab Emirates, July 26, 1993, by Hamed Nageeb.

coincidence during the initial period of the fighting. The Serbs consciously sought to keep the foreign media at arm's length in the field to minimize outside scrutiny of their policies. However, Serb spokesmen made frequent use of their ready access to international audiences through the foreign media, although with limited success, given their poor credibility.

MAKING A MORAL JUDGMENT. Clear condemnation is also a vital step to halting genocide. The international community's willingness to take a firm and public stand removes any pretext of legality on the part of the perpetrator and, at the same time, lays the legal foundation for any subsequent steps the international community may take. The case of Bosnia-Herzegovina was unusual in the broad-based popular consensus it generated. It evoked sympathy for the Muslims and disapproval of Serbian actions. Consensus was particularly evident in, but not limited to, the West and the Islamic world. Consensus also spanned the political and religious spectrum within individual countries, leading to unaccustomed alliances and novel situations. For example, traditionally more dovish liberals in countries such as the United States and France were among the strongest proponents of determined international action and the use of military force in this case.

143

Overall, the Serbs appeared to be sensitive to world opinion insofar as they attempted to screen their actions or at least to contain them, a calculated strategy intended to keep the international community from undertaking decisive measures. Serb leaders seem to have been genuinely surprised initially by the negative publicity and outrage abroad and, in later phases of their campaign, responded by toning down their tactics. At the very least, they seemed to become more sophisticated and shifted their focus of effort to less dramatic, but probably no less effective, ways to cleanse territory, such as by siege and starvation, having benefitted already from the shock value of the initial massive onslaught against the civilian population in the early phases to set the Muslim exodus in motion.

Even so, foreign reaction was not always unanimous. International dissonance was significant in that it delayed a united response, softened the sting of international condemnation for the Serb leadership, and complicated efforts to take effective multilateral concrete measures in time. This unwillingness to take timely action was especially important in the crucial early period when more options were available to help the Bosnian government and when genocide might have been derailed altogether before much of the damage had been done. Serbian officials monitored such cleavages closely. They were quick to latch on to such differing points of view within the West in shaping their information campaigns abroad and to buttress their own arguments in countering critics at home.

Some European governments, notably Greece, rejected any censure of the Serbs, while Russia held back criticism to the barest minimum. Specific domestic actors in both cases, such as the Greek Orthodox Church hierarchy in Greece and the Red-Brown coalition in Russia, were even vehemently defensive of Serbian policy. Although reinforced by long-standing cultural ties with Serbia, Greek and Russian interests centered on concrete issues, which were probably decisive in determining their benign stands. The Greek government first took into consideration the regional balance of power. The country was also positioning itself for potential territorial claims of its own in the Balkans and profited by evading the sanctions on Serbia.

For Russian hard-liners of the Right and Left Wings, Bosnia-Herzegovina was considered a convenient club to use against the Yeltsin government in their domestic power struggle. The Bosnian conflict was also viewed as a proxy war against the West and its western values, which, ironically, Russian extremists felt were championed by the Muslims and opposed by the Serbs. Beyond the domestic jockeying for influence, Russian nationalists in general may have also been anxious to ensure for Russia the great power role they believed it deserved. The Russian military, for example, goaded the Yeltsin government to show that Russia was a great power by its involvement in Bosnia-Herzegovina. After Russian peacekeepers deployed to Sarajevo, the Russian military press sought to have Moscow use the expanded military role to enhance Russian influence abroad. One military commentator asked: "Why does not the logic of a loudly proclaimed 'return of Russia to international relations as a great power' prevail at [the Russian Foreign Ministry]? If a state which knows what it wants is not behind the Russian contingent in Sarajevo. . . . the question arises: Was it worthwhile at all to get involved thus in Bosnia?"[8] Moscow probably also wanted to preclude setting an interventionist precedent by the international community. Such actions could have redounded against Moscow in its future dealings with neighboring states harboring Russian communities or in dealing with its own minorities. As for Yeltsin, his reticence to appear too visibly agreeable to western policies on Bosnia-Herzegovina was no doubt motivated by his overriding concern to avoid providing his domestic adversaries with an issue to use against him. Although it was important to Yeltsin to maintain this stance as the strength of the opposition mounted, he balanced this position with the need to avoid an abrupt break with the West.

In the Islamic world, Iraq and Libya stood apart visibly from the rest on this issue. Both countries have had long-standing arms sales and servicing relationships with Belgrade, which they no doubt wanted to continue. Moreover, on principle, both also have opposed any multilateral action, given their continuing entanglement with the UN.

While the impact of international pariahs, such as Iraq and Libya is not great, the negative role played by more respectable individuals and powerful governments has greater consequences. Denial by prominent western figures and their misreading of the situation had an effect on the speed and extent of world awareness and condemnation and, as a result, on concrete international action. Of equal significance, the reticence of certain key European governments to get involved obstructed the building of a consensus for effective measures. Although Russian foot-dragging may have made western policy makers more cautious, it also gave others an excuse to do less.

Unavoidable Concrete Measures

Although publicity and condemnation, by themselves, may be necessary as part of an overall response, in most cases they are not sufficiently substantial to halt genocide. Ultimately, any realistic strategy to stop genocide requires a readiness to take more concrete steps. Depending on the specific scenario, the strategy may include economic sanctions, political isolation, and protection, which may even extend to armed intervention on the victim's behalf or security assistance to the victimized party to provide for its own defense.

Prosecuting War Crimes

Bringing war criminals to trial is a vital deterrent to would-be perpetrators and an effective way to defuse potential calls for individual retaliation.

Self-imposed sanctions are probably not realistic in this situation. Despite their assurances, Bosnian Serb authorities are unlikely to investigate and prosecute major war crimes themselves. When the international media pressed for action in September, 1992, following the reported slaying by Serbian police of Muslims pulled from a prisoner convoy, the Bosnian Serbian police leadership claimed—after a perfunctory investigation—that "a certain number of the people who were heading for Travnik lost their lives that day," and the matter was dropped.[9] In May, 1994, two brothers who were part of the leadership of the Serbian Yellow Wasp militia were arraigned in Serbia for crimes committed against both Muslims and Serbs. This incident, however, may have been intended to deflect international criticism away from the government in Belgrade and focus on their purely criminal activities. In fact, the brothers' earlier arrest and secret release in Bosnia-Herzegovina reportedly had been a sham designed to show foreign opinion that law and order would prevail.[10]

The only reasonable alternative under such circumstances is an independent international tribunal. On February 22, 1993, the UN Security Council established a tribunal to prosecute war crimes committed in the former Yugoslavia. In early 1994 the United States government reaffirmed its commitment to seeing war criminals prosecuted. Although these efforts may develop further, the legal mechanism in place up to now suggests that prospects are dim for success in prosecuting war crimes effectively. Such an undertaking clearly requires a large staff in order to be effective. But, as one observer pointed out, the UN initially only allocated two attorneys, as compared to the 1,170 attorneys involved in preparing the proceedings at Nuremberg.[11] Barring the international community's willingness to exert its leverage, prospects for enforcing compliance on this issue are not good either. The Yugoslav government, understandably, sought to ignore the emerging tribunal by preferring not to refer to even its own claims of anti-Serb atrocities in order to avoid giving the appearance of recognizing its jurisdiction. Radomir Smiljanić, president of the Serbian nationalist White Rose, noted with some validity: "Talk about a Nuremberg trial for the Serbian people is ridiculous! First, one cannot bring the victor to trial. Gentlemen, the Serbs have won, and that small detail is being forgotten!"[12]

The mandate of the court apparently does not extend to extraditing suspects for trial. Although trials in absentia are still possible, former chief counsel for the Nuremberg trials, Drexel Sprecher, highlighted the difficulties in a February, 1993 interview. He cautioned: "It would be much [more] preferable of course if we had our hands on the people who . . . have allegedly made the offenses, gave them a preliminary opportunity to state their case or defense if they've got one, and then if we still think they're guilty we ought to invite them [to stay on]."[13]

Of course, some of the potential targets of the tribunal, such as Šešelj or Boban, have been or may be jettisoned by their patrons as political liabilities. However, even their fall from grace may not increase their legal accountability, since impartial questioning of persons who are no longer part of the system may reveal embarrassing linkages to high-ranking individuals within the political system. Thus, although Yugoslavia's minister of justice assured that those accused of war crimes could be prosecuted, he hastened to insist that prosecutions would be done only in local courts, as "we cannot accept the extradition of our citizens. . . . is it justified at all to hand over one's own citizens?"[14] Both in Serbian-controlled Bosnia and in Serbia itself, there have been frequent appearances in the state-run media by local legal experts who have argued on the Serbian authorities' behalf that any such tribunal would be illegal.

Realistically, within the current parameters, a tribunal may be able to prepare indictments that could discourage the accused from traveling abroad. At most, however, some low-level war criminals, who might be considered political rivals by those in power, may be tried discreetly in Yugoslavia, or simply handed over, as a face-saving measure. The prospects are slim, however, that principals such as Milošević, Karadžić, Boban, or General Mladić will ever be questioned, brought to trial, ostracized, or punished. When asked in February, 1993, whether being placed on a list of war criminals worried him, Karadžić responded self-confidently that he considered these charges as "all temporary."

Up to now, such leaders have been treated as valid interlocutors in the negotiations for Bosnia-Herzegovina's future, given the overriding priority of other greater political interests. However, if, in the end, they are recognized as the legal government of the emerging political entities and the consequences of their guilt in those war crimes are short-lived and far from onerous, the results would contribute to the perception that aggression and genocide do, in fact, pay.

BREAKING THE PERPETRATOR'S INFORMATION MONOPOLY. Perhaps one of the most underrated concrete means to counteract genocide is the ability to make available an accurate picture of the situation to the public in the perpetrator's community. Providing alternative information, especially through the electronic media, and jamming the offending government's domestic media, could have a significant impact on the general public. To be sure, in some instances the population may already be so indoctrinated that an outside information campaign may have only a marginal, or slow, impact on public opinion.

In the case of Serbia, nonetheless, breaking Milošević's monopoly of the electronic media early could have served as a significant supporting strategy by countering the official one-sided and inflammatory propaganda. Efforts to counter this biased reporting could have brought home to the average Serb the horrors and implications of genocide. Even if the results did not create a public outcry against Milošević's policy, in combination with other concrete measures, this approach could have accelerated the erosion of support for Belgrade's military involvement and affected Milošević's cost-benefit calculations.

PROMOTING WORKABLE POLITICAL SOLUTIONS. Ideally, outside players can also make a useful, and perhaps vital, contribution in preventing or stopping genocide by formulating and promoting political solutions to such situations. Since virtually all wars end by a negotiated agreement, the international community can play a significant role in the settlement by ensuring that provisions be made that are fair, stable, and realistic while also not rewarding genocide. Achieving such results, admittedly, is not easy.

A political plan or peace, however, should not be a goal in and of itself, especially if the end-state which it promotes merely consolidates or legitimizes the results of genocide, or even encourages it further. In Bosnia-Herzegovina, the international community faced a very real predicament. Mediators sought an agreement in order to facilitate short-term, but badly needed, humanitarian relief goals, even if the agreement hindered arriving at a long-term solution.

Plans for peace should not require the victim, as the weak party, to make the bulk of the concessions. Furthermore, they should certainly not place the victim in an equally or more vulnerable position to targeting by the perpetrator than before. To a certain extent, however, the objective of the international community in Bosnia-Herzegovina seemed to have become simply ending the fighting.

Some foreign political figures were often less than helpful in their formulation of proffered solutions for Bosnia-Herzegovina. Of course, the representatives of international organizations, as individuals, should not be made to take all responsibility for the diplomatic straits in which the outside world often placed the Muslim community. The representatives merely embodied, to a large extent, a consensus of opinion in their own and other western governments. Nevertheless, because of their vantage point and assumed expertise, such representatives of international bodies played a critical role in defining the problem and in shaping the international political response.

The input of some of these international representatives in guiding perceptions and in swaying decision makers appears to have been especially significant in the formative stages of the crisis and also at some significant early decision points. Once Western decision makers had internalized the paradigms popularized by these representatives, there appears to have been considerable resistance to reexamining the basic premises, even after the focus shifted to direct negotiations by individual governments. The influence which some of these principals exercised in the formation of opinions could be persistent indeed. For example, Major General MacKenzie had established extensive credibility among fellow-soldiers. As a result, and as the author can testify from contacts with them, many senior-level American officers long retained erroneous assumptions that were first gleaned from him. MacKenzie, however, upon leaving Sarajevo, had become a lobbyist and was being paid hefty fees by a Serbian-American political action committee while he was also meeting with the media and government officials. His affiliation with this group should have at the very least raised questions about a conflict of interest and about the potential of his providing tainted advice at crucial junctures during the conflict.[15]

In concrete terms, after Serbian military successes, international mediators often crafted ill-conceived proposals that placed the Muslims in a no-win situation. While the damage of genocide could not be undone, the "realist" school's solution of peace at any price hinged on recognizing the situation on the ground as the basis for a settlement. The operating premise for Lord Owen, for example, seems to have been that "Bosnia . . . can never be a state in which the largest population group, the Muslims, have normal democratic powers. It would simply not be accepted."[16] This opinion did little more than acquiesce to the results of genocide and, however unintentionally, rewarded its successful execution, despite repeated assurances by key policy makers to the Muslims that such a condition would be explicitly avoided.

Although, in some cases, foreign mediators and governments recognized the negative aspects of formulating such proposals, the shibboleth of "realism" repeatedly overrode their qualms. Douglas Hogg, Great Britain's Under Secretary for Foreign Affairs, in May, 1994, thus urged the Muslims in public that they "have to acknowledge military defeat when it stares them in the face" as a prelude to new negotiations.[17] Perhaps no one said it as openly as Major General MacKenzie, when he testified before Congress in May, 1993. In his characteristically blunt way, he expressed his support for partition and, with recourse to a dubious analogy, seemed to acknowledge the validity of force: "Now, obviously the critics will say this rewards force and sets a bad example. I can only say to them, read your history. Force has been rewarded since the first caveman picked up a club, occupied his neighbor's cave, and ran off with his wife."[18]

Not surprisingly, given such an outlook, the major peace plans that were proposed proceeded almost invariably from the starting point of partition along confessional lines. They were backed up by hopeful but questionable international guarantees and, conceptually, implied the recognition of the results of territorial conquest and ethnic cleansing. For example, notwithstanding the noble goals the mediators proclaimed, the Cutilheiro Plan of March, 1992, the Vance-Owen Plan of January, 1993, the "Joint Action Program" devised by the United States, Great Britain, France, Russia, and Spain in May, 1993, and the Owen-Stoltenberg formulation of the Zagreb-Belgrade partition initiative of June, 1993, and even the "contact group" plan of 1994, for all intents and purposes, placed the Bosnian government, and the Muslims overall, in an unfavorable, or even untenable, situation.

For the Muslims to have accepted a ceasefire under such conditions meant accepting defeat and a new precarious status quo. The Muslims argued that the proposed plans would reward the Serbs for their aggression, would not stop ethnic cleansing, and would leave them vulnerable to continuing pressure.[19] For the Muslims, the other option appeared to be to fight on to achieve better terms.

The Vance-Owen Plan was a watershed in that for the first time the earlier principle of a unified Bosnia-Herzegovina was reversed in favor of ethnic partition. Its central provisions seem to have been what triggered the HVO's large-scale attack against the Muslims, since the plan raised the HVO's concrete political interest in seizing the territory earmarked for Croatian control according to the plan's map. The HVO could feel secure in its belief that no help would be forthcoming to the Bosnian government and that further HVO expansion would be blessed by the international community. Although this plan resulted in the cracking of the fragile alliance between the Croatians and the Muslims and left the latter under greater pressure to negotiate, it also opened the way for more, not less, ethnic cleansing and gave impetus to increased fighting. Likewise, the Owen-Stoltenberg Plan implicitly stimulated additional ethnic cleansing, as its basic premise was the partition of Bosnia-Herzegovina into three ethnically based mini-states.

What is more, these plans actually contained a strong normative strain and, on occasion, posited an even worse position for the Muslims than they held at the time. This was certainly the case, for example, with a suggestion made by Lord Owen. Having recognized the stalemate of the earlier Vance-Owen Plan after the Bosnian Serbs had rejected it, Owen, on at least two occasions in 1993, proposed not only the division of Bosnia-Herzegovina but also the temporary partition of the heretofore undivided and as yet unconquered city of Sarajevo along ethnic lines. Although Lord Owen at the time sought to deny reports that he had called for the division of Sarajevo, his rebuttals failed to spell out what his temporary solution for the city consisted of exactly, if not partition. Despite similarly indignant denials in February of that year by Jeremy Braid, Lord Owen's special representative in Sarajevo, Braid's acknowledgement of having proposed an "extraterritorial area," negotiations on municipal borders, and a revised urban administration to Sarajevo's mayor on Lord Owen's behalf suggested otherwise.[20]

In November, 1993, Owen and Stoltenberg again raised this proposal to divide Sarajevo. By that time, with the siege still in force and winter at hand, the Bosnians had been reduced to such straits that their government considered, though under duress, the partition of Sarajevo. In response to the proposal, Muhamed Sacirbey, Bosnian ambassador to the UN, commented: "Frankly, I find any division of Sarajevo to be repugnant. . . . But on the other hand, the people of Sarajevo have to survive the consequences of the world not coming to their aid to lift the siege. . . . Death is more repugnant."[21]

Public and private pressure on the Bosnian government by the EU (through its representative Lord Owen) and the UN (through its representative Thorvald Stoltenberg) to accept these plans was significant. Almost invariably, western mediators would end up arguing the Serb position in order to induce the Bosnian side to see reason and accept the plan on the table. Lord Owen, for example, informed the Bosnian government that "it would be a tragedy if this opportunity [the original draft of the Owen-Stoltenberg Plan] was lost."[22] Likewise, Gen. Jean Cot, French commander of UNPROFOR, lamented in late 1993 that "a catastrophe" would occur unless the Muslims signed the Owen-Stoltenberg plan immediately. He insisted, instead, that "if the Muslims continue to 'draw out the rope' with the objective of gaining major territorial concessions from the Croatians and the Serbs, then all responsibility will lie on their shoulders."[23] Not surprisingly, Belgrade urged Europe, and especially France, to isolate and pressure the Bosnian government to accept the plan.

The flawed basic premise for political action by the international mediators was that this was at bottom a civil war. The war supposedly reflected long-ingrained hatreds, and all parties shared in the guilt and all had the same basic goals. Therefore, all sides had an equal right to have their interests assured. It should have been clear, on the contrary, that the Serbs did not necessarily have the same end-state in mind as the one that the foreign negotiators attributed to them. This difference was demonstrated by their ultimate rejection of the Vance-Owen Plan, since it complicated the formation of a Greater Serbia.

Essentially, although the Bosnian Serbs sought a ceasefire, their intent was a ceasefire as part of a deal which would confirm their gains and predominant position in Bosnia-Herzegovina and lead to a Greater Serbia. They furthermore wished to place any future Bosnian state in as weak a position as possible.

However, based on the analytical framework they had developed, Western representatives frequently placed the onus on the Muslims for not wanting to agree to the deals suggested. Negotiators often praised the Serbs as the ones who were flexible and desirous of ending the fighting and implied that the Muslims should be compelled to negotiate and accept what was offered to them. Testifying before Congress, Major General MacKenzie maintained: "The Serbs, at present, will talk any time, any place, any where, at any level, because they basically have what they want. . . . They are prepared to negotiate. . . . The political solution is to pull the rug of intervention out and force people to sit down and discuss. One side [the Serbs] has already said it is prepared to do that today. The other side [the Muslims] has not got the message yet. Now that is MacKenzie's point of view."[24] MacKenzie portrayed this attitude as the only policy that made sense, asserting unconvincingly, "It seems to me talking could get the Bosnian Muslims territory."[25] In fact, arguably overstepping his authority while on duty in Sarajevo, he had continuously acted to pressure President Izetbegović. Both directly and indirectly by his recommendations to other mediators, MacKenzie urged Izetbegović to accept that there would be no foreign military intervention and that the Bosnian government should therefore strike a deal with the Bosnian Serbs.[26]

Often, Western observers accused the Muslim leadership of needlessly prolonging their community's agony by continuing to fight on. Some of these observers explained the alleged intransigence simply as a way for the Bosnian leadership to create victims with which to manipulate western policy. In Major General MacKenzie's opinion: "What we now see from the Bosnian presidency's side is that it's in their interest to keep the thing going and get the Serbs to retaliate in order to convince the international community that intervention is a good idea."[27]

At times, foreign policy makers also took countervailing positions, which at the very least must have been confusing to the Muslims. Apparently some countries promised the Bosnian government that help, in the form of a lifting of the arms embargo and other guarantees, would be forthcoming.[28] At the same time, as a way to induce the Muslims to stop fighting, other countries made concerted efforts to preclude the fruition of suggestions for outside help.

Lord Owen was especially critical in public of the Clinton administration for allegedly holding out hope to the Bosnian government of international military help. Owen believed that Clinton's statements neutralized pressure on the Bosnian government to accede to the Vance-Owen Plan. Adopting a hectoring tone, he advised the United States to help, instead, to isolate the Izetbegović government: "We have a problem. We can't get the Muslims on board. And that's largely the fault of the Americans because the Muslims won't budge while they think Washington may come into it on their side any day now."[29] His guiding strategy, as he acknowledged in February, 1993, on National Public Radio in the United States, was, rather, to "shatter the Muslims' illusion" of outside aid.[30]

This approach certainly shaped Lord Owen's diplomacy. Owen and Vance, in fact, initially had demanded that the Security Council impose sanctions on any party rejecting their plan, as a way to coerce the reluctant Bosnian government to yield.[31] This action no doubt led the Serbs to believe that arming or otherwise helping the Muslims was not likely, thus further emboldening them to press on with ethnic cleansing and to hold onto the land they had seized.

As part of the effort to compel the Bosnian government to accede to the subsequent Owen-Stoltenberg Plan, the new team of mediators warned in July, 1993, that unless the Muslims accepted the partition plan, the UN would pull out. Lord Owen hastened to add, though, that "there's no attempt to blackmail the Bosnian presidency." However, this comment was clearly aimed at the Bosnian government, since the Muslims would have been harmed most if the UN would have withdrawn. He would repeat this threat often, including during the January, 1994 talks in Geneva, when he warned that UNPROFOR might leave by spring, while the arms embargo was still in place.[32]

At the summer, 1993 Geneva talks, moreover, Lord Owen threatened President Izetbegović publicly that if the Muslims continued to fight they would no longer be recognized as victims and that the world community would treat them the same way as it did the Serbs.[33] Lord Owen also suggested in December, 1993, that the Serbs had actually been restraining themselves up to now, but that the Bosnian government was trying their patience and, implicitly, that they deserved what the Serbs would do to them. He warned: "This autumn, the Serbs fought with velvet gloves in order to give the Muslims one more chance. Now they have had enough, as have the Croats. If the negotiations fail now, they [the Serbs] will go all out."[34]

According to the media, Lord Owen apparently had recourse to even more direct pressure by allegedly encouraging factions within the Bosnian government which favored accommodation to oppose President Izetbegović, thereby weakening him. First, in a break with practice up to then, Lord Owen invited the entire Bosnian collective presidency, rather than a single representative from each of the three parties, to Geneva to negotiate in July, 1993. At the same time, he selected the makeup of the subgroups negotiating each day, a move that splintered the Bosnian government ranks. Subsequently, as Muslim leader Abdić made a push for autonomy for the Bihać enclave under his own leadership, and accepted the partition plan, Lord Owen reportedly provided encouragement, while French UN peacekeepers helped to prop up the breakaway region. According to a senior UN official in Bihać, French forces were there "on agreements made with Owen, because it's Owen's will to use Abdić as a sort of joker against Izetbegović."[35]

Unsuccessful international negotiators, such as Lord Owen, faded into the background by early 1994, yielding to an increasingly visible direct political role by several western governments. Ironically, some governments appeared to be frustrated at the Bosnians' improving military capability, since that strength apparently made the Bosnians less amenable to the proposals being offered in Geneva. In early 1994, in fact, a disagreement emerged in public between the United States and France. Washington was reluctant to go along with a French proposal to coerce the Muslims to agree to the current partition plan, which Paris believed was the quickest way to end the conflict. While French Foreign Minister Alain Juppé, for example, claimed that the "United States was making a mistake by refusing to pressure Bosnia's Muslim-led government," American Secretary of State Warren Christopher "made very clear to [Juppé] that going to the aggrieved party, which has been the victim of aggression by Bosnian Serbs, and in a sense forcing a settlement on that aggrieved party, requires a very strange moral calculus."[36]

The approach of placing the blame on the Bosnian government's stubborn resistance and on U.S. support for the Muslims continued to be surprisingly resilient. Even as late as April, 1994, "two of the highest-ranking UN officials in Bosnia"—otherwise unidentified, but including a general—claimed that it was the Bosnian government which was the "greatest impediment to peace," and criticized "the United States' moral and financial support of that government [which] is prolonging the war."[37]

Yet, its concern with not rewarding ethnic cleansing notwithstanding, the United States still interpreted the situation as a civil war in which the existing basic balance of forces could not, or should not, be affected from the outside. As President Clinton expressed in a January 24, 1994 press conference: "The killing is a function of a political fight between three factions. Until they agree to quit doing it, it's going to continue. And I don't think that the international community has the capacity to stop people within the nation from their civil war until they decide to do it." At most, the President added, "we can . . . retard it [the killing], to keep it within bounds, to keep it within humanitarian limits."[38]

It appeared that the unexpected more robust NATO initiative on Sarajevo in February, 1994, marked by a threat of air strikes, might lead to a new approach by the international community to the conflict. In truth, this increased engagement was not a fair test, given that in the end the Serbs were still allowed to retain most of their gains. Moreover, in late March, 1994, when Goražde, the UN-designated safe zone enclave in eastern Bosnia, came under stepped-up Serbian military attacks, the international community seemed reluctant to make a commitment to protect it with military force. In fact, foreign policy makers initially hinted that such enclaves might be beyond the international community's defense perimeter. America's Secretary of Defense, for example, when asked whether anything would be done to prevent the fall of such towns to the Serbs, openly concluded: "We will not enter the war to stop that from happening. That is correct."[39] Such signals may have inadvertently encouraged the Serbs to step up their assault, but this reaction represented a miscalculation on their part. Their blatant challenge to the negotiations on an emerging status quo would eventually lead to the first NATO strikes against Serbian ground forces. Ultimately, however, having gauged the limited nature of outside commitment, the Serbs apparently decided that they could proceed with securing their main objectives in the enclave.

Perhaps equally importantly, however, this phase of increased American involvement may have been part of a new approach similar to that proposed by some of the European capitals. That is, the United States, in a conceptual shift, as expressed publicly, was to officially accept for the first time the possibility of partition as a guiding principle for a deal. Washington too would now put pressure on the Muslims—although recognized as the victimized party—to agree to a new status quo and to claim the right of final adjudication on the Bosnian government's goals. According to an American administration official, "Once the Muslims have stated the amount of land they desire, along with ports and land access to navigable rivers, the United States will judge whether the demands are 'realistic.'"[40] This approach, however, placed the Bosnian government in a position where its reluctance to go along with western proposals would henceforth threaten to shift the onus onto the Muslims and to isolate them from the international community if they made demands judged to be unrealistic.

In fact, while discounting any element of pressure, an unidentified administration official amplified that the new policy thrust would be one intended to "get the Bosnian Muslims to understand that we are not going to help them win the war and that within pretty small margins, they are not going to end up with much more, and [that] the international community is seriously losing patience." As a "top participant" in the administration team involved in the discussions on Bosnia further underlined, the objective was to convince the Bosnian government that U.S. support would remain circumscribed: "Look, don't over-read what we're doing here. We're not going to come back and help you win back on the battlefield."[41]

In late March, 1994, Secretary of State Christopher flatly rejected Bosnian requests for a return of all territories which had had Croatian or Muslim majorities before the war, saying that this would mean a whole new set of negotiations with the Serbs. Predictably, State Department officials began to characterize the Muslims' demands for the return of such territory as a "challenge" to efforts to "end the war in Bosnia as soon as possible through talks." Nor would the Bosnian government have international support or legitimacy if it tried to retake by military means any lost lands on their own. Instead, according to unnamed U.S. officials, "It would be best for the Muslims to aspire to modest gains at the negotiating table."[42] By early June, 1994, the United States joined the other members of the newly formed "contact group" (Russia, France, Germany, and Great Britain), which was now taking the lead in dealing with the Bosnian problem, by endorsing formally a 51-49 percent land split between, respectively, the Muslim-Croatian federation and the Bosnian Serbs.[43]

At the heart of such political solutions would lie a dilemma for the international community. Although agreements could not be anything but welcomed by the victims as a relief to their immediate plight, in the long term such well-intentioned initiatives, if based on partition, could place the Muslims in an unenviable and potentially dangerous security predicament. That is, even if a ceasefire would take hold, it would likely result in a freezing of the status quo along the front lines, with the interposed UN forces providing a buffer behind which the Bosnian Serb authorities could retain their positions with impunity. The anticipation that others would recognize the so-called possession-is-nine-tenths-of-the-law principle in a plan of this type no doubt also encouraged the Bosnian Serbs to hold onto as much territory as possible and to engage in further ethnic cleansing. They expected that these provisions would be accepted in the end as part of a global deal legitimated by the international community. At the very least, under the circumstances, the international community had to ensure that in any partition, the Muslims would be provided the best deal possible so that their areas could be viable and secure.

SANCTIONS. Sanctions can play a supporting role in promoting a political solution, but, to yield significant results, they have be applied rapidly and enforced effectively. Implementing them gradually and haphazardly, as occurred against Serbia, not only diluted their impact but allowed Belgrade time to set up a structure both at home and abroad to evade them. Although necessary as a signal of resolve against genocide, sanctions are a blunt, slow-working instrument.

They could in no way be viewed as the centerpiece of that strategy, despite the hopes of some policy makers. In practical terms, moreover, policy makers could give the impression at home and abroad that they were doing something concrete by imposing sanctions and thus deflect demands for more direct measures. In April, 1993, Great Britain's Foreign Secretary, Douglas Hurd, continued to urge that economic sanctions "be given time to work," as a substitute to lifting the arms embargo. Although sanctions certainly were successful in disrupting Serbia's economy and in causing considerable punishment to most ordinary Serbs, they did not achieve their objective of preventing Belgrade from backing aggression against the Muslim community in a timely manner.

Sanctions, by themselves, are not likely to take effect decisively and rapidly enough to stop the sweep of genocide. In Bosnia-Herzegovina, sanctions did not play the main role in slowing down the Serbian advance and in preventing the entire area from being quickly overrun. Instead, primary credit for those results should go to the increased organizational and defensive potential, however limited, that the Bosnian government forces developed. Credit should also be given to Serbian concerns not to exceed limits which, at certain junctures, might have forced the hand of the West into embarking on military intervention.

Moreover, even as the sanctions started to become more effective, with the stricter implementation mandated by UN Resolution 820 in April, 1993, pressure began to increase for their lifting, as 1993 came to a close. Some countries, such as Greece and Russia, seemed to act out of solidarity with Belgrade. Other states in the region complained about the economic losses they incurred by the disruption caused to their trade and often bypassed them.[44] Still others apparently were moved by the emerging humanitarian plight claimed by Serbia. They chose to ignore the conscious political decision in Belgrade to continue financing a costly war in Bosnia-Herzegovina and a military buildup within Serbia, two situations which were in themselves major contributors to the economic distress. A lifting of the sanctions was a key component of the November, 1993 Franco-German proposal. In 1994, paradoxically, this issue was raised too by Western policy makers as an inducement to convince the Bosnian Serbs to halt their assault on the safe zone enclave of Goražde. Again, the lifting of sanctions was used as a way of putting pressure on the Bosnian government to accept a solution formulated by the "contact group." French officials warned that if the Bosnians rejected the forthcoming proposal, the "Western countries would probably call for an easing of economic sanctions against Yugoslavia—the Bosnian Serbs' chief source of supply."[45]

The pressure for an easing of the sanctions underlined the inherent contradiction of this strategy. That is, effective sanctions are likely to cause so much pain to the civilian population of the targeted country that the international community may find it difficult to go through with them to the bitter end. Once sanctions begin to erode or are removed, however, it is considerably more difficult to reapply them.

MILITARY MEASURES. The threat, or use, of military force by the international community, in certain scenarios, can be an especially powerful factor in countering genocide. In the case of Bosnia-Herzegovina, what military force could do, if not provide a global solution, was to at least change the terms of reference for negotiations. If used early, force could have removed part of the incentive for territorial grabs, which provided much of the impetus for ethnic cleansing.

To a certain extent, the assessment that this was a civil war was often used in the West as a rationale for not acting militarily on behalf of the Muslims, since intervention could have been construed as "taking sides." This concern, perhaps key in a benign peacekeeping mission monitoring an agreement accepted by all parties, should have been less important if stopping genocide had had a higher priority. Even a case of civil war would not necessarily preclude the existence of a guilty party and a victim, nor need it prevent the international community from taking sides and helping one party to defend itself from another. Similar cases occurred when the UN decided to support South Korea in 1950, or when the United States backed the Greek government against the Communist insurgency in the late 1940s. Proponents of the civil war paradigm often buttressed their arguments, however, by the depicting all parties as equally guilty. This insistence on "neutrality" implicitly equated the goals and methods of the Muslims and the Serbs and was to be reiterated time and again. Perhaps nowhere was this position clearer than when the Serbs stepped up their attack on Goražde. In response, President Clinton in his April 15, 1994 press conference, went out of his way to stress that the "United States has no interest in having NATO become involved in this war and trying to gain some advantage for one side over the other."[46]

Great Britain and France, as well as some lesser players, for their part, were particularly anxious to downplay the gravity of the situation for a long time in order to avoid committing themselves to any greater direct involvement. The British Foreign Secretary pointed out that Great Britain had only been somewhat more "open and honest" in its refusal to take any military action than had others, as no one was particularly anxious to get involved.[47]

Some influential observers discouraged any military steps at all, however limited, with the prediction of dire consequences. Although proven wrong by subsequent events, Major General MacKenzie warned in early 1993 that even establishing a no-fly zone would result in direct retaliation against UN peacekeepers on the ground.[48]

The use of air strikes, in particular, was a hotly debated option. Doubters argued that the effectiveness of air power would be limited because targets such as artillery positions would be difficult to hit. Critics also focused on other considerations, such as a desire to avoid broadening the war and to avoid risking retaliation against the peacekeepers on the ground. Representatives of some member states, such as Great Britain's Foreign Secretary, for example, questioned the utility of air strikes at all, asking rhetorically "Will this improve the situation of the [UN] Blue Helmets? Will this save Bosnian lives?"[49]

Although a powerful tool, air strikes, by themselves, admittedly would not have been decisive in stopping genocide. They would have been ineffective especially if limited either to tactical targets such as the artillery positions surrounding Sarajevo or to isolated instances for demonstration effect. Despite the message that such air strikes could send, the greatest value of air power, instead, would have been as a supporting arm within a broader sustained campaign. Rather than seeking to maintain access open to cities or to target every mortar position or vehicle, air power could have been used to disrupt the Bosnian Serbian Army's command and control and logistics. Air power could have been effective by thwarting heavy Bosnian Serb units' ability to mass, move, communicate, or resupply from Serbia, particularly if carried out in conjunction with a lifting of the arms embargo. Such an application of air power would have had a much more decisive impact by enabling the Bosnian government to mount a successful campaign to secure its own territory.

In particular, there was considerable reluctance to using force to roll back Serbian gains. Asked whether UNPROFOR would consider using force to compel the Serbs to withdraw from their recent gains around Goražde, the commander, Lieutenant General Rose, categorically answered, "Absolutely not." He showed little sympathy for the Bosnian government's demand that the Serbs pull back to their departure lines and categorized this condition as "clearly . . . the requirement of one side."[50]

Yet the Serbs were more responsive to realistic and significant outside military pressure than was predicted. A key correlation in Serbian behavior was the degree of the credibility of foreign participants to implement the threatened military action. After having seized the key terrain surrounding Sarajevo in the summer of 1993 in preparation to strangle the city, General Mladić had initially claimed that the international community would be reluctant to carry out its announced threats. He chuckled: "I am not afraid of anything. You have been threatening me for more than a year and nothing has happened. What are you going to do?"[51] He subsequently concluded, however, that a continued refusal to retreat could indeed elicit a more forceful response, in the form of air strikes. This shift in attitude led to somewhat greater flexibility on his part as he pulled his forces back at least tactically to remove a potential rallying point for outside action, while not sacrificing recently achieved territorial positions which tightened the noose around Sarajevo.

As a result of its timid overall approach, however, by the time of its January, 1994 summit, NATO's credibility had eroded significantly. Unable to reach a consensus on a broader application of power and agreeing to the most that they could agree to, several European countries urged NATO to use air power, an action that would maintain the lines of communication to some of the besieged cities and provide tactical force protection for UNPROFOR personnel carrying out their humanitarian mission.

Not surprisingly, the Serbs were becoming increasingly contemptuous of NATO threats and, according to Maj. Gen. Manojlo Milovanović, Chief of Staff of the Bosnian Serb Army, "We have been threatened for two years now, but these threats are not feasible." He was sure that as long as the French had personnel on the ground Paris would not agree to air strikes. "These new threats of air strikes by NATO are no more than a tempest in a teacup," he responded confidently.[52] Over time, the Serbs believed that they had become adept at assessing the limits of foreign reaction. They were prone, however, to miscalculate through some especially egregious act, such as the deadly February 5, 1994 mortar attack on Sarajevo—a UN-designated safe zone—which would come to represent a litmus test of western resolve.

The incident sparked an outrage abroad. After some hesitation, reaction to the incident led to a consensus within NATO to use military force unless the Serbs pulled back their heavy equipment. Ominous hints and preparations gave the projected air strikes unprecedented credibility. President Clinton himself warned that, as far as options were concerned, "we rule out nothing." Potential targets extended far beyond the immediate artillery positions surrounding Sarajevo. Despite initial posturing, the Bosnian Serbs ultimately agreed to comply before the deadline set by NATO had expired, although, they refused to yield their strategic gains. Their compliance indicated a fairly realistic Serbian calculation of the potential benefits and losses in a direct military confrontation with NATO. Not surprisingly, the Serbs viewed the United States' stance as a bellwether for the international community's actions and were confident that without American leadership the rest of the world would not be able to do much (fig. 4).

The alternation between threats and backing down by the West over many months no doubt emboldened the Serbs to expand the parameters of their freedom of action toward the international community. They were convinced that consistent western military response would be unlikely, especially with a more assertive Moscow. A decision to provide for genuine "peace enforcement" to ensure the Serbs stop ethnic cleansing and return lands they seized almost certainly would have required a substantial force on the ground, perhaps for a lengthy period of time. Mobilizing domestic support for such a commitment, especially in light of the casualties that were likely to be incurred, was viewed as problematic in the West and was rejected. Both Bosnian Serb and Belgrade representatives were very adept at latching on to themes to which they felt Western leaders would be sensitive—be it the prospect of a long commitment with high casualties, danger to the peacekeepers on the ground, or an expanded war—and incorporated them in their information campaigns abroad.

In the United States, serious concerns were repeatedly voiced by the administration, Congress, and many in the media about the possibility of an open-ended military commitment, which could be potentially costly in lives and money and result in a quagmire. Especially with the discouraging results in Somalia looming in the background, American military intervention

162

The cartoon shows the United States far outweighing all the other major powers, highlighting Washington's central role in international action. Published in *Vojska,* the Yugoslav military's official journal, Belgrade, May 27, 1993, by Nikola Otaš.

on the ground would take the form of peacekeeping rather than peace enforcement. That is, any American military participation would take place only with the concurrence of all the parties, after the fighting had stopped and a political settlement had been brokered, not to roll back Serbian gains by force. This approach was reflected in the U.S. government's insistence that American ground forces would be committed to Bosnia-Herzegovina only when, and if, all sides agreed to peace.[53]

Given the United States' attitude, it was disingenuous for Lord Owen to suggest in mid-1994 that American military force would be available for the implementation of an agreement if the Serbs reneged on any promise they made. Yet, as a way to induce the Muslims to stop fighting, he said: "Give the Muslims, particularly, but also the Croats, a guarantee with a credible implementation force—and this is where the United States comes in—that they [the Serbs] will be rolled back and that they will honor their agreements."[54]

Ultimately, an appropriate coupling with sensible political goals is vital to the success of the military element of power. Arguably, undertaking even vigorous action is questionable if the political objective that military power is intended to support is the freezing of a status quo that is unfavorable to the victim. The problem all along, however, had been whether there would be sufficient long-term resolve in the West to push for a major rollback of Serb gains as part of a campaign threatening or using military force. Without that resolve, the effects of ethnic cleansing might be mitigated, but its basic course would be neither diverted nor prevented from the outside.

The Essential Factor of Time

Timeliness, in particular, is a crucial element if condemnation or concrete measures are to be effective against genocide. Understanding and responding to such a situation early is not only less costly in resources required, but is likely to be more successful in avoiding or limiting the number of victims and in broadening the policy options available to the international community.

A stern admonishment to Milošević by the international community early on during Serbian expansion might have been sufficient to preempt what subsequently occurred in Bosnia-Herzegovina, provided it had been backed up with credible will. A vigorous reaction was certainly appropriate after any number of egregious acts against Croatia. After the assault on Dubrovnik or the destruction of the city of Vukovar, a timely reaction could have included the effective enforcement of tight economic, political, and communications sanctions on Serbia and the simultaneous lifting of the arms embargo on Croatia.

More aggressive condemnations would have sent an unambiguous message. Instead, the initial restrained criticism created the impression that the international community would act slowly and ineffectively, or not at all. The longer the world did nothing concrete about Bosnia-Herzegovina, the more unlikely it became that the situation would be reversed, as the country was torn apart and its population scattered or killed. The very fact that month after month passed without an effective foreign reaction increased the likelihood that, in the end, a new status quo would take hold. Lack of appropriate reaction increased the chances that such distasteful solutions as ethnic partition and an acceptance of territorial conquest would eventually be considered rational and convenient options around which to form an international consensus. In geopolitical terms, the West's room for maneuver would certainly have been far greater early in the crisis, not least because of the appearance of Russia's Zhirinovskiy on the political scene and the hardening of Russian opinion overall. If the hard-liners' influence in Moscow continues to grow, the window of opportunity to affect the situation in Bosnia-Herzegovina in the future can be expected to shrink apace.

Early warning is especially important in identifying and monitoring a potential genocide situation as it begins to emerge and subsequently unfold. For Bosnia-Herzegovina, the lengthy preparatory campaign in Serbia was clearly an unhealthy development. While not leading inexorably to genocide, it nevertheless was bound to seriously escalate communal tensions. Its implicit message—that Serbia's leadership saw the Muslims, and other non-Serbs, as expendable obstacles—significantly raised the potential for the occurrence of genocide.

Timely foreign pressure on Milošević to desist from his inflammatory propaganda campaign against non-Serbs might have convinced him to lower the tension and, at the very least, could have stimulated a mobilization of world opinion much earlier. In addition to providing warning, collection and analysis of information is crucial in establishing a clear and sound basis for any assessment and policy formulation before the crisis assumes unmanageable proportions. The burden for guiding the collection effort for such information ultimately lies squarely on the policy maker, who must indicate a sufficient proactive interest in this area of policy rather than merely reacting to events.

11. Must a Victim Remain Defenseless?

A Case for Self-Defense

As the experience in Bosnia-Herzegovina illustrated, the measures that the international community is willing to take may simply not be enough to prevent or stop genocide. In certain scenarios, providing security assistance in order to enable the victims to protect themselves and to offer effective resistance to their victimizers may be the most effective, and the only realistic, means of inhibiting or stopping genocide. There is nothing that says that victims must remain defenseless.

The Arms Embargo's Unequal Equality

The continuation of the blanket arms embargo imposed on Yugoslavia in September, 1991, made it impossible for the Bosnian government to obtain significant amounts of weapons and ammunition. The Bosnian Serbs, however, were not affected by the arms embargo, thanks to the arsenal transferred to them by the departing Yugoslav People's Army and the continued resupply of arms and munitions from neighboring rump Yugoslavia (Serbia and Montenegro).

The embargo, although initially intended to reduce the level of violence, implicitly placed the victim and perpetrator on an equal moral plane and unquestionably favored the well-armed Serbian aggressor. In moral and practical terms, to have treated the two parties equally made little sense, certainly no more so than to have slapped an embargo on both Britain and Nazi Germany in 1940 to induce the belligerents to stop fighting. All the arms embargo did was to help ensure that the Bosnian authorities could not get what they needed to protect their territory and population adequately. As a result, the Yugoslav Army and the Bosnian Serb Army were able to use napalm, artillery, cluster bombs, and surface-to-surface missiles with impunity. Ultimately, however noble the goal, this policy represented a type of involvement by the international community whose impact clearly benefitted one of the parties to the detriment of the other.

Thanks to their preponderance of military power, the Serbs found the Muslims to be a relatively easy target at first. Initially, the Serbs could conduct operations at a low cost in terms of their own casualties, while the Muslims found it difficult to defend themselves effectively no matter what casualties they were willing to incur. To be sure, some observers, such as Major General MacKenzie, had created an erroneous impression that this imbalance was not a factor, when he had testified before Congress. He stated that "there is no shortage of weapons over there," even for the Bosnians, a view he continued to propagate in his public appearances.[1] However, throughout the war, and even after the Muslim-Croatian rapprochement of 1994, the military balance was heavily tilted toward the Serbs, although in relative terms the Bosnians' combat capabilities did improve over time.

Forging a Consensus—At What Price?

Initially, the United States had been openly reluctant to press for a lifting of the arms embargo. But when the new Clinton administration came into office in January, 1993, it revised U.S. policy by viewing a lifting of the embargo on the Bosnian government as the most effective approach to stopping the genocide. In October, 1993, President Clinton disclosed in an interview, "I felt very strongly that the United Nations made a grave error by applying the arms embargo on Yugoslavia to Bosnia after they recognized Bosnia. . . . I still think it is wrong."[2]

However, attempts to marshal a consensus within NATO to lift the arms embargo produced no results at the time and foundered largely because of British and French foot-dragging. Notwithstanding considerable popular domestic support in both Great Britain and France for more resolute action on Bosnia-Herzegovina, a reluctance on this score by both governments was highlighted during the unsuccessful visit to Europe by United States Secretary of State Warren Christopher in May, 1993. During that visit, it became clear that the administration in Washington had underestimated the resistance among some key allies to removing the arms embargo. According to President Clinton: "I had the feeling that the British and French felt it was far more important to avoid lifting the arms embargo than to save the country. I mean, that's just the way they felt."[3] The administration's response at the time to this refusal was surprisingly tepid, and the administration may have found the European refusal a convenient way to avoid pursuing the issue.

Among the European allies, Germany was the most forceful proponent for lifting the embargo, while the British government seems to have played a central role in opposing it. Returning again and again to an assertion that the conflict was a "civil war" caused by "centuries of ethnic hatred," Prime Minister Major's government sought to shape western policy on the embargo with a view to obstructing any change in the international position. Great Britain's actions in support of a continued embargo took various forms, including opposition at the UN, where Britain had already worked to block the General Assembly's recommendation to lift the embargo in December, 1992. Great Britain again exerted considerable effort, along with France and Russia, to derail a similar motion at the Security Council in June, 1993.[4] In the end, in the interest of a united European position, Germany's Chancellor Kohl also retreated reluctantly from his position. As a result, the initiative languished and was shelved, much to the chagrin of not only many in the West but to public opinion in most Muslim countries (fig. 5). In the United States, despite calls by many lawmakers to lift the embargo, the Clinton administration continued to be reluctant to do so unilaterally and lobbied with Congress on behalf of retaining the embargo. Congress, however, was also split on this issue. Despite a June, 1994 vote by the House of Representatives in favor of lifting the arms embargo unilaterally, the vote was only advisory and could be ignored or easily bypassed due to the narrow majority it received. Moreover, this bill was a stand-alone measure, rather than being attached as a rider to some other important piece of legislation, increasing the likelihood that it could be vetoed easily. As it was, even some of those in Congress who had voted in favor of lifting the embargo apparently did so with the understanding that the measure would not be put into effect. The following month the Senate rejected a motion to lift the embargo unilaterally.[5] Sensitivity about not jeopardizing other countries' support for embargoes against Iraq, Libya,

The cartoon depicts Margaret Thatcher as a man for proposing that the arms embargo against the Muslims be lifted. Other world leaders are portrayed as too irresolute to take the same action. The papers held by Thatcher read "Thatcher: 'Arm Bosnia's Muslims.'" Published in *Al-Sharq Al-Awsat*, London (Saudi-owned), April 15, 1993, by Mahmud Kahil.

and Iran played a key role in the international community's not wishing to thwart European policy on Bosnia, and administration officials argued that lifting the embargo unilaterally would "fracture the NATO alliance and put us at odds with Russia."[6] However, it was questionable whether it was either fair or sensible to equate Bosnia-Herzegovina to such pariah states and to force the Bosnians to pay for the misdeeds which had led to the other embargoes.

Arguing to Keep the Embargo

Supporters of a continued embargo based their case on several key points, as did France's foreign minister, Alain Juppé. In May, 1994, he stated that a lifting of the embargo would have meant the end of humanitarian aid, the renewed shelling of cities, the creation of more refugees, the taking of revenge by the Bosnians, and even the mutually exclusive "trigger[ing of] the crushing" of the Bosnians, and transforming the conflict into an endless "Hundred Years' War." All these events would thereby derail peace, according to Juppé, "a peace that I would not characterize necessarily as a just one—is there ever anything like a truly just compromise?—but one that can be balanced and stable."[7] A key point was that allowing the Bosnian government to arm would prolong the fighting. A representative for the U.S. Joint Chiefs of Staff, testifying before Congress in January, 1993, against lifting the embargo, offered a blanket judgment that the result of such a move "would be continued chaos . . . it would just be contributing to the violence."[8] In general, countries with peacekeeping personnel in the country—especially Great Britain, France, and Canada, but also others—contended that lifting the embargo would place their forces at greater risk, whether from expanded combat conditions or from direct retaliation. A related argument was that humanitarian efforts would also suffer as a result of the increased fighting and retaliation that were expected to follow.

However, it is questionable that by preventing one side from defending itself chaos was averted. Neither can it be assumed that the peacekeepers would have been at greater risk if the Bosnian side had been able to match the Serbs in firepower rather than being kept at the mercy of Serbian forces. The Serbs' targeting of the peacekeepers, presumably out of spite, would have been far from inevitable. The Serbs would have only gained a potential military response or, at best, the peacekeepers' departure, thus removing those potential targets and at the same time alienating the international community, without reversing the arms flow to Bosnia. Moreover, such a high number of peacekeepers supporting humanitarian operations would probably not have been needed in the first place if the Bosnian government had been able to take care of itself militarily. If anything, fewer regions and civilians would have been placed at risk and in need of humanitarian relief if the Bosnian government had been able to provide for its own defense.

Nor was it the embargo that reduced the killing. There is no evidence that hamstringing the Bosnian government's defense reduced the level of fighting. It only increased the number of Muslim casualties and the area over which Serbian forces were able to hold sway. It was the Muslims' improving military capability and their success in raising the cost of further Serb expansion that convinced the latter to slow down and consolidate their gains.

Yet, in April, 1993, negotiator Lord Owen explained his personal opposition to lifting the arms ban by arguing that the Serbs would then also have been free to acquire more weapons. Although he insisted that then the "danger is that you will unleash 1990s sophisticated armament if the Russians supply the Serbs," it was difficult to see what other arms the Serbs needed that they could not already obtain from Belgrade's domestic arsenals or why Moscow would donate advanced weaponry, which the Bosnian Serbs could not absorb easily in any event.[9] Lord Owen inexplicably also argued that "lifting the embargo should not be assumed to be in the Muslim interest." Instead, in his view, the Bosnian government should have seen its retention in a positive light, for, thanks to the embargo, supposedly the Serbs were prevented from acquiring advanced Russian systems. He contended, somewhat lamely, that the other parties had actually benefitted positively from the embargo, as they had somehow been better placed to bypass the controls than had the Serbs, allowing them to allegedly manufacture and import arms.[10] On the contrary, if the Bosnian government did improve its relative military position, it would occur despite the intent and implementation of the embargo, not because of it.

Lord Owen remained adamantly opposed to lifting the embargo and saw the Bosnian government's campaign to end the embargo as little more than a stratagem by which the Bosnian government hoped to draw the U.S. into the fray. He assumed that if the embargo were lifted the situation would deteriorate for the Muslims. He claimed the Muslims hoped worsening conditions would then lead to outside intervention in order to save them from the desperate situation which lifting the embargo would create.[11]

Major General MacKenzie had argued before Congress on May 26, 1993, that lifting the embargo would involve a gap of time before arms began flowing in any case. He went on to claim that the "Bosnian Serbs and Croats would take advantage of the delay, and they certainly haven't used all their resources yet and they would take everything they could as quickly and as violently as possible."[12] However, that "delay" was to occur anyhow, which the Serbs used to try to seize as much land as possible, committing to the limit whatever resources they had, rather than holding back even as the embargo remained in force.

The rationale against lifting the embargo often also hinged on a dubious antithetical apposition of fighting and "a political solution." This Manichaean paradigm lay at the root, for example, of Cyrus Vance's reproach to those who believed that the use of force by the international community might become necessary: "Frankly I'm getting fed up with this mindless criticism that doesn't face up to a central fact. . . . In Bosnia there is no viable alternative to a negotiated settlement."[13] That is, what was uppermost was obtaining a settlement, with the provisions flowing from such a deal almost as an afterthought. As Lord Owen and others saw it, such a settlement could not be achieved as easily if the Bosnian government were in a better position to defend itself, since the Bosnians, realistically, might then be less likely to negotiate and accept partition, the Serbs' seizure of territory, and the displacement of the Muslim population as conditions of the political solution offered to them.

However, the two phenomena of conflict and political negotiation are not mutually exclusive. Rather, they are complementary and interactive parts of a single process, for, as the Prussian military strategist Karl von Clausewitz had observed, war is "a continuation of politics." Wars are fought for political ends, and virtually all wars end politically, with a negotiated settlement. Usually, negotiations, in whatever form, even continue between two belligerents while fighting is occurring, rather than the two being mutually exclusive categories of interaction. The Serbs were particularly adept at the simultaneous fight-and-talk strategy. What fighting may do, however, is ensure better terms for that eventual political solution. For Bosnia-Herzegovina, what even a limited ability to continue fighting did was to help the Muslims avoid a more disastrous end-state, including even more complete genocide and the total dismemberment of the state. Without a secure source of arms, however, there was a limit to what the Muslims could accomplish on the battlefield. The deficiency in arms was reflected at the negotiating table too. In July, 1994, as a direct result of a recent military victory—due largely to their advantage in artillery—the Bosnian Serbs' negotiating position on the "contact group" peace plan hardened.[14]

Foreign initiatives on retaining the embargo in place inevitably strengthened, however unintentionally, the Serbs' negotiating position by ensuring the latter a lopsided advantage on the battlefield. Nevertheless, British Foreign Secretary Douglas Hurd quixotically opposed lifting the arms embargo specifically in order to prevent the creation of what he termed a "level killing field," an argument he first tested in a letter to the London *Daily Telegraph* on April 5, 1993. Yet a putative desire to be even-handed could only be to the disadvantage of the Bosnian government. Lord Owen, too, had resisted this option because, in his mind, it would have constituted "an irresponsible tilting of the balance," presumably away from the Serbs, although it is difficult to justify in either political or moral terms why that balance should have been maintained. In retrospect, however, he maintained, somewhat unconvincingly, that helping the Bosnian government to find just this military balance had been a goal of the EU all along. He contended, "We have tried to level the differences and discrepancies between the armed forces," although all he could cite as proof was the enactment of the no-fly zone.[15]

The falling out between the Muslims and the Croatians in the spring of 1993 provided a convenient rationale to retain the embargo, for outsiders could now argue, and did, that everyone was now fighting everyone and that the situation had become too complex. Douglas Hogg, Great Britain's Under Secretary for Foreign Affairs, tried to convince a Croatian journalist of this chaotic view when the latter asked him why the embargo had not been lifted. Hogg responded, "I believe that you too will agree that if we supply arms to the Muslims to fight against you [Croatians] and then, as a result, also armed you, that would make little sense." Undeterred, the interviewer persisted in asking why then the embargo had not been lifted earlier, when there had been no such Croatian-Muslim fighting to serve as an obstacle, or rationalization. In his reply, Hogg highlighted that the objective in any event had been all along to avoid changing the military balance or, as he put it: "The international community took the decision at that [earlier] time that we had to be committed to seeking a political solution instead of supplying arms and thereby making the situation worse. That is my belief."[16]

Finally, those opposed to lifting the embargo often surfaced "practical" considerations, such as Bosnia-Herzegovina's geographic isolation or difficulties with training the Bosnian Army. Had the international community determined that the Bosnian government, as the legally elected authority in Bosnia-Herzegovina, did merit its direct support, security assistance in the form of arms, training, logistic support, and intelligence could have been provided easily. Finding a route, given the will, would not have been insurmountable, especially while the Croatian-Bosnian alliance held—at which time small quantities of smuggled light arms did get through to Bosnia-Herzegovina via Croatia—and again after cooperation was reestablished in early 1994.

Even if the international community did not want to get involved directly, obtaining arms and training would not have presented a major problem, once the legal barriers and physical controls of the embargo were lifted. With the sanctions removed, the Bosnian government could have dealt on its own with private suppliers of its choice. Most men in former Yugoslavia have had basic military training already and the Islamic countries, in particular, might have made available the necessary facilities for additional training on their territory. As it was, had the Islamic countries been more supportive, they could have provided a "halfway house" from the very first.

Even while the arms embargo was still in effect, they could have taken Bosnian refugees to their countries and formed them into military units, ready to deploy to Bosnia when the embargo was lifted. However, they too, by and large appear to have been reluctant to help materially despite their verbal support.

Would Arming the Bosnians Have Mattered?

But would arming the Bosnian government forces have led to a different outcome? Evidence suggests that it would have. It would be difficult to see how lifting the embargo would have made the situation worse operationally, as Hogg had feared, at least insofar as the Muslims were concerned, since the Serbs' military situation would have deteriorated. On the contrary, it may have been precisely the achievement of a greater military balance, the "tilting of the balance" in the form of an increased capability for the Bosnian government forces, that prevented the further disintegration of the Bosnian government and the continued destruction of the Muslim community. Even as late as the end of 1993, the acquisition of small amounts of light arms by capture and on the black market—along with better organization and leadership—improved the Bosnian government's situation on the battlefield and, consequently, its bargaining position significantly.

If the Serbian cost-benefit assessment had been forced to shift dramatically, it is more likely that the Serbs would have sought to stop the conflict and have finally sat down to negotiate and compromise in good faith. Just such a revision in the correlation of forces on the battlefield early in the crisis, very likely, could have led to a shorter war and more just termination, with fewer victims. Ultimately, it may have led to a more stable end-state, as was highlighted by the Croatians' turnaround in February, 1994, in relation to the Bosnian government after the Bosnian government forces had defeated the Bosnian Croatians.

Even the simple possibility of lifting the arms embargo had a decided impact on the political situation. As President Clinton correctly assessed, "the closest we ever were to settling that [politically] was when the Serbs and the Croats thought that the Europeans were going to go along with my proposal to lift the arms embargo and to make standby air power to enforce no use of Serbian artillery against the government . . . while the arms embargo was being lifted."[17] Recognizing this factor, Hurd, in July, 1994, raised the possibility—although reluctantly and vaguely—of ending the embargo in order to exert leverage on the Bosnian Serbs to accept the new peace plan. If the Bosnian Serbs rejected the plan, he hinted, "lifting of the arms embargo may become unavoidable." In a similar move to apply pressure, in August, 1994, the U.S. Congress and President Clinton also expressed their intention to work to lift the embargo if there were no progress on the peace plan, although disagreement continued among policy makers whether the U.S. should ignore the embargo unilaterally.[18]

Had the Bosnian government been able to build up its military power quickly and to create a capability to protect its citizens and territory, most of the Croatians, and even many of the Serbs, would very likely have rallied to the government out of conviction and self-interest, as was the case during the early days of the crisis. Instead, as the Bosnian government, constrained by the embargo, found itself hard put to cope with the security situation, Bosnian Croats and Serbs saw it more difficult to avoid cooperating with the radical leadership within their communities, since these leaders had the coercive power and could dangle before them the lure of being on the winning side. Working in such uneven circumstances, even some Muslims ultimately sought to make separate deals with the Serbian authorities in a desperate attempt to survive.

As it was, general war-weariness induced by even the limited capability which the Bosnian Army was able to establish eventually succeeded in helping to convince the Bosnian Serbs by mid-1993 that they had reached their culminating point and that further major territorial gains would have to come at an unacceptable human and economic cost. The Bosnian Serb and the Serbian leadership, significantly, were very sensitive about taking casualties and, despite the firepower overmatch their forces enjoyed, had a difficult time convincing all the Bosnian Serbs to fight for what many saw as simple territorial expansion.

National will in Serbia itself was considerably more fragile than conventional wisdom often assumed, although some in the West held out the specter of an open-ended and wholesale commitment in Bosnia-Herzegovina on Belgrade's part to forestall foreign intervention. On the contrary, while supporting the notion of Greater Serbia in the abstract, many Serbs in Serbia apparently had no desire to fight for it. Milošević would have been hard-pressed to make a major long-term manpower commitment to Bosnia-Herzegovina, particularly if that involved the call-up of reluctant reserves and the prospect of high casualties.

There is ample evidence to suggest that, in fact, many Serbs from both Bosnia-Herzegovina and Serbia did their best to avoid serving in the military even in a situation that entailed only moderate personal risk. Yugoslav Army sources railed against the emigration of "intellectuals" and military-age men from even safe areas in Bosnia-Herzegovina, who often left behind older family members to take care of their property. The Yugoslav Army openly called them traitors. As of early 1993, at least 53,000 registered, and many more unregistered, draft-age Serbs from Croatia and Bosnia-Herzegovina were living in Serbia, despite continuing pressure and roundups to return them home to take up arms. A Serbian official in the city of Novi Sad accused many Bosnian Serbs of not registering with the authorities with the expressed intention of avoiding the draft and of "not behaving like people who are threatened."[19]

According to Bosnian Serb general Lisica, motivating his troops became increasingly difficult. In his experience, appeals to Serbian Orthodoxy were only met by "shaking with fear" and those to the state by wisecracks that "our state [Yugoslavia] has collapsed."[20] Morale on the battlefield was often questionable and better not tested. In one case, General Lisica personally confronted a Bosnian Serb artillery unit which had abandoned its position and tried to shame its personnel by offering them the choice of either returning to duty or doffing their uniforms. All except one chose to shed their uniforms and walk home bare rather than stay at the front.[21] Even Bosnian Serbs allegedly involved in atrocities were disinclined to actually take part in combat, which presented greater risks than ethnic cleansing operations. Thus, Dušan Tadić, the Bosnian Serb arrested in Germany in February, 1994, on charges of war crimes, had come there after deserting from his unit in the Bosnian Serb Army. A Serb official who was acquainted with him described him as someone who was "never able to hide his fear; he was exceptionally afraid of combat."[22] An unwillingness to make themselves liable for the draft at the hands of the Bosnian Serb authorities also led to difficulties in convincing other Serbs to settle in newly cleansed areas in Bosnia-Herzegovina, even outside the war zones, "despite so much liberated and unpopulated space," as the Yugoslav Army termed it.[23]

Once large-scale violence had begun against them, the Muslims, on the contrary, seemed to become more willing to fight, no doubt spurred by the instinct for survival. In fact, Bosnia-Herzegovina Army units often attracted more volunteers than they had weapons to provide. Had the Bosnian government been allowed to obtain sufficient arms, not only would the Serbs not have had a free hand in dealing with Muslim civilians, but the cost of the Serbian policy would have risen dramatically in terms of casualties, thereby limiting or derailing ethnic cleansing.

This analysis also suggests that, should the international community have decided on military intervention, the prospect of a quagmire may not have been as automatic as was usually assumed, especially if the intervention had occurred in conjunction with a lifting of the arms embargo on the Bosnian government. A neutralization of the Bosnian Serb heavy weapons capability by international forces would have enabled a larger, now armed and better motivated, Bosnian government army to play the main role in dealing militarily and politically with the remaining Bosnian Serb forces and to restore security and stability.

Timing, again, is a crucial variable in such situations. An early lifting of the embargo could have stopped ethnic cleansing before much of the damage had been done. With the Bosnian government holding less territory, greater numbers of people being removed from their homes, and the Croatian allies shifting sides, conditions deteriorated, requiring greater amounts of arms. Their delivery would have become more problematic and the ensuing combat to retake occupied areas and to return the expelled population would have taken proportionately longer and been more costly and disruptive. Nevertheless, even at later stages in the war, this option seemed more realistic in halting and reversing the effects of genocide than the successive plans which the international community crafted but was reluctant to back up.

An Armed Bosnian Government—Latent Aggressor?

Once armed, would the Muslims have taken revenge for the injuries they had suffered; would they themselves have engaged, in sum, in reverse ethnic cleansing on a mass scale? Major General MacKenzie, for one, openly fostered this view.[24] More to the point, some policy makers, such as Alain Juppé, also latched on to this view as a rationalization for not lifting the embargo.[25]

No doubt, the Bosnian government, at least early in the war, would have tried to reestablish its authority over all of the republic's territory, or at least over those areas which did not have a Serb majority before April, 1992. At worst, a Bosnian Serb defeat would probably only have led to a reintegration of Bosnia-Herzegovina. Nevertheless, the absence of any official government doctrine calling for ethnic purity or exclusivity suggests it unlikely that the Muslim power structure would have instituted a policy of revenge or provided the legal or moral framework for others to do so.

On the contrary, Muslim leaders had called for a pluralistic secular society—not an Islamic state—with the continued inclusion of the Serbian and Croatian communities, a position from which they never officially diverged. In an interview given in April, 1991, Izetbegović underlined his position: "I reiterate that no one here has any intention of creating an Islamic Bosnia. Our goal is, and we hope to get the agreement of the Serbian and Croatian peoples, that we gradually create a secular state out of Bosnia-Herzegovina." As he repeated to a Serbian nationalist periodical later that year, with the intent of reassuring the Serbs:

> From the first day that I entered on the political scene up to now, I have repeated like a parrot, not only repeated but also acted accordingly: "We want to set up a secular republic here in Bosnia-Herzegovina." No Islamic or Muslim republic is possible in Bosnia-Herzegovina. . . . We were offered a [reduced] Muslim republic. I could have gotten that easily had I prolonged the negotiations in Split [with Milošević and Tudjman] instead of breaking them off. . . . But I knew very well that that would not be an acceptable solution for Bosnia-Herzegovina.[26]

One should remember that even the case against Izetbegović in his 1983 trial for "fundamentalism" had included charges that he had called for a multiparty democratic system like that of Austria for Bosnia-Herzegovina, which, of course, was a crime in the eyes of the then-ruling Communist Party.[27]

Other Bosnian opinion makers, including leading clerics, also continued to call for a multiconfessional society rather than an Islamic state or ethnic-based partition, notwithstanding the mounting international pressure to accept the latter. When asked about his vision for his native Bosnia-Herzegovina, Ševko Omerbašić, Director of the Islamic Council of Croatia and Slovenia, aware that his comments would be printed in a newspaper destined to be read largely by his countrymen, stressed: "There is no dilemma there. Bosnia-Herzegovina must remain free, united, sovereign, and multiconfessional. . . . I believe in a shared life in Bosnia-Herzegovina."[28] Moreover, representatives continued to carry the same message even in Muslim forums abroad, where one would have expected them to exploit Islamic exclusivity to curry favor if that had actually been Bosnian government policy. Bosnia's ambassador to Croatia told the Arab press, "There was never a plan for Bosnia to be an Islamic state."[29] Similarly, at a press conference in Doha, Qatar, the religious head of Bosnia-Herzegovina's Islamic community called for "a just peace" in which members of all nationalities could return to their homes.[30] This desire was true even in late 1993, when Irfan Ljubijankić, the Minister for Foreign Affairs, visiting the UAE, called for saving "our multicultural identity," at a time when partition looked increasingly unavoidable.[31] Whatever skepticism about political expediency one might raise, it would be difficult for any leadership to mobilize popular support for an "Islamic state" while arguing and working so systematically and vigorously against the concept in public, including among key potential backers at home and abroad.

Moreover, Bosnian representatives purposely differentiated between ordinary Serbs and Croatians and those individuals who had specifically engaged in war crimes, rather than lumping all of them indiscriminately into a single category, as their opponents had often done with the Muslims. The situation in Sarajevo, Tuzla, or other areas which the government controlled directly could have served as a telling indicator. There, even under exceedingly trying conditions, the predominantly Muslim authorities had not turned on the Serb and Croatian communities, an attitude they could have easily assumed from the very first, given their local superiority.[32]

However, if partition were imposed irrespective of the desires of the Bosnian government, based on international pressure to accept a strategically and politically inviable territorial situation, the likelihood of the situation degenerating into reverse ethnic cleansing at some time would have been heightened. The longer the phenomenon of anti-Muslim ethnic cleansing and the sense of international abandonment continued and as increasing numbers suffered at the hands of the Serbs and, later, the Croatians, the greater the number of individual Muslims who would have felt they had scores to settle. By mid-1993, in a bid to ensure their state's survival and security, Bosnian forces had begun to retaliate by pushing Croatians out of their homes in central Bosnia until the rapprochement of February, 1994.

Undoubtedly, individual Muslims would have been tempted to exact retribution, and a battered Bosnian government structure might have been challenged to prevent that everywhere, as it regained lost ground in a fluid situation. In such scenarios, legal redress against the perpetrators of war crimes, in the form of a tribunal, is an essential and usually effective factor in preventing revenge that might otherwise occur on a wide and indiscriminate scale by the victimized party.

Overall, moreover, a Bosnian government with the wherewithal to defend itself would have had more incentive, as well as a greater physical and moral ability, to control whatever radical elements might arise within its own ranks bent on revenge, rather than a weaker one unable to offer any credible alternative to a policy of despair. At the same time, a situation in which the Bosnian government had the means to protect the country's territory and to deal with opposing forces would have led to significant numbers of Bosnian Croatians and Serbs rallying once it became clearly in their interest to do so. Just such a shift in allegiances occurred during World War II, as many Ustaše and Chetniks, including entire organized military units, went over to the Partisans as they saw the balance of power in Bosnia-Herzegovina shifting. The bloodless absorption of the HVO forces in Sarajevo into the Bosnian Army in November, 1993, as well as the formation of the Croatian-Muslim federation, could well have served as the model for this type of integration. To facilitate and ensure such a process, a phased lifting of the arms embargo, linked to the government's commitment to avoid retaliation, could have been a workable option.

12. Heading for the End-State

The Continuing Humanitarian Dilemma

Unable to match the Serbs' firepower, the Muslims increasingly came to face-to-face with the bleak choice of either continuing a desperate struggle for a united state or of accepting partition on the best conditions offered. The latter option entailed trying to survive in camp-like cantonments dependent on foreign largesse. With hundreds of thousands of its citizens unable to return to their homes and forced into what seemed an inviable patchwork of territories, the Bosnian government oscillated between the two options. Even into 1994, the leadership's avowed ideal remained a united, multiconfessional Bosnia-Herzegovina, with the Bosnian government appearing willing to compromise if others were.

With the military situation having at least stabilized in much of Bosnia-Herzegovina by late 1993, the Bosnian government was encouraged to try to hold on in order to improve the terms of future negotiations toward an end-state. Yet, by the end of 1993, Bosnian leadership appeared increasingly, but reluctantly, less hopeful that achieving a completely reunified country was feasible. Leaders seemed resigned to the inevitability of partition in some form. However distasteful and fraught with uncertainty it might be, partition could at least offer a respite for the Muslims over a particularly difficult period. Gradually, in light of the international community's apparent reluctance to become involved more directly or to lift the arms embargo, the ultimate goal evolved into the establishment of some type of Bosnian state. This proposed state, although smaller, was at no time intended to be exclusively Muslim, much less organized along the principles of political Islam. Quite to the contrary, leaders demonstrated a renewed willingness to envision a federation with the largely Croatian Herceg-Bosna entity and even a confederation with neighboring Croatia. At the same time, an increasingly key concern was to get a just share of the territory in order to establish a viable and defensible entity, even if all the losses of territory could not be reversed.

By late 1993, most of the Bosnian Serbs, and certainly Milošević, had come to believe that they had reached their culminating point. They had achieved most of what was feasible for now without incurring costs far exceeding the likely benefits or seeing the momentum shift to the other side. By that time, the Bosnian government had reorganized and improved its military, which went in tandem with problems with the Bosnian Serbs' capabilities and morale. Even this modest shift in the balance of power placed Milošević in what some would say was a well-deserved dilemma. It forced him to either stand by and risk seeing the Bosnian Serb position erode and open himself up to accusations of betraying the Serb cause, or to step up Serbia's support and involvement.

At least initially, in January, 1994, reports indicated that Milošević was stepping up his commitment, with the deployment of additional regular Yugoslav Army forces across the Drina. Perhaps he hoped that a quick, decisive intervention would still enable the Serbs to seize additional key territory before a negotiated settlement.[1] But, perhaps for Milošević, a calculating pragmatist rather than a rigid visionary, what matters most is his personal political position. The escalation option had all the potential for a military quagmire in Bosnia-Herzegovina and risked causing more casualties, which could have had serious ramifications for his domestic support in Serbia. Facing the possibility of a more costly military situation, he most likely would seek to stop the conflict through an accord, but one that would allow the Serbs to hold on to as much territory as possible.

The Bosnian government's improved situation on the battlefield also represented a dilemma for the Bosnian Serb leadership. The latter wanted both to retain the territory they had taken and to also convince the Bosnian government to stop fighting. Realistically, however, they would have to choose between the two options.

As of this writing, the "contact group" plan appears to be the basis for negotiations for peace in Bosnia-Herzegovina. A final version of the plan remains to be hammered out. However, one of the basic provisions is a return by the Bosnian Serbs of some, but not all, of the land which had a non-

Serb majority before the war. If the plan also recognizes the principle of territorial continuity for the Bosnian Serbs, it would reward the present power balance situation on the ground rather than reflect pre-war ethnic realities. Moreover, what will remain key is the Bosnian government's need to place trust in international guarantees for its future security as part of the plan.

Although predicting specific events in such a volatile situation as that of war-torn Bosnia-Herzegovina is fraught with uncertainty, certain scenarios and their implications, nevertheless, may have more realistic potential than others. Eventually, a political settlement may be concluded in which all sides accept the results of the recent conflict and decide, though grudgingly, that Bosnia-Herzegovina has seen enough turmoil. Perhaps leaders on both sides may decide to operate based on a new status quo and to accept recent changes in territory, but that scenario is problematic. Even if all parties accept an agreement based on formal or de facto partition, that agreement may not usher in a period of peace and stability and, in and of itself, not necessarily be a solid guarantee against a resumption of genocide at some later date. Unless the reshaped Bosnian state is made viable and the existing balance of power is further modified, additional rounds of aggression and ethnic cleansing remain likely. For the Bosnian Serbs, a diplomatic agreement among all sides may be only a temporary expedient that permits them to not only consolidate their gains under the guise of the new status quo but also to reconstitute their strained military establishment. Indeed, they may pause to work out a more permanent political relationship and probable eventual union with Serbia, which itself is in need of rebuilding its battered economy and international political position.

Under the circumstances, whatever compromise the Serbian side may be willing to make in negotiations, such as the concession under international pressure to recognize a certain percentage of territory to the Bosnian state, the solution may well turn out to be either cosmetic or temporary. According to one Serbian representative at Geneva: "All of us on the Serbian negotiating team had erasers and pencils in our hands, and we sought to reduce that [territory to be allotted to the Muslims]. Whenever there were modifications of the map, these were [only] symbolic. There was always less than that famous 30 percent."[2]

According to some hard-liners, such as General Mladić, the Serbian state in Bosnia even ought to expand to the sea at the expense of Croatia, either by the latter's concession or by force. He warned: "Mr. Tudjman must think that over seriously. Croatia has two thousand kilometers of coastline. It would be best if we come to an agreement about our access to the sea peacefully, rather than having me resolve it. Everyone knows what that would mean."[3]

Of course, some of this posturing was no doubt maximalist rhetoric, as the Bosnian Serbs were willing to give up some territory in exchange for a recognition of their other gains. Whatever agreement resulted, the Bosnian Serb leadership sought to block a return of the ousted non-Serb inhabitants in order to ensure that the territory now under Serbian control would henceforth be ethnically homogeneous. What appeared as a key negotiating point to them, however, was retaining the strategically dominant position they had achieved, including a coterminous territory having direct links with Serbian-held areas in Croatia and with Serbia. In particular, in order to enable them to set up a consolidated Greater Serbia, the Bosnian Serbs regarded as crucial their control over the Posavina Corridor in northern Bosnia-Herzegovina. At the same time, Serbian control over so much key territory would leave a Bosnian state weak, with its configuration a patchwork of unconnected territories. If, however, the basis of an agreement was that of pre-war ethnic boundaries—with the subsequent results of ethnic cleansing ignored—the ethnically Serbian territories would have been scattered, and the Bosnian Serbs would have found it hard to avoid being reintegrated into a unified Bosnia-Herzegovina.

Although the goals of the Serbian negotiators were constant, their credibility remained suspect. Diplomacy, as General Mladić noted, was just one more tool to achieve unchanged objectives: "In order to succeed, you have to be devious; tell them one thing one time, another thing at another time."[4] Likewise, as Karadžić reassured Bosnian Serb military personnel: "Pay no attention to what we do at the conferences, as all the maps are transient, and only what you hold is eternal. Hold every village of ours, and do not worry."[5] Ultimately, in the Bosnian Serbs' view, military power would continue to be critical in determining the future, for as General Mladić reiterated in a speech in Belgrade in late 1993, his guiding concept of intercommunal relations in Bosnia-Herzegovina was that "as long as planet Earth has been in existence, borders between states and peoples have been determined by the shedding of blood and by the cutting off of heads."[6]

Even with an agreement, the Muslims' vulnerability is likely to continue for the foreseeable future unless they can acquire more arms. They will simply be unable to defend themselves against their better armed neighbors, barring a lifting of the arms embargo or the disarming and neutralization of their tormentors.

If their neighbors remain stronger, they may be tempted to take advantage of the Muslims. Predictably, anger and opposition prevailed among leaders across the Serbian political spectrum to the Croatian-Muslim agreement, which degraded the correlation of forces for the Serbs. The Serbs hope that it will fall apart, reopening possibilities for increased Serbian pressure on the Muslims.

In particular, the Bosnian Serbs appeared determined to eliminate the exposed Muslim enclaves if the chance arose. According to Momčilo Krajišnik, speaker of the Bosnian Serb Parliament: "No deal will be considered which would mean splitting up Serbian ethnic space. There will be no concessions to the Muslims in eastern Bosnia." Instead, he suggested that the Bosnian government should trade away their enclaves in eastern Bosnia for other territory, although he was also quick to add that the Serbs would not give up territory in western Bosnia in exchange either.[7]

Other Serbian nationalists, such as Gojko Djogo, prominent author and president of the Union of Bosnia-Herzegovina Serbs in Serbia, maintained pressure to eliminate these remnants of the Muslims' presence, arguing in both ideological and security terms. According to Djogo, "I would cleanse the pockets in the Podrinje [region of eastern Bosnia] . . . of the madmen infected with the Asiatic plague, who hold a knife at our backs." Speaking candidly, Djogo claimed that ultimately there would be no room at all for the Muslims in Bosnia-Herzegovina: "The final solution of the Yugoslav and Serbian questions is the division of Bosnia between the Serbs and Croatians into two parts. Anything else is like piling ashes over a fire which tomorrow will flare up again. The creation of new peoples [the Muslims] and states [Bosnia-Herzegovina] was [just] Communist metaphysics."[8] In Serbia itself, in November, 1993, the Yugoslav Army, government agencies, and a few think tanks held a seminar to discuss the Serbs' future boundaries. One participant concluded that in this region "borders have always been drawn by rifles." Another, speculating on the prospects for the survival of ethnic enclaves, used an analogy that such a "'leopard skin' quickly disappears or is transformed, as the consequence of ethnic wars."[9]

More broadly, Karadžić's continued view that the Muslims were essentially an artificial entity of a transient nature was unsettling. In August, 1993, at the time that an agreement was being hammered out in Geneva, he claimed that the Muslims had been created as a nation in the former Yugoslavia according to the plans of foreign forces in order to limit Serbian influence. He concluded, therefore, that, by rejecting their alleged true Ser-

185

bian identity, the Muslims were now "vulnerable to marginalization and even to the danger of annihilation. . . . The Muslims could have mattered only if they were part of the Serbian nation. As it is, I do not see a future for the Muslim nation."[10] That Karadžić's basic outlook had not evolved significantly stood out clearly as he shared with a domestic audience in February, 1994, his longstanding assessment that the outside world still did not understand. He summarized his unchanged long-range plans for the Muslims by stating:

Europe wants us to remain in a common country with the Muslims so as to control them. That European calculation is extremely wrong since in about fifteen years the Muslims would be in the majority, and they would create pressure, as in Kosovo, for the Serbs and the Croats to move out. Then it would become a great Muslim state in Europe. Trying to avoid a small Muslim state in Europe, Europe is creating a great Muslim state, because of its miscalculations. Europe does not know that, though. We will not accept that. We have nothing against a small Muslim state, but we also have nothing against dividing Bosnia in two parts between the Serbs and the Croats.[11]

At some time in the future, having solidified their domestic and diplomatic position, the Serbs may well resume their pressure against the vulnerable Bosnian—and Croatian—territories, especially if international guarantees waver. Next time, of course, the Serbs may go about their task in a more effective manner if they succeed in assimilating the lessons learned from the current round on how to deal with the international community.

Zhirinovskiy's cavalier promises to Belgrade of future Russian support may act as an especially potent encouragement to the Serbs. Within a few years, Moscow's political and military backing may spur the Serbs to renew the drive for an even larger Greater Serbia, if Zhirinovskiy, or someone like him, comes to power. Šešelj has come out openly in favor of consolidating recent gains and postponing further advances until later: "Due to the unfavorable international environment, they [other territories] will have to await better days. We must wait for someone like Zhirinovskiy to become president of Russia."[12] Russia has already signaled its intention to play a greater role in the region with its more active involvement in shaping and implementing the February, 1994 Sarajevo ceasefire agreement. But no matter who is in charge, an increasingly nationalist Russian government may become less cooperative on foreign policy issues in general. That situation makes it less likely that an international consensus can be reached to take long-term decisive action in the future on Bosnia-Herzegovina, particularly if that risk means a potential confrontation with a more assertive Moscow.

The Muslims, too, face a dilemma. On the one hand, an agreement might be considered realistic if it reflected the existing balance of power at the time it was signed. On the other hand, it could encourage renewed fighting later if the Muslims feel that its provisions are weighted heavily against them. If an agreement ratifies a precarious situation and mandates their continued vulnerability, those conditions could contain the seeds for more confrontations. If the Muslims perceive themselves as the aggrieved party, their overriding sense of injustice may compel them to use any ceasefire or agreement as a breathing spell to prepare for further rounds of war. As Clausewitz pointed out: "Even the ultimate outcome of a war is not always to be regarded as final. The defeated state often considers the outcome merely as a transitory evil, for which a remedy may still be found in political conditions at some later date."[13] In the real world, the end-state of a war is seldom, if ever, definitive. Like a receding horizon, the result desired by the victorious belligerent may be elusive, and all the more so if the other party believes the outcome to be unjust and reversible. Under the circumstances, in the absence of a just settlement and compensation, the result of negotiations may well be continued instability in the region. Access to a seaport, in particular, would finally provide the Bosnian state with a reliable conduit for arms, thus changing the balance of power against its Serbian neighbors, and making the retrieval of lost lands more feasible and attractive no matter what the outside world thought. Moreover, barring a just settlement, some Muslims might become radicalized by their wartime experience. The creation of a nearly insoluble diaspora dilemma could potentially add to the international refugee and terrorist problems beyond the desires and control of the present Bosnian leadership.

Even in a post-agreement period, the international community will need to remain deeply involved for a long time. The provision of humanitarian aid will retain its importance in the post-agreement period in order to help people survive what is likely to be a traumatic and lengthy dislocation. To ensure the viability of a redefined Bosnian state as projected, extensive long-term economic aid would also be needed. Otherwise, faced with the prospects of living in what could become for all intents and purposes a series of inhospitable mammoth refugee camps, many people would seek to leave eventually, hoping for a normal life elsewhere. As long as the Serbs avoid high-visibility acts of violence which could outrage and galvanize foreign opinion, a freezing of the status quo in and of itself might exert enough pressure on the Muslim inhabitants to promote continued ethnic cleansing, perhaps at a slower rate, from areas that remain under Serbian control. The

UN has already had to deal with the predicament of wanting to help people leave occupied zones in order to save them but thereby facilitating a form of unintentional "managed ethnic cleansing." Following verbal protests by the international community after the April, 1994 killing of seventeen Muslims and two Croatians in the Serbian-controlled town of Prijedor, Karadžić sought to exploit the situation. He offered to the International Red Cross to "guarantee the safe evacuation of the non-Serb population from the Bosnian Serb Republic."[14]

Even a solid agreement—if it is based on the premise of partition—is likely to spur additional ethnic cleansing by the Serbs rather than stop it, unless resolute steps are taken to discourage it. If local leaders feel they have international acquiescence to consolidate their control in ethnic terms over their allotted areas, or if they feel that there are no effective sanctions forthcoming, they are likely to take advantage of the situation by forcing more people to leave. Past experience in the occupied territories in Croatia—where the Serbs continued to expel non-Serbs behind a UN buffer of peacekeepers—suggests that, barring the provision of a considerably stronger mandate, UN forces may not have the capability to prevent more ethnic cleansing from occurring over the long term.

In order to ensure the safety of the Muslims within whatever new borders emerge from partition and to provide some chance for stability, the international community may have to deal in the future with the same dilemma it has faced up to now, namely whether or not to provide guarantees which could entail military intervention or to allow the Bosnians to provide for their own defense. While more assertive responses, such as those that took place in 1994, could build up UN credibility, UN willingness to act forcefully, consistently, and punitively will ultimately be decisive. However, as current political trends in participating countries suggest, Muslims at the least may have legitimate concerns about the credibility of such protection over the long term.

Even with the presence of peacekeeping forces, unless there is an institutionalized mandate allowing them to exercise greater involvement than they have had under the relatively toothless Chapter 6 of the UN Charter, the peacekeepers' ability to act effectively will remain limited. Peacekeeping assumes a largely pro forma presence, one desired by all parties to monitor and confirm an agreed-to disengagement. By default, the UN peacekeepers did at times engage in "aggravated peacekeeping" (sometimes alluded to as "Chapter 6½" operations), which was marked by a willingness to use force for self-defense or to carry out their humanitarian mandate. However, this approach does not envision the active "peace enforcement" found in the charter's Chapter 7, which may be needed in order to impose the world community's will on rogue actors, such as the Bosnian Serbs, by force if necessary. As Lt. Gen. Michael Rose, UNPROFOR military commander in Sarajevo, explained in March, 1994, when he discussed the mission, "We're not in the business of imposing a peace through force."[15] In fact, for some, including Lt. Gen. Michael Rose, peace enforcement appeared incompatible with "our first priority . . . to make sure humanitarian aid comes through." "As soon," Rose stressed, "as we become combatants—see what happened in Somalia—we become helpless."[16]

Western countries have shown considerable reluctance to engage in sustained peace enforcement actions that are intended to compel aggressive parties to comply. This wariness is likely to only be heightened, as enthusiasm for such missions is further dampened by the negative experience of Somalia. The prospects are poor for effective protection for the Muslims, much less for a roll-back of Serbian gains. These indications have been based not only on past practice but also on declarations, such as the one made by Great Britain's Under Secretary for Foreign Affairs, Douglas Hogg, in October, 1993. He stated, "We are not prepared to expel the Serbs by force from the areas which they have seized."[17] Likewise, the announcement in April, 1994, by "two of the highest-ranking UN officials in Bosnia" seemed to suggest a willingness to write off hard-to-defend areas, such as the three UN-designated Muslim safe areas in eastern Bosnia. As the two officials commented in an interview, "their [the Muslims'] only option is to be moved out or to submit to living under Serbian rule."[18]

In addition, the reliability of the control mechanisms placed over the Serbs' armaments and forces will be key to the effectiveness of any UN guarantees in Bosnia-Herzegovina. Apparently, some players, such as Rose, had initially favored minimal controls as part of the ceasefire agreement on Sarajevo in February, 1994. Although he was later overruled in favor of tighter measures, he declared himself satisfied as long as he could observe Serbian weapons.[19] Whether practical controls can be established countrywide or even whether controls in the Sarajevo area can be maintained over time will be a crucial variable. The increasing involvement of Russian troops as peacekeepers, given their outright pro-Serb partisanship, is likely to complicate UN monitoring and controls to an even greater degree.

Past acquiescence of some participants in the UN peace support mission to pressure from Belgrade and the Bosnian Serb authorities may impede maintaining their credibility. For example, obstacles by Belgrade made the UN Nordic Battalion's attempts to bring its tanks into Bosnia-Herzegovina from staging areas in Serbia a drawn-out ordeal. Harassment included demands for the prior payment of so-called road taxes and Belgrade's classification of the vehicles as offensive equipment. The Bosnian Serbs also imposed a delay on the replacement of the Canadian unit by Dutch troops in the UN-designated safe zone enclave of Srebrenica. These and other types of obstacles are clearly detriments to UN peacekeepers. Although a willingness to exercise greater authority could help establish greater credibility for UN forces, their resolve will likely continue to be tested by means of harassment.

Whether the peacekeeping process, with or without an accompanying blanket settlement, goes smoothly or not, the length of a UN commitment remains an issue. When would UN forces leave? Would the establishment of a secure, defensible Bosnia-Herzegovina be the necessary measure of success without which UN forces would remain in place? Or, would the commitment be tied to a time-driven deadline? Would a large force be stationed there for five years, ten years, or even forever? The commitment of a large force could be exceptionally onerous, not only in financial terms, but also in degrading the overall combat readiness of a participating country's military.

In case of an unsteady ceasefire or of mounting casualties, in particular, serious questions may arise about the foreign peacekeeping forces' staying power before participating governments decide that the cost is not worth the objective. Some countries—especially the United States—have been reluctant to provide ground forces for anything but a peacekeeping mission in a benign environment. Although many countries may initially assume that the mission of foreign military forces can be confined to peacekeeping, the environment during the truce could shift rapidly and dramatically to a more hostile one, marked by flagrant cheating or violent opposition, despite an agreement. Peace enforcement, resembling combat operations in all but name, may be required in order to prevent a truce from unraveling to its previous state. Such escalated peace enforcement operations may result in casualties among UN forces, as the experience in Somalia illustrated, creating pressures to withdraw.

Potentially for any American forces deployed, the threshold of the casualties that could be incurred before domestic calls to pull out are heard could be fairly low indeed, unless the public back home can be convinced of the value of the sacrifices. In early 1994, when the United States was considering contributing ground forces to the peacekeeping effort, a high-ranking American military officer commented pessimistically, but realistically: "We very clearly know that there are certain points in this plan where if it's not working we would just have to leave. If it's not working and we're not going to put any more effort into it, we'd have to do a Somalia, I guess."[20] Contingents from other countries would be hard-pressed to stay behind if the United States took the lead in withdrawing or in scaling back the mission significantly.

By late 1993, some countries were already increasingly loath to continue a protracted and frustrating peacekeeping mission. Douglas Hogg, correcting his earlier statement that Great Britain planned to pull out its contingent from UNPROFOR, noted that his comments had reflected only his personal view, rather than government policy. However, he modified his previous statement only to emphasize that London would not be the first to pull out.[21] Incidents such as the December, 1993 mock execution by Serb gunmen of Canadian peacekeepers are likely to erode further support abroad for a continued presence of foreign personnel and to increase calls for their withdrawal at signs of trouble. Despite the limitations imposed on UNPROFOR which often made it appear ineffective, UNPROFOR's presence nevertheless did hinder the Serbs' strategy and limited their excesses on the ground. An eventual removal of UNPROFOR, without an accompanying lifting of the arms embargo on the Bosnian government, would likely not only serve to convince the Serbs that the world was finally tiring and abandoning Bosnia to its fate but also make it easier for them to resume doing as they liked with fewer witnesses.

Regional Implications

Rump Yugoslavia: More of the Same?
At another level, the fallout from Bosnia-Herzegovina may eventually encourage a similar process elsewhere in the rump Yugoslavia and pose further, and even more serious, challenges to regional stability. If a settlement appears to reward genocide, the Serbian leadership could conclude that, after consolidation and a decent interval, it may use whatever means necessary, including ethnic cleansing, in pursuit of its strategic political objectives without risking significant military intervention or unmanageable cost.

Even if it decides to wash its hands of Bosnia-Herzegovina, the international community may face the same dilemma again, especially in the majority-Albanian areas controlled by Serbia and Montenegro. Apparently, the Serbian political elite, encompassing both the Milošević government as well as the opposition and other national institutions—including the Serbian Orthodox Church—are still committed to creating a Greater Serbia in the long term in which there is little or no room for non-Serbs.

The academic Mihailo Marković, reputed to be one of Milošević's closest advisors, in April, 1994, shared his vision of the future enlarged Serbian state. According to his analysis, it ought to be an ethnically exclusivist state, entailing the domination or elimination of non-Serbs, rather than including them in a plural society. In an interview with a Belgrade daily, he openly suggested that the presence of a significant number of non-Serbs would not be desirable for the effective functioning of a Greater Serbia: "What is in question is a historical law of modern civilization. A significant degree of ethnic homogeneity has always been a precondition for the development of democracy, in order to make possible the implementation of the democratic principle of 'one man-one vote' instead of [having] a multiplicity of complicated methods of collective representation. As a result of [collective representation], as we saw in [the former] Yugoslavia, an insoluble problem arises of how to represent large and small ethnic groups on the basis of proportional or equal representation."[22] Velibor Ostojić, president of the executive council of the dominant Bosnian Serb party, the SDS, put it even more bluntly in March, 1994, when he said the final goal must be "to create a Serbian nationalist state such as only the Orthodox have. . . . to build a new national state. . . . to finally establish a Serbia. . . . in which we would bit by bit assertively express our Serbianness [srbovati] and, essentially, live like Serbs."[23] Barring the rollback of recent gains, the Serbs are likely to resume the pursuit of their geopolitical interests, using a strategy in which a key component will continue to be ethnic cleansing. In the future, within rump Yugoslavia itself, their tactics are likely to be more refined, with the intention of avoiding some of the public relations blunders and miscalculations committed in Bosnia-Herzegovina. The process of delegitimizing the presence of other communities, for example, has continued in Serbia's media and political system and among intellectuals. And, although taking a different form than in Bosnia-Herzegovina, quiet ethnic cleansing has already been occurring among the non-Serb population in Serbia (in the Sandžak, Kosovo, Vojvodina, and Serbia proper) and Montenegro.

In Kosovo, the nearly two million Albanians, as well as the Croatian minority, have been under a state of virtual martial law for almost a decade and a half. However, the pressure has been increasing in recent years, as the authorities have made it nearly impossible for non-Serbs to have access to jobs, schooling, and medical care. At the same time, Serbian militias and the security forces have stepped up their intimidation of the majority Albanians, many of whom have already started to flee abroad. Numerous attacks have occurred against Muslims in the Sandžak, including arrests, kidnapping, the burning of houses, and killings.[24] As justification for its crackdown in the Sandžak, the Yugoslav military press has accused the West, allegedly spurred by the Catholic Church, of encouraging separatism there.[25]

The spillover is likely to affect Montenegro, Serbia's junior partner in the rump Yugoslavia, too, despite a disquiet among many Montenegrins about the international isolation that Belgrade's policies have caused. In the Montenegrin portion of the Sandžak, for example, harassment of Muslims has been significant. In September, 1992, armed Chetniks sought to force the Muslims of Pljevlja to leave, hurling slogans such as "Turks leave" and "This is Serbia," and destroying their shops and houses. By mid-1993, the Muslims in that area had been victims of over a hundred bomb attacks, kidnappings, expulsions, and shootings by Serb militias, and even the firing of bullets to form a cross on the mosque's minaret by the city's police.[26] In other towns in Montenegro, Serbian militias reportedly have carried out several hundred attacks against Muslims, including blowing up the mosque in the town of Nikšić.[27]

In Serbia and Montenegro, even most of the political parties which view themselves as democratic so far appear to differ only in degree from the government in their stance on the Muslim minorities. Asked about the Muslims in Montenegro's part of the Sandžak, Novak Kilibarda, leader of the Montenegrin People's Party, dismissed the possibility of autonomy for the Muslim minority in the Sandžak as absurd. Likewise, reacting to requests for autonomy for the Sandžak, the local branch of the SPO, one of the more moderate Serbian Chetnik parties, instead threatened the Muslims with expulsion. It menaced, "If there is any country in the world in which it is permitted to create another state on its territory, then go there!"[28]

Pressure on other communities in Serbia and Montenegro is already significant, and many individuals have been forced out. Those still at risk include the Hungarians in Vojvodina, the Croatians there and in Kosovo and Montenegro, the Gypsies, and other smaller ethnic groups. Serbia's Gypsies, many of whom are also Muslim, are burdened with double discrimination and are especially vulnerable. Although grossly undercounted in censuses, as they are forced to "pass" for statistical purposes, large communities of Muslim Gypsies exist in most cities in Serbia. According to experts, they number tens of thousands in Belgrade alone.[29]

The Serbian authorities feel that the example of recent instances of devastating violence will be useful in intimidating others into passivity. Thus, when Serbian forces leveled the Croatian city of Vukovar, Belgrade Television compared the destruction to Hiroshima. Authorities concluded that, in light of this experience, the "Albanians have no stomach to open a southern front."[30] Milošević, of course, should benefit further from the world's slow reaction in Bosnia-Herzegovina to cow the minorities in the rump Yugoslavia into non-resistance as they are cleansed. The Serbian authorities are already following this tack with the Muslims in the Sandžak. As reinforcements of military and security forces flowed into the Sandžak, the Yugoslav Army journal threatened that "these people [the Muslims of the Sandžak] . . . know that the Serbs and the Army will not allow Croatia and Bosnia to happen again and that they [the Serbs and the Army] are ready to defend themselves."[31]

If the current process of cleansing is not rapid or extensive enough to achieve the desired objectives, Belgrade may be tempted to escalate the tempo to a faster pace, as influential circles within Serbia have urged. Or, again, Milošević may resort to such actions in order to divert attention from political and economic difficulties and to reactivate his domestic support if he feels it is flagging. In particular, Belgrade may be encouraged to escalate its ethnic cleansing as it balances the results against the relatively low long-term cost exacted for its policies in Bosnia-Herzegovina. Despite frequent threats, the international community was slow to react, and the delay contributed to the recognition of a new status quo. A key variable to preventing genocide elsewhere will be what measure of success the international community adopts in relation to Bosnia-Herzegovina. Future developments may be influenced by whether the international community is satisfied with recognizing essentially a new state of affairs benefiting the Serbs or whether it succeeds in rolling back Serbian gains.

Even if Belgrade's intent is to manage ethnic cleansing in Yugoslavia, the situation in the Sandžak or in Kosovo may worsen. The Belgrade government and other Serbian political actors—especially the militias and the Serbian Orthodox Church—may increase the pressure on the local

populations to an unbearable level, possibly pushing them to take desperate actions. Many Serbian hard-liners no doubt seek to spark just such a
reaction so that the state will have a rationale to launch full-scale repression. As the leader of one of the most extreme parties, Jović—whose
militia has been marauding in Kosovo—admitted, his objective was specifically to provoke such an Albanian reaction. He stated: "The issue of the
occupation [by the Albanians] of Kosovo and Metohija cannot be solved
except by inducing the Shiptars [a pejorative Serbian term for the Alba-
nians] to start an uprising."[32]

Belgrade would likely bank on its lessons learned from the West's divisions to stress that the situation in the rump Yugoslavia itself was an internal
problem, as opposed to that in the internationally recognized independent
state of Bosnia-Herzegovina. Belgrade could thereby hope that this additional complicating factor and its greater direct control would preclude
outside access and be enough to deter international intervention, despite
the West's having drawn a metaphoric line in Kosovo.

If the international community, however, does eventually react militarily
in response to egregious violations that overstep acceptable bounds, in a way
this reaction too will have been the result of Serbian miscalculation, induced
by a lack of the international community's credibility as established by the
course of events in Bosnia-Herzegovina. In the end, the cost of putting a
stop to another outburst of ethnic cleansing may well be higher than if the
international community had deterred it in the first place through more
effective action in Bosnia-Herzegovina, or even earlier in Croatia.

Regional Spillover?

In the wider region, some countries may be incensed if Serbia is allowed to
get away with ethnic cleansing, thus encouraging others to also pursue this
policy. Kosovo, even more so than Bosnia-Herzegovina, could, of course,
ignite broader spillover regional instability, because of its implications for
Albania and Macedonia and, as a result, for Bulgaria, Greece, and Turkey.

In Macedonia, too, although the Serbs make up only 2.1 percent of the
population, Serb nationalists from outside have kept the national issue alive.
They have oscillated between menacing Macedonia with partition on behalf
of the allegedly threatened Serb minority and suggesting that the entire
country be annexed to Serbia in order for Macedonia ostensibly to protect
itself from its own Albanian minority. Karadžić, for example, has pressed
Macedonia to unite with Serbia, since "Macedonia cannot defend itself and

survive without Yugoslavia. This is obvious. . . . The Albanians greatly want to seize control of a substantial part of Macedonia. The best thing for Macedonia is for it to join Yugoslavia." Expecting the Macedonians and Albanians to live together, for him, was "like putting a cat and dog together." Instead, viewing ethnic partition as an established and accepted procedure, Karadžić even offered the Serbs' own experience in Bosnia-Herzegovina as a guide, suggesting that "if the Macedonians are threatened with attack by the Albanians and blood is shed, I would recommend them to act like us and sit down at the conference table and arrange the life of their ethnic communities without bloodshed."[33] Such encouragement and Serbian involvement could only promote further violence and, potentially, genocide. Bulgaria would not likely stand by passively to a threat to the Macedonians, whom most Bulgarians consider as members of their own nation, while Greece too might intervene to claim its own share of the spoils.

Likewise, ethnic cleansing carried out by the Serbs against the Hungarians in Vojvodina and in the occupied territories in Croatia has at times raised tensions. Despite the Budapest government's efforts to calm passions, others, such as the for-now marginal political figure Istvan Csurka, a Hungarian hard-liner, take a different approach on the Serbs' treatment of the Hungarians. He asserts: "The question arises. What must others do? What must we Hungarians do? Be silent or talk aimlessly? Should we not defend ourselves? When one can see on our doorstep what is happening to others, and what is happening to our brothers and sisters, can one really criticize us for attempting to find effective means for self-defense?"[34]

At the same time, Belgrade's success has eroded the self-restraint others might have felt about pursuing an aggressive policy of their own. For example, considering the "return of territories formerly belonging to Hungary," Csurka claimed that the only obstacle to retaking territories formerly under Hungarian rule was Hungary's current lack of sufficient military and economic means, for "Milošević is passed over in silence and tolerated because he has the military means, built up over decades."[35]

Even in Slovenia, gadfly ultranationalist politician Zmago Jelinčić has found encouragement for his quest for a Greater Slovenia in Serbia's success at redrawing the traditional borders. Jelinčić believes he now has a good chance of challenging the existing inherited borders with Croatia. He asked Croatia rhetorically, "Do you have such a border [the traditional border] with Serbia?" as he dismissed the possibility that Serbia would be made to retreat from its territorial gains.[36]

Global Implications

Copycat Genocides?

The international community's record of irresoluteness in dealing with genocide in Bosnia-Herzegovina may have other unintended consequences. If violent partition were based on ethnicity and the West's acceptance of the validity of both this goal and the accompanying ethnic cleansing process, this principle would have a significant impact on how the international community views what is politically and ethically legitimate. This effect could result even if the international community rationalized its stance in terms of realism.

Within this context, copycat cases could likely increase elsewhere, spurred by the demonstrated effect of the international community's inability to guarantee a group's safety and survival in Bosnia-Herzegovina. The credibility of individual nations and of international institutions such as the UN has likely become tarnished already as a result of their record in Bosnia-Herzegovina (fig. 6). The deterrent capability of the international community as a whole may erode further in the wake of this crisis, and other would-be offenders could embark on a path similar to that of the Serbs against their weaker neighbors or domestic minorities. Potential perpetrators would assume that they could manage any likely reaction, provided that the vital interests of the international community are not threatened.

Multiethnic societies around the world are already being challenged in an unstable political environment. The probability of interethnic conflict stepping over the boundary into violence and genocide may be considerably higher now after the experience of Bosnia-Herzegovina. How far the lesson may extend was highlighted in a speech by Chief Mangusutho Buthelezi, leader of the Inkatha Freedom Party in South Africa, who boasted that his Zulu nation would have to be reckoned with because they are the "Serbs of South Africa, [since] we are the most numerous."[37]

Beyond the phenomenon of genocide itself, the erosion in the credibility of international organizations and of the will of some western countries may well affect the readiness of others to challenge the status quo on a range of issues in the future (fig. 7). This credibility will continue to be tested even with an agreement in Bosnia-Herzegovina, as the potential for continued violations and renewed victimization requires a resolute response for years to come. Seeing in the United States' slow initial reaction a lessened credibility (which may contribute to future miscalculations by Tehran), a leading

The cartoon underscores the UN's slow and ineffective help to Bosnia-Herzegovina's Muslims. The inscription on the woman reads "Bosnia's Muslims," the inscription on the man reads "Serbs." The sign on the ground reads "Bosnia," the one on the lifesaver reads "aid." Published in *Al-Ra'y Al-'Amm,* Kuwait, April 4, 1993.

Iranian ayatollah remarked: "Did the Serbs listen to them [the Americans]? You said: 'O Serbs, this is a no-fly zone.' And around three hundred times the Serbs told you: 'To hell with you!'"[38]

If a just solution is not found, the reputation of the West in the Islamic world could also suffer from the perception, correct or not, that the West was indifferent because the victims were Muslims. Even now this image is prevalent across the spectrum of public opinion in the Islamic world, not only in radical circles, but also among moderates, including such friends of the West as the Gulf countries, Egypt, Malaysia, and Turkey.

These results are especially worrisome now. Since the breakup of the Soviet empire across Eastern Europe and Central Asia, the potential for ethnically based strife that arises from the disintegration of such polyglot entities is of great concern. Equally disturbing is the questioning of existing international borders and of the legitimacy of the presence of other communities within a national state. The appearance on the political scene of a demagogue like Russia's Zhirinovskiy, with his racist and expansionist views,

The cartoon portrays the United Nations as a soldier with a white flag and an olive branch, instead of a bayonet, casting a shadow of a timid rabbit with a carrot. The caption reads: "Bosnia." Published in *Al-Sharq,* Doha, Qatar, Feb. 6, 1994.

raises the specter of a Milošević with nuclear weapons, someone, moreover, who would have already been able to take the measure of the international community's lack of resolve on such issues. Should he or somebody similar come to power in Moscow, the lessons learned from Bosnia-Herzegovina could tempt him to undertake his own expansion, justifying the strategy by the need to protect Russians who settled in the now-independent neighboring republics. He could implement his own version of ethnic cleansing on a massive scale. Zhirinovskiy has already contributed to a heightening state of anxiety by proposing to redraw borders in Eastern Europe, a plan that includes the disappearance of some countries. He has also established linkages with Right-Wing and Left-Wing revisionist circles throughout the region. Such plans have strong implications for the potential of ethnic cleansing and for regional security.

States and communities that feel threatened and abandoned could be encouraged to arm further—possibly with weapons of mass destruction. They may desire their own deterrents in order to protect themselves, calculating that they cannot depend on the international community for security in a situation where their very survival may be at stake. In the post-Bosnia environment, such threatened entities are less likely to trust in compromises with others, lacking faith in an outside guarantee when the chips are down.

Viewing realpolitik and morality as either completely distinct or as mutually competitive is misleading. In the final analysis, the result of underestimating the importance of moral interests may be an erosion of the very national interests that should be guidelines for foreign policy. Moral values, in the long term, may be as much a hardheaded political interest as any other. If principles such as the unacceptability of aggression, the promotion of democracy, collective security, and peaceful change erode, the world becomes less stable, less safe, and less just—a situation which certainly runs counter to the United States' enduring national interests.

Fraying Morality?

Ultimately, the greatest cost of the genocide in Bosnia-Herzegovina may well be to the world's value system. In moral terms, this case implies a disturbing vision of the future. Although in retrospect one could plausibly use ignorance as an argument for not having done more to prevent the Jewish holocaust, experience with Bosnia-Herzegovina suggests otherwise. Perhaps even greater awareness may not have affected international response to either the holocaust or future instances of genocide. In Bosnia-Herzegovina, awareness was unavoidable, as seldom has there been an incident of genocide with more real-time exposure to so many people. What Bosnia-Herzegovina measured was the cost that the international community was willing to bear in order to prevent or stop genocide. However sensible the cost-benefit analysis may have turned out to be to policy makers, and however genuine the anguish these policy makers may have felt, the result was that they finally assessed that stopping genocide was not worth the cost. The real danger is that this attitude significantly affects future situations in which society's sense of outrage becomes gradually diminished and desensitized by its willingness, however reluctant, to accept genocide as part of a political process. If so, each nation, institution, and individual will share in the moral responsibility for allowing such tragedies to occur.

Appendix A

Political Organizations

HDZ: Hrvatska Demokratska Zajednica (Croatian Democratic Union). Ruling party in Croatia, led by Franjo Tudjman.

HSLS: Hrvatska Socialno–Liberalna Stranka (Croatian Social–Liberal Party). Largest opposition party in Croatia, led by Dražen Budiša.

HVO: Hrvatsko Vijeće Obrane (Croatian Defense Council). Croatian political organization in Bosnia-Herzegovina, formerly led by Mate Boban.

SDA: Stranka Demokratske Akcije (Democratic Action Party). Main Muslim political party in Bosnia-Herzegovina and the Sandžak, led by Alija Izetbegović.

SDS: Srpska Demokratska Stranka (Serbian Democratic Party). Main Serbian political party in Bosnia-Herzegovina, led by Radovan Karadžić.

SNO: Stranka Narodne Obnove (Party of National Renewal). Chetnik party, led by Mirko Jović. Its militia, the White Eagles, is commanded by Dragoslav Bokan.

SPO: Srpski Pokret Obnove (Serbian Renewal Movement). Chetnik party, led by Vuk Drašković. Its militia is the Serbian Guard.

SPS: Socijalistička Partija Srbije (Socialist Party of Serbia), formerly the League of Communists of Serbia. Ruling party in Serbia, led by Slobodan Milošević.

SRS: Srpska Radikalna Stranka (Serbian Radical Party). Chetnik party, led by Vojislav Šešelj.

Appendix B

Local Leadership

Mate Boban: Head of the pro-Tudjman wing of the Bosnia-Herzegovina Croatian Democratic Union and leader of the Croatian Defense Council (HVO) in Bosnia-Herzegovina until February, 1994.

Dobrica Ćosić: Author and early leader in the Serbian nationalist movement. He became president of Yugoslavia in 1992 but was subsequently pressured by Milošević to quit.

Vuk Drašković: Herzegovina-born writer and leader of the Chetnik Serbian Renewal Movement (SPO).

Danica Drašković: Wife of Vuk Drašković and an official in the Chetnik Serbian Renewal Movement, as well as the director of its official magazine, *Srpska reč*.

Alija Izetbegović: Leader of the Muslim SDA party; he was elected president of Bosnia-Herzegovina in November, 1990.

Mirko Jović: Leader of the Chetnik Stranka Narodne Obnove (SNO).

Radovan Karadžić: Montenegrin-born psychiatrist, leader of the Bosnian Serb movement, and president of the Serbian Republic of Bosnia.

Slobodan Milošević: Leader of the transformed Serbian League of Communists, renamed the Socialist Party of Serbia (SPS).

Ratko Mladić: Former Yugoslav People's Army general who became commander of the Bosnian Serb Army in May, 1992.

Milan Panić: U.S. businessman of Serbian origin who returned to become

Premier of Yugoslavia in 1992; by year's end he was ousted by Milošević.

Pavle: Patriarch of the Serbian Orthodox Church since 1990.

Željko Raznatović (Arkan): Reputed former petty criminal who became leader of the Serbian Tigers militia, which allegedly has been responsible for numerous atrocities.

Vojislav Šešelj: Bosnian-born leader of the Chetnik Serbian Radical Party (SRS), one of the main Serbian opposition parties. Allied to Milošević until mid-1993, he broke over Milošević's willingness to accept a negotiated solution in Bosnia-Herzegovina. Their disagreement was accompanied by an escalation of competition for power.

Gojko Šušak: Croatian émigré, originally from Bosnia-Herzegovina, who was an early supporter of Tudjman. After his return from Canada, Šušak became Croatia's Minister of Defense. In that post, he has managed Croatia's policy toward Bosnia-Herzegovina.

Franjo Tudjman: Former Partisan general, dissident, and subsequently leader of the Croatian Democratic Union (HDZ). He became president of Croatia in 1990.

Appendix C

The Local Press

BiH Ekskluziv, Split, Croatia: Weekly, published by émigrés from Bosnia-Herzegovina. It favors a united, multiconfessional, state.

Borba, Belgrade: Daily, originally the organ of the League of Communists of Yugoslavia, now independent and critical of the Serbian government.

Danas, Zagreb: Weekly, initially independent but now reflective of the Croatian government's views.

Duga, Belgrade: Hard-line nationalist fortnightly.

Evropske Novosti, Frankfurt, Germany: European edition of the Belgrade daily *Večernje novosti,* published for the Serbian community in Europe in order to bypass the embargo on Yugoslavia. It is favorable to Milošević's government.

Glas Koncila, Zagreb: Weekly, official organ of the Catholic Church in Croatia.

Globus, Zagreb: Weekly, independent; critical of the Croatian government.

Ilustrovana Politika, Belgrade: Weekly which reflects the Serbian government's views. Slobodan Milošević has been on its editorial board since mid-1990.

Intervju, Belgrade: Weekly which reflects the Serbian government's views; noted for its hard-line nationalism.

Ljiljan, Ljubljana: Weekly published by émigrés from Bosnia-Herzegovina, with a religious Islamic bent. It was published in Zagreb until its criticism of Croatia led to its closing there in 1993.

Monitor, Podgorica, Montenegro. Weekly liberal publication which favors an independent Montenegro.

Narodna armija, Belgrade: Weekly official organ of the Yugoslav People's Army and, later, with a changed name of *Vojska,* of the revamped Yugoslav Army.

Nedjeljna Dalmacija, Split, Croatia: Weekly with somewhat greater independence than its daily counterpart, *Slobodna Dalmacija,* which was initially independent, but now reflects the Croatian government's views.

NIN, Belgrade: Weekly mouthpiece for Milošević in the late 1980s, but later moved into the opposition.

Oslobodjenje, Ljubljana, Slovenia: Originally a pro-Yugoslav Sarajevo daily, it is now published as a weekly in Slovenia. It favors a unified, multi-confessional Bosnia-Herzegovina.

Pogledi, Kragujevac, Serbia: Weekly published by the Chetnik Serbian People's Renewal (SNO); noted for its hard-line nationalism.

Politika and *Politika ekspres,* Belgrade: Dailies which reflect the Serbian government's views.

Posavski Glasnik, Zagreb: Weekly published by émigrés from the Posavina area of northern Bosnia. It favors a united, multiconfessional state for Bosnia-Herzegovina.

Pravoslavlje, Belgrade: Fortnightly published by the Serbian Orthodox Church.

Pravoslavni misionar, Belgrade: Monthly published by the Serbian Orthodox Church.

Spona, Frankfurt, Germany: Independent weekly published for the Serbian community in Western Europe to bypass the embargo on Yugoslavia. It ceased publication in December, 1993.

Srbija, Belgrade: Monthly organ of the Serbian Radical Party (SRS); noted for its hard-line nationalism.

Srpska reč, Belgrade: Weekly organ of the Chetnik Serbian Renewal Movement (SPO); Danica Drašković is its director.

Srpska stvarnost, Santa Monica, California: Weekly, begun in 1993, published by "an independent news agency," named Serbian News Today, dedicated to "information in the USA." However, the magazine shares the same address and fax number as the local bureau of

Radio-Television Serbia, Serbia's state-run system which is part of the Ministry of Information. The publication is apparently linked to the latter. It is aimed at the Serbian community in North America to bypass the embargo on Yugoslavia.

Stav, Novi Sad, Vojvodina, Serbia: Relatively liberal weekly, supporting autonomy for Vojvodina.

Večernji list, Zagreb: Daily, closely aligned to Croatian government views.

Vesti, Frankfurt, Germany: Daily published by the Serbian Renewal Movement (SPO) for the Serbian community in Europe to bypass the embargo on Yugoslavia.

Vjesnik, Zagreb: Leading daily.

Vreme, Belgrade: Liberal weekly, critical of the Milošević government.

Notes

Chapter 1

1. See Ervin Staub, *The Roots of Evil: The Origins of Genocide and Other Group Violence* (Cambridge: Cambridge University Press, 1989); John L. P. Thompson and Gail A. Quets, "Genocide and Social Conflict: A Partial Theory and a Comparison," *Research in Social Movements, Conflict and Change* 12 (1990): 245–66; Herbert C. Kelman, "Violence without Moral Restraint: Reflections on the Dehumanization of Victims and Victimizers," *Journal of Social Issues* 29 (1973): 25–61; Isidor Wallimann and Michael N. Dobkowski, eds., *Genocide and the Modern Age: Etiology and Case Studies of Mass Death* (New York: Greenwood Press, 1987); Barbara Harff and Ted Robert Gurr, "Toward Empirical Theory of Genocides and Politicides: Identification and Measurement of Cases since 1945," *International Studies Quarterly* 32 (1988): 359–71; Michael R. Marrus, *The Holocaust in History* (Hanover, Conn.: University Press of New England, 1987); and Israel W. Charny and Chanan Rapaport, *How Can We Commit the Unthinkable? Genocide: The Human Cancer* (Boulder: Westview Press, 1982).

2. Violence, as measured by the homicide rate, for example, was over 5.7 times lower in Yugoslavia in the late 1980s than in the United States (2.4 per 100,000 population versus 13.7, respectively). See *Statistički Godišnjak Jugoslavije, 1991 (Statistical Yearbook of Yugoslavia, 1991)* (Belgrade: Federal Statistics Institute, 1991), table 104–28; and *State and Metropolitan Area Data Book, 1991* (Washington, D.C.: U.S. Dept. of Commerce, Aug., 1991), p. 215. By comparison, Sweden's rate in 1988 was 2.6 per 100,000, and Finland's 3.4. See *Yearbook of Nordic Statistics, 1993* (Copenhagen: Nordic Statistical Secretariat, 1993), tables 232, 334.

3. U.S. Secretary of Defense William Perry, for example, explained the situation in terms of the old "scorpion-and-frog" joke, in which a scorpion carrying a frog across

a river drowns the frog out of spite, even at the cost of itself committing suicide. "Well, this is the Balkans" he concluded. See his March 10, 1994 speech, "Determining Appropriate Use of Force in Bosnia," *Defense Issues* 9 (Washington, D.C., Department of Defense, 1994): 4.

4. Office of United States Chief Counsel for Prosecution of Axis Criminality, *Nazi Conspiracy and Aggression: Opinion and Judgment* (Washington, D.C.: Government Printing Office, 1947), pp. 3–4. For information on other relevant international conventions on genocide, see Helsinki Watch, *War Crimes in Bosnia-Hercegovina*, vol. 1 (New York: Aug., 1992), pp. 199–227.

5. See Thompson and Quets, "Genocide and Social Conflict," pp. 247–48.

6. Several government and non-government agencies have published reports chronicling the human rights situation in Bosnia-Herzegovina, including the U.S. Senate, Committee on Foreign Relations, *Staff Report: The Ethnic Cleansing of Bosnia-Hercegovina*, Aug. 15, 1992 (Washington, D.C.: U.S. Government Printing Office, 1992), which includes some riveting testimony by victims; and the U.S. Dept. of State, *Submission of Information to the United Nations Security Council in Accordance with Paragraph 5 of Resolution 771 (1992) and Paragraph 1 of Resolution 780 (1992)* (up to eight reports as of this writing). Among the most thorough and best-documented records is the two-volume report in Helsinki Watch, *War Crimes in Bosnia-Hercegovina*, 2 vols. (New York: Aug., 1992–Apr., 1993).

7. His lucid and compelling reports are contained in *A Witness to Genocide* (New York: Macmillan, 1993).

Chapter 2

1. Katherine McIntire, "Centuries of Hatred Mark Bosnian Conflict," *Army Times*, May 24, 1993, p. 12.

2. Thomas Butler, "The Ends of History: Balkan Culture and Catastrophe," *Washington Post*, Aug. 30, 1992, p. C3.

3. Interview with Lord David Owen by Charlie Rose on the *Charlie Rose Show*, Public Broadcasting System (PBS), June 14, 1994.

4. U.S. Senate, Committee on Armed Services, *Situation in Bosnia and Appropriate U.S. and Western Responses*, Hearing, Aug. 11, 1992 (Washington, D.C.: U.S. Government Printing Office, 1992), p. 29.

5. U.S. Senate, Committee on Armed Services, *Joint Chiefs of Staff Briefing on Current Military Operations in Somalia, Iraq, and Yugoslavia*, Hearing, Jan. 29, 1993 (Washington, D.C.: U.S. Government Printing Office, 1993), pp. 95–96.

6. Speech at Gazimestan, "Kosovo i sloga" (Kosovo and Unity), *NIN*, July 2, 1989, p. 6.

7. Speech at the First Conference of the League of Communists of Yugoslavia's Central Committee, Belgrade, June, 1988, reprinted in the collection of Slobodan Milošević's speeches, *Godine raspleta (Years of Unravelling)*, 4th ed. (Belgrade: Beogradski izdavačko-grafički zavod, 1989), p. 215.

8. For an insightful overview of the Muslim community's history and ethno-

graphy, see Vatro Murvar, *Nation and Religion in Central Europe and the Western Balkans; The Muslims in Bosnia, Hercegovina, and Sandžak: A Sociological Analysis* (Brookfield: University of Wisconsin, 1989). In fact, many Serbs may have considerably more Turkish ancestry than the Muslims, for the family names of such Serbian leaders as Radovan Karadžić and Dobrica Ćosić are of Turkish origin.

9. Significantly, Zrinski and Frankopan have been viewed subsequently as national martyrs in Croatia and hold a place of honor in the Zagreb cathedral's gallery of heroes. At times, even members of a single family could belong to different religions, as was the case of a seventeenth century Croatian Franciscan from Bosnia who was considered for an appointment as a Catholic bishop, although three of his brothers were Muslims, according to documents quoted in Dominik Mandić, *Etnička povijest Bosne i Hercegovine* (*The Ethnic History of Bosnia-Herzegovina*) (Toronto: Ziral, 1982), p. 239.

10. Orthodox Montenegrins continued to immigrate to Ottoman Bosnia-Herzegovina in the nineteenth century, even after their own country had become independent. Se Djordjije Djoko Pejović, *Iseljavanja Crnogoraca u XIX vijeku* (*The Emigration of the Montenegrins in the Nineteenth Century*) (Titograd, Montenegro: Istorijski Institut Republike Crne Gore, 1962), pp. 109–11, 207.

11. On this period of Ottoman history, see Kemal Karpat, *An Inquiry into the Social Foundations of Nationalism in the Ottoman State: From Social Estates to Classes, From Millets to Nations* (Princeton: Princeton University, 1973), pp. 57–93, especially pp. 80–83; and Stanford J. Shaw and Ezel Kural Shaw, *History of the Ottoman Empire and Modern Turkey*, vol. 2 (Cambridge: Cambridge University Press, 1977), pp. 13–15, 147–49.

12. The contemporary Serb historian Vuk Karadžić, for example, chronicles such incidents of expulsion, forced conversion, or killing as Serbia established its state in the nineteenth century, in *Istorijski spisi* (*Historical Records*), ed. Radovan Samardžić (Belgrade: Prosveta, 1987), pp. 56, 274. An official history of the 1804 Serbian uprising also records contemporary accounts of this process of cleansing, Stojan Novaković, *Ustanak na dahije* (*The Revolt against the Janissary Notables*) (Belgrade: State Printing Office, 1904), especially pp. 121, 175. Stevan Ignjić analyzes the same process in one part of Serbia in the 1860s, in "Muslimanska imanja u Užicu" (Muslim Property in Užice), *Oslobodjenje gradova u Srbiji od Turaka 1862–1867. god.* (*The Liberation of Serbia's Cities from the Turks in 1862–1867*), ed. Vasa Ćubrilović (Belgrade: Srpska Akademija Nauka i Umetnosti, 1970), pp. 377–87.

13. On Serbia's policy of ethnic cleansing in the provinces conquered during the Balkan Wars, see Carnegie Endowment for International Peace, *Report of the International Commission to Inquire into the Causes and Conduct of the Balkan Wars* (Washington, D.C.: Carnegie Endowment, 1914), pp. 148–86.

14. This incident is related by sculptor Ivan Meštrović, one of the architects of the first Yugoslavia, *Uspomene na političke ljude i dogadjaje* (*Memoirs about Political Personages and Events*), ed. Dubravko Horvatić (Zagreb: Matica Hrvatska, 1993), pp. 65–66.

15. See Ivo Banac, *The National Question in Yugoslavia: Origins, History, Politics*

(Ithaca: Cornell University Press, 1984), p. 368. This study is the best overall analysis of the early period of Yugoslavia's history.

16. Meštrović, (*Memoirs*), p. 213.

17. The relevant Chetnik documents were published in *Zbornik dokumenata i podataka o narodnooslobodilačkom ratu naroda Jugoslavije* (*Collection of Documents and Data on the National-Liberation War of the Peoples of Yugoslavia*), vol. 14, part 1 (Belgrade: Institute of Military History, 1981), especially pp. 1–7, 101–103.

18. This document is reproduced in *Dokumenti o izdajstvu Draže Mihailovića* (*Documents on the Treason of Draža Mihailović*), vol. 1 (Belgrade: State Commission for the Documentation of Crimes by the Occupiers and their Collaborators, 1945), pp. 10–13.

19. Ibid., document number 523, p. 505.

20. For example, in a 1969 survey, Serbs (and Montenegrins), accounted for 42.2 percent of the population but held 78.9 percent of the higher-level federal government posts; see *Ekonomska Politika* (Belgrade: Jan. 27, 1969), table on p. 12. In the military in the early 1980s, Serbs accounted for 66.2 percent of all officers and in 1991 for 70.0 percent of all officers with the rank of major and above; see Vlatko Cvrtila, "Tko je što u Armiji" (Who Is What in the Army), *Danas*, Feb. 5, 1991, pp. 16–17.

21. Churchill Lecture before the English-Speaking Union, Guildhall, London, Nov. 26, 1993. My thanks to the English-Speaking Union for providing a transcript of the speech.

Chapter 3

1. Leo Kuper, *Genocide: Its Political Use in the Twentieth Century* (New Haven: Yale University Press, 1981), p. 84.

2. The text of the *Serbian Memorandum* has been published in Bože Čović, ed., *Izvori velikosrpske agresije* (*The Sources of Great Serbian Aggression*) (Zagreb: Školska Knjiga, 1991), especially pp. 291, 297.

3. Ivan Stambolić, *Rasprave o SR Srbiji* (*Debates on the Socialist Republic of Serbia*) (Zagreb: Globus, 1987), pp. 218–19.

4. Edward W. Said, *Orientalism* (New York: Vintage, 1979).

5. Vuk Drašković, "Šta menjati u Ustavu" (What to Change in the Constitution), speech to the Union of Serbian Writers, Feb. 5, 1988, in *Koekude, Srbijo* (*Quo Vadis, Serbia?*), 4th ed. (Belgrade: Nova knjiga and Glas Crkve, [1990]), p. 74.

6. Branislav Lainović quoted in Duška Jovanić, "Heroj bez ordena" (Hero without Medals), *Duga*, June 11–24, 1994, p. 25.

7. Goran Babić, "Vrh bijelog minareta" (The Top of the White Minaret), *Duga*, Sept. 3–16, 1988, pp. 36–37. Although the author was a "Yugoslav" from Croatia, he had been unable to find an outlet for his attacks there.

8. Articles highlighting the threat, such as those by Nataša Jokić, "Pouke za vernike i nevernike" (Lessons for Believers and Unbelievers), *Intervju*, June 20, 1986, pp. 16–17; and by Svetislav Spasojević, "Potkopana Makedonija" (Buried Macedonia), *NIN*, January 7, 1990, pp. 26–27, were typical.

9. Dragoš Kalajić, "Kvazi Arapi protiv Evropljana" (The Semi-Arabs against the Europeans), *Duga*, Sept. 13–19, 1987, pp. 14–15.

10. Interview with Jovan Rašković by Mira Ružić, "O etnokarakterima; Edipovci i kastrati" (On Ethnic Characteristics; Sufferers of the Oedipus and Castration Complexes), *Intervju*, Sept. 15, 1989, p. 15.

11. Miroljub Jevtić, "Rezervisti alahove vojske" (The Reservists of Allah's Army), *Duga*, Dec. 9–22, 1989, p. 21.

12. Ibid., pp. 20, 22.

13. Miroljub Jevtić, *Savremeni džihad kao rat* (*The Contemporary Jihad as War*) (Belgrade: Narodna Biblioteka Srbije, 1989), pp. 316–17.

14. Miroljub Jevtić, "Šta se krije iza groblja; Islam juriša na Srbiju" (What Is Hidden behind the Cemetery? Islam Is Attacking Serbia), *Ilustrovana Politika*, Dec. 18, 1990, p. 25.

15. Miroljub Jevtić, "Turci (opet) žele Srbiju" (The Turks [Again] Want Serbia), *Srpska reč*, Aug. 19, 1991, p. 64.

16. Darko Tanasković, "Nacija i vera, izmedju *m* i *M*" (The Nation and Religion: Between a Small and Capital *M*), *NIN*, Sept. 24, 1989, p. 25.

17. Jevtić, ("Allah's Army"), p. 23. Tanasković also notes that "for many, [Islam] still is felt as alien, and even inimical;" see ("Nation and Religion"), p. 25.

18. Jevtić, ("Allah's Army"), p. 23.

19. Interview with Miroljub Jevtić by Slavoljub Kačarević, "Islam bez maske" (Islam without a Mask), *Intervju*, Sept. 15, 1989, p. 11.

20. Interview with Atanasije Jevtić in Rajka Radivojić, "Zavodjenja za Goleš-planinu" (Leading Astray to Mount Goleš), *Intervju*, Dec. 9, 1988, p. 27.

21. Spasojević, "Buried Macedonia," p. 41.

22. Dragomir Ubiparipović, "Pismo jednovernoj i jednokrvnoj braći" (A Letter to Brothers of the Same Faith and Blood), *Glas Crkve*, Valjevo, Serbia, 2, 1991, p. 56.

23. Miroslav Radovanović, "O potrebi donošenja nacionalnog programa" (On the Need to Draft a National Program), *Glas Crkve*, 4, 1991, pp. 52–54.

24. [Deacon] Radovan Bigović, "Povodom pisanja sarajevskog lista Novi Vox" (On the Occasion of What the Sarajevo Newspaper *Novi Vox* Has Written), *Pravoslavlje*, Nov. 15, 1991, p. 5.

25. Thompson and Quets, "Genocide and Social Conflict," pp. 254–55.

26. Božidar Mijač, "Mir, da, ali kakav?" (Peace, Yes, But What Kind of Peace?), *Pravoslavlje*, March 15, 1992, p. 5.

27. For an incisive assessment of this key figure, see Sabrina P. Ramet, "Serbia's Slobodan Milošević: A Profile," *Orbis*, (Winter, 1991), pp. 93–105.

28. An excellent analysis of Milošević's rhetoric and praxis of violence is to be found in Nebojša Popov, *Srpski populizam; Od marginalne do dominantne pojave* (*Serbian Populism: From a Marginal to a Dominant Phenomenon*), supplement to *Vreme*, May 24, 1993, especially pp. 22–23.

29. Ibid. The Serbian activists from Kosovo who had spearheaded Milošević's rise to power, in fact, later complained that he had used them for his own narrow ends and that he had then abandoned them when they were no longer needed (Sandra Petrušić, "Kolevku srpstva prevrnuli Srbi" [It Is the Serbs Themselves

Who Have Overturned the Cradle of Serbianism], *Srpska reč*, March 2, 1992, pp. 38–40).

30. Jevrem Brković, "Šušteća šutnja" (A Rustling Silence), *Danas*, Feb. 7, 1989, p. 33.

31. Ibid.; and Vlado Mićunović, "Mitinzi solidarnosti u Nikšiću i Cetinju" (Solidarity Meetings in Nikšić and Cetinje), *Intervju*, Sept. 30, 1988, p. 17.

32. Muharem Durić and Mirko Carić, "Kako srpski nacionalisti odmažu srpskom narodu i šta prati mošti kneza Lazara" (How Serbian Nationalists Are Revenging the Serbian People and What Bathes the Relics of Prince Lazar), *Politika*, Sept. 17, 1988, p. 7.

33. "Predlog programa Stranke Srpska Narodna Obnova (SNO)" (Draft Program for the Serbian Popular Renewal [SNO]), January, 1990, in (*Quo Vadis, Serbia?*), pp. 127–41.

34. Interview in "Novoosnovani, a ne opozicija" (Newly Established, But Not the Opposition), *Danas*, June 19, 1990, p. 16.

35. Interview with Arkan by Toma Džadžić, "Već imam kuću na Dedinju" (I Already Have a House on Dedinje), *NIN*, Dec. 13, 1991, p. 11.

36. Rajko Djurdjević, "Bajram 1409. u Beogradu" (Bairam 1409 in Belgrade), *Duga*, May 13–19, 1989, p. 75; and "Ni mi nismo znali: Pokušaj paljenja beogradske džamije" (Even We Did Not Know: An Attempt to Set the Belgrade Mosque on Fire), *Preporod*, Sept. 15, 1989, p. 20. *Preporod* was the Islamic community's official newspaper.

37. Nedžad Latić and Mensur Brdar, "Jesu li selakovljani sačuvali novopodignutu munaru od rušenja" (Have the People of Selakovac Saved their Newly Built Minaret from Destruction?), *Preporod*, Aug. 15, 1989, p. 10; and Mirko Popovac, "Novi Pazar: Vruće leto u senci minareta" (Novi Pazar: A Hot Summer in the Shadow of the Minarets), *Duga*, Sept. 16, 1989, p. 76. Novi Pazar, of which Selakovac is a suburb, had eighteen mosques (including the new one), down from a pre-World War II total of twenty-seven.

38. "Ko to tamo svira" (Who Plays the Tune There?), *Borba*, Oct. 30, 1990, p. 12.

39. Dada Vujasinović, "Država koja se razmnožava" (A State Which is Multiplying Itself), *Duga*, Oct. 26–Nov. 10, 1991, p. 19.

Chapter 4

1. In the referendum, 1.6 million votes were cast, representing 63.4 percent of the registered voters, with a 99.43 percent vote in favor of independence. Evidently, it was not only Muslims and Croatians who had voted for independence. For well-informed and insightful analyses of the political background of this period, see Alan F. Fogelquist, *The Breakup of Yugoslavia, International Policy, and the War In Bosnia-Hercegovina* (Los Angeles: Institute of South Central European and Balkan Affairs, 1993); and Sabrina Petra Ramet, *Balkan Babel* (Boulder: Westview Press, 1992).

2. Huda Al-Husayni, "Mushkilatna ann al-sirb yaraun khasarathum fi al-khutta

wa-ann al-muslimin yazunnun annaha lam tunsifhum" (Our Problem Is That the Serbs Believe the Plan is Damaging to Them While the Muslims Believe It Is Not Fair to Them), *Al-Sharq Al-Awsat,* Mar. 19, 1993, p. 10.

3. "Yes, Serb Rights," *Washington Post,* Apr. 30, 1993, p. A25.

4. Angelo Ferrari, *Il Giorno,* reprinted as "Patrijarh Pavle: Svi smo krivi" (Patriarch Pavle: We Are All Guilty) in *Politika,* Frankfurt, Germany, Jan. 28, 1994, p. 6.

5. Predrag Aleksijević, "Politika kao porodična sudbina" (Politics as the Family Fate), *Ilustrovana Politika,* Jan. 20, 1992, p. 3. Karadjordje was one of the two principal Serbian leaders of the first Serbian revolt against the Ottomans, and the ancestor of the Serbian dynasty of that name, on whose behalf Mihailović's wartime Chetnik movement had sought to create Greater Serbia.

6. "Spor oko 'ako'" (The Dispute Over "If"), *Vreme,* Jan. 13, 1992, p. 17.

7. Dobrica Ćosić interview in *Avanti,* Mar. 3, 1992, reprinted in *Srpsko pitanje; Demokratsko pitanje (The Serbian Question: The Democratic Question)* (Belgrade: Politika, 1992), pp. 228, 230.

8. Speech of Dec. 8, 1991, "Ovde je njiva—tamo je saksija" (The Field Is Here, the Flowerpot Is There), *Srpska reč,* Dec. 23, 1991, p. 12.

9. Predrag Milošević, *Sveti ratnici (Holy Warriors)* (Gornji Milanovac and Priština: Dečje Novine and Jedinstvo, 1989), p. 164.

10. "Bogami ćemo da se tučemo" (By God, We Will Fight), *NIN,* Apr. 12, 1991, pp. 40–41.

11. Mirjana Bobić-Mojsilović, "Fašista sam, tim se divim" (I Am a Fascist and Proud of It), *NIN,* Apr. 10, 1992, p. 24.

12. M. Bažić, "Germansko-katolička 'operacija' za uništenje Srba u BiH: Islamska tvrdjava usred Evrope" (The German-Catholic "Operation" to Wipe Out the Serbs of Bosnia-Herzegovina: An Islamic Fortress in the Heart of Europe), *Politika ekspres,* Mar. 9, 1992, p. 7; and Milan Mijalkovski, "Epizodna uloga Makedonije" (Macedonia's Episodic Role), *Narodna armija,* Feb. 6, 1992, p. 54.

13. Dragoš Kalajić, "Usamljeni, kao Nemci" (Isolated, Like the Germans), *Duga,* Feb. 1–14, 1992, pp. 34–35.

14. "U Srbiju, ili u rat" (Either into Serbia, or to War), *Danas,* Oct. 29, 1991, p. 15.

15. "Rekli su" (They Said), *Vreme,* Feb. 8, 1992, pp. 8–9.

16. As reported, for example, by Lt. Col. Gen. Nikola Uzelac, commander of the Yugoslav People's Army Banja Luka Corps in Budo Simović, "Ovde se neće ponoviti Slovenija" (Slovenia Will Not Be Repeated), *Ilustrovana Politika,* Nov. 4, 1991, p. 7.

17. D. Ružić, "Jajce strahuje od Šipova" (Jajce Is Frightened by Šipovo), *As,* Sarajevo, Oct. 18, 1991, p. 4.

18. His account was originally published in the Warsaw *Gazeta Wiborczoj* and also published as "Bio sam srpski plaćenik" (I Was a Serbian Mercenary), Lana Petošević, transl., *Vreme,* Oct. 5, 1992, pp. 30–31.

19. Dada Vujasinović, "Ero sa srcem u Zemunu" (Ero Has His Heart in Zemun), *Duga,* Feb. 1–14, 1992, p. 26.

20. Nebojša Jevrić, "Svanulo je, laku noć" (The Sun Has Risen, Good Night), *Duga,* Mar. 15–28, 1992, p. 5.

21. Blagica Stojanović, "Kriv što je živ" (Guilty of Being Alive), *Srpska reč,* May 24, 1993, p. 49.

22. On the war, see Norman Cigar, "The Serbo-Croatian War of 1991: Political and Military Dimensions," *Journal of Strategic Studies* 16 (Sept., 1993): 297–338.

23. Speech reported by D. Stevanović, "Jović: JNA je korišćena za zaštitu Srba" (Jović: The JNA Was Used to Defend the Serbs), *Politika,* Mar. 4, 1992, p. 1.

24. Col. Nedeljko Popara, "Sedam stotina dana rata" (Seven Hundred Days of War), *Vojska,* Aug. 26, 1993, p. 16.

Chapter 5

1. Interview, "Bezbolna amputacija Hrvatske" (The Painless Amputation of Croatia), *Srbija,* Jan., 1992, p. 29.

2. "Borba nije okončana" (The Struggle Is Not Over), *Vesti,* May 12, 1993, p. 6.

3. Quoted in Gordana Igrić, "Beda etničkog sna" (The Calamity of the Ethnic Dream), *Vreme,* Nov. 15, 1993, p. 30.

4. Faik Tafro, "Fočansko leto 1992; Znalo se" (The Foča Summer of 1992: It Was Known), part 4, *Srpska reč,* Aug. 2, 1992, p. 51.

5. UN Security Council, *Final Report of the Commission of Experts Established Pursuant to Security Council Resolution 780 (1992),* UN document S/1994/674 (New York: United Nations, 1994), pp. 38–39, 42–43.

6. Reported by Nebojša Jevrić, "Krivci iz plavo-crveno-sivog rukava" (The Guilty Ones with the Blue, Red, and Gray Sleeve), *Duga,* June 25–July 8, 1994, p. 26.

7. Mary Battiata, "New Wave of Terror in Bosnia Described to UN, EC Envoys," Washington Post, Sept. 26, 1992, p. A16.

8. Dragan Cicić, "Prosperitet u ratnoj zoni" (Prosperity in the War Zone), *NIN,* reprinted in *Vesti,* Dec. 21, 1993, p. 17.

9. Mary Battiata, "A Town's Bloody 'Cleansing,'" *Washington Post,* Nov. 2, 1992, p. A19.

10. Faik Tafro, "Ljudi umiru gledajući" (People Die Looking On), part 1, *Srpska reč,* May 10, 1993, p. 46.

11. Gutman, *Witness to Genocide,* pp. 157–163.

12. Agence France Presse, Mar. 9, 1993, in *Foreign Broadcast Information Service (FBIS)-East Europe (EEU)-93-045,* Mar. 10, 1993, p. 78.

13. Marco Ventura, "Bosnia: Ora i grandi hanno deciso" (Bosnia: The Powerful Have Now Decided), *Epoca,* Milan, July 17, 1994, p. 129.

14. UN Security Council, *Final Report,* p. 53.

15. Interview by Branko Bucalo with Peter van Hugh, "Proljeće donosi mir" (Spring Brings Peace), *BiH Ekskluziv,* Apr. 1, 1994, p. 2.

16. Michael Palaich, "Man or Monster: Confessions of a Serb War Criminal," *Soldier of Fortune,* Aug., 1993, pp. 62–64.

17. John Pomfret, "Serbs Start Pulling Back Big Guns around Sarajevo," *Washington Post,* Feb. 18, 1994, p. A31.

18. Patrick Quinn, "Serbs, Croats Demand Tolls from UN, Slam Muslims," *Wash-

ington Times, Jul. 2, 1993, p. A7; and Dejan Jelovac, "Za dom, za kralja, napred!" (For the Homeland, for the King, Forward!), *Vreme,* July 5, 1993, pp. 32–33. Among combined Bosnian Serbian-Croatian operations against the Muslims were offensives against Žepče and Maglaj; see John Pomfret, "Fighting Intensifies across Bosnia," *Washington Post,* July 2, 1993, p. A26; and John F. Burns, "Bosnia Serbs Drive to Take Sarajevo: UN Is Kept Back," *New York Times,* July 22, 1993, p. A8.

19. For example, an HVO officer, Stipe Stojanović, in an interview by Patrik Maček, reported that the Serbs treated HVO personnel "surprisingly well;" see "Emirat pakla" (Emirate of Hell), *Slobodna Dalmacija,* Split, June 24, 1993, p. 7. A Croatian refugee from the Travnik area noted that the "Serbs did take good care of us, both the children and the baby, that I cannot deny;" see M. Sarić, "Bez ičega na svijetu" (Having Nothing at All in This World), *Večernji list,* Zagreb, June 22–23, 1993, p. 23.

20. Jelovac, ("For the Homeland"), p. 33.

21. Interview on Belgrade Radio, Nov. 26, 1993, in *FBIS-EEU-93-227,* Nov. 29, 1993, p. 28.

22. TANJUG, Belgrade, Oct. 19, 1993, in *FBIS-EEU-93-201,* Oct. 20, 1993, p. 35; Sarajevo Radio, Nov. 5, 1993, in *FBIS-EEU-93-214,* Nov. 8, 1993, p. 27; and Paris Agence France Presse in English, Dec. 5, 1993, in *FBIS-EEU-93-232,* Dec. 6, 1993, p. 43.

23. Tafro, ("Foča Summer"), p. 51.

24. Vedran Srdjić, "Grad u izgnanstvu" (A City in Exile), *BiH Ekskluziv,* Aug. 27, 1993, p. 7.

25. John Pomfret, "Serbs Said to Block Return of Muslims," *Washington Post,* May 12, 1993, p. A21; also see Blaine Harden, "Refugee 'Witnessed Massacres Every Day' at the Bridges on the Drina," *Washington Post,* Aug. 7, 1992, p. A18; Battiata, "A Town's Bloody 'Cleansing,'" p. A19; and Jonathan C. Randal, "Serbs Turn Focus on West Bosnia," *Washington Post,* Mar. 6, 1993, p. A26.

26. Such as the killing of 2,000 to 3,000 people in the Brčko area of northern Bosnia, "US Aides Cite 'Eyewitness Accounts' in Mass Killings of Muslims by Serbs," *Washington Post,* Sept. 27, 1992, p. A43.

27. According to the minutes by the Serbian Defense Minister's former staff secretary, Dobrica Gajić-Glišić, "Iz kabineta ministra vojnog" (From the Defense Minister's Office), part 2, *NIN,* Apr. 24, 1992, p. 27.

28. Interview with Vojislav Šešelj by C[vijetin] M[ilivojević] and M. M., "Spreman čekam hapšenje" (I Am Ready as I Wait to Be Arrested), *Spona,* Nov. 18, 1993, p. 15; and Jonathan S. Landay, "Belgrade Regime Tied to Alleged War Crimes," *Christian Science Monitor,* Nov. 26, 1993, p. 6.

29. From the minutes of the session, "'Osma sednica' Srpskog pokreta obnove; Pokušaj samoubistva" (The "Eighth Session" of the Serbian Renewal Movement: A Suicide Attempt), *Srpska reč,* May 10, 1993, p. 23.

30. Details are provided in Danica Drašković, "U Srebrenici je gorela zemlja" (In Srebrenica the Earth Was on Fire), *Srpska reč,* May 10, 1993, p. 23.

31. Karlo Jeger, "Oklopno-mehanizirana brigada Užičkog korpusa napada Goražde iz Srbije" (A Mechanized Infantry Brigade from the Užice Corps is Attacking Goražde from Serbia), *Globus,* Apr. 15, 1994, pp. 7–8.

32. Slavko Aleksić, quoted in "Ljudi i vreme" (People and Time), *Vreme,* May 31, 1993, p. 54.

33. See Yitzhak Arad, Shmuel Krakowski, and Shmuel Spector, eds., *The Einsatzgruppen Reports* (New York: Holocaust Library, 1989).

34. Battiata, "A Town's Bloody 'Cleansing,'" p. A19.

35. Tafro, ("People Die Looking On"), p. 48.

36. See Jonathan C. Randal, "Serbs Ending '700 Years of Muslim Presence' in Bosanska Dubica," *Washington Post,* Mar. 19, 1993, p. A52; Peter Maass, "UN Says Serbs Use Beatings, Arrests to Spur Muslims' Flight", *Washington Post,* July 23, 1992, p. A22; Jonathan C. Randal, "28,000 Facing Eviction in Bosnia," *Washington Post,* Aug. 12, 1992, p. A24; and Peter Maass, "Serbs Strike Fear in a Bosnian City," *Washington Post,* Aug. 12, 1992, pp. A1, A25.

37. Anna Husarka, "City of Fear," *New Republic,* Sept. 21, 1992, p. 18.

38. See especially Mary Battiata, "Town's Muslims Caught in Psychological Noose," *Washington Post,* Sept. 30, 1992, p. A25.

39. This account of the situation in Banja Luka is based on reporting by Roger Thurow, "Forced from Home, Muslims Must Turn to Serbs for Passage," *Wall Street Journal,* Nov. 22, 1993, pp. A1, A5.

40. Ibid.

41. David B. Ottoway, "'Ethnic Cleansing' by Scam: Bosnian Serbs Take Muslims for a Ride," *Washington Post,* June 21, 1994, p. A10.

42. Filip Švarm, "Pred strašni sud" (Before the Last Judgment), *Vreme,* Apr. 5, 1993, p. 33.

43. Agence France Presse, Mar. 18, 1993, in *FBIS-EEU-93-052,* Mar. 19, 1993, pp. 27–28.

44. Anthony Lewis, "The Guilty Men," *New York Times,* Oct. 29, 1993, p. A15. In the case of Srebrenica, the cutting off of the town's water supply and the halting of aid convoys had violated an accord, signed only a week earlier, not to interfere with humanitarian aid; James Rupert, "E. Bosnian Town Loses Water Plant," *Washington Post,* June 27, 1993, p. A14.

45. Quoted in John Pomfret, "Bosnian Serb Rebuffs NATO on Demands for UN Access," *Washington Post,* Jan. 15, 1994, p. A16.

46. Battiata, "A Town's Bloody 'Cleansing,'" pp. A1, A19. A similar process also happened, among other places, in Trebinje, according to Alija Resulović, "Dan dugih noževa" (The Day of the Long Knives), *BiH Ekskluziv,* July 9, 1993, p. 5; also see Helsinki Watch, *War Crimes,* vol. 2, p. 147, and Gutman, *Witness to Genocide,* pp. 109–117.

47. U.S. Dept. of State, *Submission,* second submission (Oct., 1992), p. 7.

48. On life in the detention camps, see Gutman, *Witness to Genocide,* pp. 44–76, 90–101, 137–43.

49. See, for example, Peter Maass, "In Bosnia, a Treacherous Trek to Safety," *Washington Post,* Oct. 31, 1992, p. A1; Battiata, "A Town's Bloody 'Cleansing,'" p. A19; Jonathan C. Randal, "Serbs Turn Focus on West Bosnia," *Washington Post,* Mar. 3, 1993, p. A26; and Jonathan C. Randal, "In Bosnia, One Woman's Tale of Terror, Tragedy and Pain," *Washington Post,* Mar. 27, 1993, p. A20.

50. Randal, "Serbs Ending '700 Years,'" p. A52.

51. U.S. Senate, *Staff Report,* pp. 15, 16; Helsinki Watch, *War Crimes,* vol. 2, p. 118; and Peter Maass, "Muslims Tell of 'Gladiator' Punishments," *Washington Post,* Nov. 3, 1992, p. A15. In more severe cases, crosses have reportedly been carved into the faces of Muslims; see Georg Reissmuller, "Beaten until the Entire Body Was Black," *Frankfurter Allgemeine,* Dec. 30, 1992, in *FBIS-EEU-93-001,* Jan. 4, 1993, p. 74.

52. Edina Žunić reports about coercion in the city of Bijeljina in "Metropola švercera i terora: Bijeljina" (Metropolis of Black Marketeers and of Terror: Bijeljina), *BiH Ekskluziv,* Dec. 3, 1993, p. 7; and Thurow, "Forced from Home," p. A1.

53. Quoted in "Ljudi" (People) section, *Monitor,* Feb. 4, 1994, p. 25.

54. Andrija Tunjić, "Preko reda dolaze ranjenici, ali i oni iz kafića" (The Wounded, But Also Those from the Café Have Priority in Line), *Vjesnik,* July 6, 1993, p. 7. On this issue, also see Slavenka Drakulić, "Women Hide behind a Wall of Silence," *Nation,* Mar. 1, 1993, pp. 253–54; Philippe Granjon and Pascal Deloche, "Rape as a Weapon of War," *Refugees* (UN High Commissioner for Refugees), Oct., 1993, pp. 42–44; and Gutman, *Witness to Genocide,* pp. 68–76, 144–49, 164–67; and UN Security Council, *Final Report,* pp. 55–60. For accounts by the victims themselves, see Alexander Stiglmayer, ed., *The War against Women in Bosnia-Herzegovina,* Marion Faber, transl. (Lincoln: University of Nebraska Press, 1994).

55. As reported by Alessandra Morelli, a field officer for the UN High Commissioner for Refugees, "UN Reports New Abuses by Serbs," *Washington Post,* June 10, 1994, p. A24.

56. For accounts of destroyed mosques, see Maass, "Serbs Use Beatings," p. A22; A. D. Horne, "Muslims in Serb-Run Town Tell of Repression and Worry," *Washington Post,* Aug. 17, 1992, p. A10; Dušan Stojanović, "Laughter as Houses Burn," *Washington Post,* May 8, 1993, p. A16; David B. Ottoway, "A Muslim Town Is Emptied by Fear," *Washington Post,* May 18, 1993, p. A17; and "U Bijeljini srušeno pet džamija" (Five Mosques Demolished in Bijeljina), *Evropske Novosti,* Frankfurt, Mar. 20, 1993, p. 12.

57. Jonathan C. Randal, "Bosnian Serbs Increase the Pressure on Muslims, Croats in Banja Luka," *Washington Post,* May 11, 1993, p. A14.

58. Petošević, ("Serbian Mercenary"), p. 31.

59. Aleksandar Ćirić, "Rukopis mrtvih" (Manuscript of the Dead), *Vreme,* Apr. 5, 1993, p. 32.

60. Vojislav Maksimović, "Podseća na robovanje" (It Is Remindful of Slavery), *Evropske Novosti,* Jan. 27, 1994, p. 18.

Chapter 6

1. Interview with Momčilo Krajišnik by Jovan Janjić, "Država kao devojčica" (The State As a Little Girl) *Srpska stvarnost,* Sept. 25, 1993, p. 5.

2. Patrick Quinn, "Offer to End Sanctions Fails to Sway Serbs on Peace Plan," *Washington Times,* July 15, 1994, p. A15.

3. Blaine Harden, "The Yugoslav Gulag," *Washington Post*, Aug. 7, 1992, p. A18. On detention camps also see "Bosnian Camps Interest Activists," *Washington Times*, Aug. 3, 1992, p. A7; Peter Maass, "Bosnian Refugees Tell of Random Serb Terror," *Washington Post*, Aug. 5, 1992, p. A27; Mary Battiata, "Former Prisoners Allege Wholesale Serb Atrocities," *Washington Post*, Oct. 6, 1992, p. A1, A18; and Seth Faison, "Bosnian in U.S., Horror Behind and New Life Ahead," *New York Times*, July 25, 1993, p. A8.

4. For example, a U.S. Marine Corps veteran of the World War II Pacific theater remembers that "we came across at least one hundred more wounded and dead Japs. . . . I hate to tell this, but I saw our guys killing them all, taking their flags, pictures, sabers, and knocking out their gold teeth for souvenirs." He continued, "Our captain, I think, hated Japs more than anyone. On several occasions, when the men brought in the prisoners, always wounded, he would call me over and say, 'Doc, give this bastard a couple of shots.' I would, then he'd call another [medical] corpsman over and say, 'Doc, give this bastard a couple of shots.' He would. That much morphine put the poor bastard to sleep for good;" Stanley Bowen, "Saipan to Tinian," *Follow Me* (Camp Lejeune, N.C.: May–June, 1994), p. 25. Similarly, a British soldier remembered of D-Day in Normandy, "If a German soldier appeared, everybody fired at him. It was no bother, we didn't think of them as human beings;" Russell Miller, "We Didn't Think of Jerries as Human, " *The Times*, London, Sept. 24, 1993, p. 16.

5. Kelman, "Violence without Moral Restraint," p. 39.

6. Reported by Evgeniy Vostrukhov, "Umeret' v Yugoslavii" (To Die in Yugoslavia), *Izvestiya*, Nov. 25, 1992, p. 3.

7. Blaine Harden, "Serb Forces Overwhelm Key Town," *Washington Post*, Apr. 15, 1992, p. A33.

8. Nebojša Jevrić, "Živo meso i krompiri" (Live Meat and Potatoes), *Duga*, May 9–22, 1992, p. 7.

9. Speech reported by TANJUG Domestic Service, Belgrade, July 19, 1993, in *FBIS-EEU-93-138*, July 21, 1993, p. 41.

10. Peter Maass, "Bosnian Serbs Say They're Fighting Against Islamic Fundamentalism," *Washington Post*, Aug. 11, 1992, p. A13.

11. Interview in *Pogledi*, Nov. 12, 1993, in *FBIS-EEU-93-228*, Nov. 30, 1993, p. 41.

12. O. Kesar, "Vlasti reaguju jer je i osveta zločin" (The Authorities React, for Even Revenge Is a Crime), *Politika*, Apr. 6, 1994, p. 11.

13. This claim was made by Prijedor's police chief; see Gutman, *Witness to Genocide*, p. 113.

14. Ejub Štitković, "Kur'an po SRNI" (The Qur'an According to the Serbian Republic Information Agency), *Vreme*, Apr. 27, 1992, p. 33.

15. Asked subsequently about the incident, the individual replied that it was a "hypothetical question" he could not answer; see David B. Ottoway, "Defiance Moves Serbs in Bosnia," *Washington Post*, May 8, 1993, p. A16.

16. Thus Dragoš Kalajić warned that the "plan to set up an Islamic jamahiriyya" threatens Europe, and European and Christian culture, civilization, and traditions; see "Džamahirijom protiv Evrope" (With a Jamahiriyya against Europe), *Duga*, Mar. 15–28, 1992, p. 18.

17. According to the political figure Nikola Milošević, "Osuda režima" (Condemning the Regime), *Srpska reč,* June 7, 1993, p. 45. Although he also accused Slobodan Milošević and Franjo Tudjman of the same fault, to equate Izetbegović with the other two leaders was in itself a distortion of the goals and methods they supported.

18. See "Karadžićeva poruka" (Karadžić's Message), *Spona,* June 3, 1993, p. 19.

19. "Crkveni vrh ne priznaje Drinu" (The Church's Top Leadership Does Not Recognize the Drina), *Spona,* June 3, 1993, p. 19.

20. "Narod blagosiljao vladike" (The People Blessed the Bishops), *Evropske Novosti,* Apr. 9, 1993, p. 4.

21. Patriarch Pavle on Belgrade TV, Oct. 16, 1992, and interview by Branimir Brljević, "Bezboštvo je kriv za rat" (Atheism Is Responsible for the War) *Globus,* Nov. 26, 1993, p. 35.

22. Interview by M. Ć., "Narod u vlasti politike" (The People in Charge of Policy), *Evropske Novosti,* Mar. 4, 1993, p. 10.

23. Interview with Dimitrije Kaležić by Dragana Panić, "Sloga je stanje duha" (Unity is a State of Mind), *Vojska,* Aug. 5, 1993, pp. 11–12.

24. Interview with Bella Stumbo, "Slobo and Mira," *Vanity Fair,* June, 1994, p. 171.

25. Žika Antić, "Mauzerovi panteri" (Mauzer's Panthers), *Vojska,* Apr. 29, 1993, p. 51.

26. Belgrade TV Daily News, Jan. 14, 1993.

27. Resulović, ("Long Knives"), p. 5.

28. Jovan Janjić, "Spas od pakla" (Rescue from Hell) *NIN,* May 22, 1992, p. 13; and shown on Belgrade TV Daily News, Dec. 8, 1992.

29. Interview in *Pogledi,* Nov. 12, 1993, in *FBIS-EEU-93-228,* Nov. 30, 1993, p. 41.

30. Dragan Terzić, "Vodi li se u Bosni i Hercegovini verski rat?" (Is a Religious War Being Fought in Bosnia-Herzegovina?), *Pravoslavlje,* Nov. 15, 1992, p. 3.

31. Mile Nedeljković, *Krst i polumesec (The Cross and the Crescent)* (Belgrade: Politika, 1993), p. 105.

32. Interview with Darko Tanasković by Aleksandra Tomić, "Evropa neće izbeći demografski džihad" (Europe Will Not Avoid the Demographic Jihad), *Vojska,* Sept. 23, 1993, p. 9.

33. Belgrade TV Daily News, Dec. 6, 1992.

34. Miroljub Jevtić, "Oproštaj bez milosti" (Parting without Mercy), *Evropske Novosti,* July 7, 1993, p. 2.

35. Miroljub Jevtić, quoted in "Ljudi i vreme" (People and Time), *Vreme,* May 24, 1993, p. 54.

36. Miroljub Jevtić, "Nema mira u Bosni" (There Is No Peace in Bosnia), *Evropske Novosti,* Dec. 28, 1993, p. 4.

37. Interview with Nada Todorov by [Col.] Nikola Ostojić, "Genocidne poruke iz '1001 noći'" (The Genocidical Messages from "The Thousand and One Nights"), *Vojska,* Apr. 8, 1993, pp. 20–21.

38. Commentary by Miroslav Stefanović, Belgrade TV Daily News, Nov. 15, 1992.

39. Tomić, ("Europe Will Not Avoid"), p. 8.

40. Milan Mijalkovski, "Opasne iluzije" (Dangerous Illusions), *Vojska,* Nov. 25, 1993, p. 18.

41. Vojislav Lubarda, writing in *Javnost,* Sarajevo, quoted in "Ljudi i vreme" (People and Time), *Vreme,* Dec. 13, 1993, p. 57.

42. Quoted in M. Radetić, "Srbi i bez krsta" (Serbs Even without a Cross), *Evropske Novosti,* June 22, 1994, p. 11.

43. Slavko Aleksić, quoted in "Ljudi i vreme" (People and Time), *Vreme,* May 31, 1993, p. 54.

44. Blaine Harden, "Serbian Bid for Bosnia Alleged," *Washington Post,* April 11, 1992, p. A17.

45. Gaja Petković, "Guarantees fo the Almighty," *NIN,* Mar. 11, 1994, *FBIS-EEU-94-067,* Apr. 7, 1994, p. 62.

46. See the "Jokes" section in *Srpska reč,* Aug. 2, 1993, p. 43.

47. Kelman, "Violence without Moral Restraint," p. 49.

48. Interview in "Ko je Dafina Milanović? Suze u cvećari" (Who is Dafina Milanović? The Flowerseller Has Tears), *Evropske Novosti,* Mar. 24, 1993, p. 4.

49. Speech of June 28, 1989 (Kosovo and Unity), in *NIN,* July 2, 1989, p. 6.

50. Speech of Dec. 8, 1991 ("The Field Is Here"), p. 13.

51. Kalajić, ("With a Jamahiriyya against Europe"), p. 15.

52. ("Painless Amputation"), p. 30.

53. Quoted in Popov (*Serbian Populism*], p. 18.

54. "Ljudi i vreme," (People and Time), *Vreme,* Apr. 13, 1992, p. 50.

55. Vladimir Cvetković, quoted in "Ljudi i vreme" (People and Time), *Vreme,* May 24, 1993, p. 55.

56. Quoted in B. Lazukić, "Srbi su čudo nebesko" (The Serbs Are a Heavenly Wonder), *Borba,* Mar. 23, 1994, p. 11.

57. Speech in Podgorica reported in "Na Balkanu dva jezika" (Two Languages in the Balkans), *Evropske Novosti,* Feb. 3, 1994, p. 6.

58. Reported by Jevrem Damjanović, "Ko mrzi Srbe; Razbijena zavera ćutanja" (Who Hates the Serbs: The Conspiracy of Silence Is Broken), *Ilustrovana Politika,* Jan. 17, 1989, p. 15.

59. Interview with Dr. Jovan Striković, director of Belgrade's Sveti Sava Hospital, by Zoran Sekulić, "Vlada li kod nas 'virus umora'?" (Is the Virus of Fatigue Prevalent among Us?), *Ilustrovana Politika,* Dec. 4, 1990, p. 18. By July, 1992, Milošević's name was added to the magazine's masthead.

60. See (*Sources of Great Serbian Aggression*), p. 294.

61. Speech by Vuk Drašković on Sept. 11, 1988, "Svi Nabukodonosori roda srpskoga" (All the Nebuchadnezzars of Serbian Origin) in (*Quo Vadis, Serbia?*), p. 82.

62. Quoted in ("They Said"), p. 9.

63. Dragoš Kalajić, "Usamljeni, kao Nemci" (Isolated, Like the Germans], *Duga,* Feb. 1–14, 1992, p. 34.

64. Dragoš Kalajić, "Blokada oslobadja" (The Blockade Liberates), *Duga,* May 28–June 10, 1994, p. 85.

65. Tihomir Stojanović, "Opasnost četvrtog rajha" (The Danger of a Fourth Reich), *Narodna armija,* Nov. 2, 1991, p. 27.

66. Interview by Momir Djoković, "Srbi na ivici istorije" (The Serbs on the Brink of History), *Spona,* March 25, 1993, p. 12.

67. Jevtić, ("The Turks [Again]"), p. 65. In fact, he stressed, "We hope that all of that is clear enough to the highest holders of power in the land."

68. Interview on Belgrade Television, in *FBIS-EEU-92-230*, Nov. 30, 1992, p. 43.

69. A summary of the synod's report appeared in *Pravoslavlje*, Feb. 1, 1992, p. 2.

70. Quoted in Popov, (*Serbian Populism*), p. 18.

71. Ćosić interview, *Avanti*, pp. 228–29.

72. Memorandum of the Holy Episcopal Synod's session of May 14–20, 1992, *Pravoslavlje*, June 1, 1992, p. 2.

73. Interview by Milomir Marić, "General Ratko Mladić: Kako sam postao najveći Srbin" (General Ratko Mladić: How I Became the Greatest Serb), part 4, *Vesti*, Apr. 16, 1993, p. 18.

74. Ervin Staub, *Roots of Evil*, pp. 18–19.

75. Ibid., p. 55.

76. Interview in *Der Spiegel*, Hamburg, Apr. 26, 1993, in *FBIS-EEU-93-078*, Apr. 26, 1993, p. 41.

77. Speech in Bijeljina, Pale Radio-Televizija Republike Srpske, Studio-S Radio, Jan. 31, 1994, in *FBIS-EEU-94-021*, Feb. 1, 1994, p. 33; and speech in Podgorica, reported in *Evropske Novosti*, Feb. 3, 1994, p. 6.

78. Stojan Adašević, *Politika Ekspres*, quoted in "Ljudi i Vreme" (People and Time), *Vreme*, Apr. 19, 1993, p. 55.

79. Interview in *Javnost* (Priština, Kosovo), quoted in "Ljudi i Vreme" (People and Time), *Vreme*, Aug. 23, 1993, p. 59.

80. Ljubiša Rajić, "Natalitet i mortalitet; Koliko naroda, toliko neba" (Natality and Mortality: The More People, The More Heaven), *Vreme*, May 31, 1993, p. 32.

81. Vasilije, Bishop of Zvornik-Tuzla, "Odbranimo svetinju života" (We Are Defending the Sanctity of Life), *Pravoslavlje*, May 1, 1993, p. 5.

82. Interview with Sabina Izetbegović-Berberić, Alija Izetbegović's daughter, by Sina Karli, "Pad kuće Alije Izetbegovića" (The Fall of the House of Alija Izetbegović), *Globus*, Dec. 18, 1992, p. 32. Among Serbs who have promoted this argument is the Orientalist scholar Miroljub Jevtić, quoted in Miroslav Filipović, "Sandžak, zemlja Alahova?" (The Sandžak, Land of Allah?), *Stav*, Feb. 21, 1992, p. 20.

83. Interview by Marić, ("Gen. Ratko Mladić"), p. 18.

84. Quoted in Nenad Stefanović, "Znate li gde je vase sklonište" (Do You Know Where Your Shelter Is?), *Vreme*, May 24, 1993, p. 13.

85. Col. Ljubomir Stojadinović, TANJUG Domestic Service, Belgrade, in *FBIS-EEU-94-019*, Jan. 27, 1994, p. 25.

86. Quoted in Aleksandar Zelenkov, "Klopka za svete ratnike" (A Trap for the Holy Warriors), *Evropske Novosti*, Feb. 23, 1993, p. 10.

87. Arte Television, Paris, France, 8½ program, Jan. 14, 1993.

88. Igrić, ("The Calamity"), p. 30.

89. This incident is mentioned in Drašković's open letter to Herzegovina's Orthodox Bishop Atanasije, "Izdržaću" (I Will Hold Out), *Srpska reč*, Aug. 2, 1993, p. 29.

90. Dušan Stojanović, "Laughter as Houses Burn," *Washington Post*, May 8, 1993, p. A16.

91. Faik Tafro, "Fočansko leto 1992: Ubiti kao popiti čašu vode" (Foča Summer of 1992: To Kill As Easily As Drinking a Glass of Water), part 2, *Srpska reč*, May 24, 1993, p. 53.

92. Reported by Aleksijević from his interview with Karadžić, ("Politics as the Family Fate"), p. 3.

93. See Helsinki Watch, *War Crimes*, vol. 1, pp. 132–34, and vol. 2; also Harden, "Yugoslav Gulag," p. A18.

94. Mary Battiata, "Serbs, Absent UN, Press Bosnian Drive," *Washington Post*, Dec. 7, 1992, p. A25.

95. Resulović, ("Long Knives"), p. 5.

96. Randal, "Serbs Ending '700 Years,'" p. A52.

97. Jovan Janjić, "Kolektivno samoubistvo" (Collective Suicide), *NIN*, May 22, 1992, p. 12.

98. Tafro, ("People Die Looking On"), p. 45.

99. "The Camps: Death with No Rules," *Vreme*, Aug. 17, 1992, in *FBIS-EEU-92-174*, Sept. 8, 1992, p. 33; and Resulović, who mentions a similar case in Trebinje, in ("Long Knives"), p. 5.

100. Quoted in Edita Hadžić, "Put bez povratka" (Path with No Return), *BiH Ekskluziv*, Sept. 17, 1993, p. 6.

101. Srdjić, ("City in Exile"), p. 7.

102. Ahmed Bosnić, "Užasi Grbavice" (The Horrors of Grbavica), *BiH Ekskluziv*, July 8, 1994, p. 9.

103. T. D. Allman, "Serbia's Blood War," *Vanity Fair*, March, 1993, p. 100.

104. David Cray, "Serb Details Rape, Killing of Muslims," *Washington Times*, Mar. 14, 1993, p. A10.

105. Quoted in G. Rošić, "Sin of Those Written Off a Long Time Ago," *Borba*, Aug. 10, 1993, in *FBIS-EEU-93-154*, Aug. 12, 1993, p. 29.

Chapter 7

1. Zoran Bingulac, quoted in "Ljudi i vreme" (People and Time), *Vreme*, Nov. 29, 1993, p. 56.

2. Interview with Radovan Karadžić by A. Aleksandrović, "Na pragu pravednog mira" (On the Threshold of a Just Peace), *Evropske Novosti*, Aug. 18, 1993, p. 12.

3. Interview by Daniel Schiffer, "Dividiamoci da buoni nemici" (Let Us Part as Good Enemies), *L'Espresso*, Nov. 8, 1992, p. 92; and interview on RTB Television Network, Belgrade, Sept. 22, 1992, in *FBIS-EEU-92-189*, Sept. 29, 1992, p. 27.

4. Peter Maass, "Serbs Chase 14,000 Muslims," p. A18.

5. Interview with Maj. Vojkan Djurković by Slavisa Lekić, "Ljudi i vreme" (People and Time), *Vreme*, Oct. 11, 1993, p. 51.

6. Roger Thurow, "Forced from Home," p. A5.

7. Interview with RTB Television Network, Aug. 28, 1992, in *FBIS-EEU-92-169*, Aug. 31, 1992, p. 41. Ćosić likewise dismissed the issue off handedly: "I do not know

about such concentration camps;" interview by Olaf Ihlau and Renate Flottau, *Der Spiegel*, Aug. 10, 1992, in *FBIS-EEU-92-155*, Aug. 11, 1992, p. 35.

8. Tanjug Domestic Service, Aug. 6, 1992, in *FBIS-EEU-92-153*, Aug. 6, 1992, p. 44.

9. Peter Maass, "The Search for a Secret Prison Camp," *Washington Post*, Aug. 13, 1992, p. A18. A Polish mercenary, who served as a guard at one of the Serbian-run camps, has left an account in which he details some of the mistreatment inflicted on the detainees, and notes that the press was not allowed access. For this account, see Petošević, ("Serbian Mercenary"), p. 31.

10. Statement in "Vanredno zasedanja svetog arhijerejskog sabora SPC povodom laznih optužbi protiv srpskog naroda u Bosni i Hercegovini" (The Extraordinary Session of the Holy Episcopal Synod of the Serbian Orthodox Church in Response to the False Accusations against the Serbian People in Bosnia-Herzegovina) *Pravoslavni misionar*, June, 1992, pp. 250–51.

11. Interview by Ferrari, ("Patriarch Pavle"), p. 6.

12. Interview by Schiffer, ("Let Us Part"), p. 92.

13. Mary Battiata, "Muslims Flee Renewed Drive by Serb Forces," *Washington Post*, Oct. 11, 1992, p. A1.

14. U.S. Senate, *Staff Report*, p. 10. One reporter called the process "a shell game," see Maass, "Secret Prison Camp," p. A18. Also see "U.S. Says Serbs Shift Prisoners to Avoid Detection by Red Cross," *Washington Post*, Aug. 13, 1992, p. A20; and A. D. Horne, "UN Inspection Team Barred from Serb-Run Prison Camp in Bosnia," *Washington Post*, Aug. 25, 1992, p. A10.

15. Allman, "Serbia's Blood War," p. 100.

16. U.S. Senate, *Staff Report*, p. 26.

17. Dragan Terzić, ed., "Istina i pravda na zapadni način" (The Western Version of Accuracy and Truth), *Pravoslavlje*, Sept. 1, 1992, p. 3.

18. U.S. Senate, *Staff Report*, p. 22.

19. O. Kesar, "Vlasti reaguju jer je i osveta zločin" (The Authorities React, for Even Revenge Is a Crime), *Politika*, Apr. 6, 1994, p. 11.

20. Interview by Sebnem Senyener, *Sabah*, Istanbul, Feb. 10, 1993, in *FBIS-EEU-93-030*, Feb. 17, 1993, p. 34.

21. Statement by the Holy Episcopal Synod, *Pravoslavni misionar* (June, 1992), p. 250.

22. Interview with Milošević, BBC *Panorama* documentary by Stephen Bradshaw, broadcast in Washington, D.C., Apr. 18, 1994.

23. Article by Mirko Babić, in a Bosnian Serb military publication, *Bilten Prve Majevičke Brigade*, reprinted in *Borba*, Dec. 30, 1992 and in *FBIS-EEU-93-105*, Jan. 26, 1993, p. 43.

24. Ibid.

25. Interview by Milić od Mačve, in *Javnost* (Priština, Kosovo), quoted in "Ljudi i Vreme" (People and Time), *Vreme*, Aug. 23, 1993, p. 59.

26. Interview by Željko Garmaz, "Srpska Bela Ruža prijeti: Izazvat ćemo nezapamćen kaos u Njemackoj!" (The White Rose Threatens: We Will Create Unprecedented Chaos in Germany!), *Globus*, Sept. 10, 1993, p. 51.

27. Milić, ("People and Time"), p. 59.

28. Reported by G. Borović and M. Tadić, "Ratne prijetnje uz amanet vlasti" (Military Threats with the Government's Blessing), *Monitor*, Feb. 11, 1994, p. 8.

29. Gutman, *Witness to Genocide*, pp. ix–x.

30. Babić, *FBIS-EEU-93-105*, p. 44.

31. Interview by Juan Carlos Azcue in *ABC*, Madrid, Jan. 17, 1993, in *FBIS-EEU-93-013*, Jan. 22, 1993, p. 53.

32. Giovanni Porta, "Dentro il bunker serbo" (Inside the Serbian Bunker), *Panorama*, Milan, Aug. 22, 1993, p. 80.

33. Interview with German Radio, reprinted in "Ista mera za sve" (The Same Measure for All), *Spona*, Aug. 12, 1993, p. 23.

34. Interview with Dr. Jovan Marić by Snežana Djokić, "Plovidba do ostrva zdravlja" (Sailing to the Island of Health), *Vojska*, Oct. 21, 1993, p. 16.

35. Patrick Quinn, "Serbs, Croats Press Bosnia Drives," *Washington Times*, July 5, 1993, p. A9. This incident was similar to the case of the mosques destroyed in Bijeljina; see ("Five Mosques"), p. 12.

36. Peter Maass, "UN Officials Denounce Bosnian Serb Barrage," *Washington Post*, Apr. 14, 1993, p. A23.

37. George J. Church, "This Time We Mean It," *Time*, Feb. 21, 1994, p. 28.

38. John Pomfret, "U.S. Says Serbs Plan to Fake Arms 'Airdrop,'" *Washington Post*, Feb. 10, 1994, p. A23.

39. Interview by Azcue in *FBIS-EEU-93-013*, p. 53; and Belgrade TANJUG, Sarajevo Market Kills 66, Wounds Hundreds," *Washington Post*, Feb. 6, 1994, p. A1; Radovan Kovačević and Radovan Pavlović, "Minobacač nije mogao da izazove takvu tragediju" (A Mortar Could Not Have Caused Such a Tragedy), *Politika*, Feb. 9, 1994, p. 9.

40. Peter Maass, "Bosnian Serbs Bar UN Pleace Plan," *Washington Post*, Apr. 3, 1993, p. A17.

41. Miroljub Jevtić, "Samo goli interes" (Only Naked Interest), *Evropske Novosti*, July 1, 1993, p. 2.

42. Gen. Ratko Mladić, quoted in "Vreme i ljudi" (People and Time), *Vreme*, Dec. 6, 1993, p. 56.

43. Interview by Ljiljana Vajagić, "Kopča za novi mirotvorni plan" (A Buckle for the New Peace Plan), *Spona*, June 3, 1993, p. 9.

44. Interview with Slobodan Milošević by Daniel Schiffer, "Musulmani, vi proteggo io" (Muslims, I Will Protect You), *L'Espresso*, Jan. 17, 1993, p. 76.

45. Andrew Borowiec, "Prime Minister Says He's 'Only Hope' for Yugoslavia," *Washington Times*, Sept. 25, 1992, p. A10.

46. Interview with Milan Panić by Branimir Brljević, "Ovdje, u Budimpešti, razgovaram o balkanskoj ekonomskoj uniji!" (Here, in Budapest, I Am Discussing a Balkan Economic Union!), *Globus*, Feb. 4, 1993, p. 12.

47. Dejan Lukić, "'Užasavanje' Eli Vizela" (Eli Wiesel's "Repulsion"), *Srpska Stvarnost*, Sept. 25, 1993, p. 21.

48. Raja Thomas, "Jevreji, Srbi i jugoslovenski sukob" (The Jews, the Serbs, and

the Yugoslav Conflict), part 8, "Sumnjivi dokazi i prevare" (Dubious Proof and Deception), *Politika*, Apr. 27, 1994, p. 25.

49. For example, Thomas, ("The Jews"), *Politika*, part 9, "Igra sa brojem slučajeva silovanja" (Playing with the Numbers of Rape Cases), Apr. 28, 1994, p. 27; part 13, "Veći Hrvati od stvarnih Hrvata" (More Croatian than the Real Croatians), May 5, 1994, p. 19; part 15, "Razlika izmedju američkih Jevreja i Izraelaca" (The Difference between American Jews and the Israelis), May 7, 1994, p. 25; and part 18, "Trojni gradjanski rat" (Three-Way Civil War), May 11, 1994, p. 23 (Frankfurt edition).

50. Eugene Robinson, "Balkan Parties' Ability to Stop Bosnian War Questioned," *Washington Post*, Aug. 29, 1992, p. A15.

51. Schiffer, ("Let Us Part"), p. 91. Karadžić continued to promote this view notwithstanding the evidence to the contrary, claiming: "We do not keep [a] siege on Sarajevo. We just protect our own suburbs in Sarajevo, and those suburbs happen to be around the Muslim quarters of the city." See Jerusalem Qol Yisra'el Radio, Aug. 3, 1993, in *FBIS-EEU-93-148*, Aug. 4, 1993, p. 35.

52. All these officials are quoted in M. Gutić, "U Goraždu panika" (Panic in Goražde), *Evropske Novosti*, Apr. 5, 1994, p. 4.

53. Harden, "Key Town," p. A33, and U.S. Senate, *Staff Report*, p. 7.

54. Allman, "Serbia's Blood War," p. 100. Likewise, in the Manjača camp, authorities insisted to reporters that those detained were "armed rebels and war criminals," although the detainees maintained they had been unarmed civilians; see "Life Inside Camps," *Washington Times*, Aug. 10, 1992, p. A8.

55. Allman, "Serbia's Blood War," p. 102.

56. V. Mitrić, "Žrtve svoje komande" (Victims of their Own Commanders), *Večernje Novosti*, Frankfurt, June 9, 1992, p. 5.

57. As reported by a Serb militia commander, Aleksandar Zelenkov, ("Holy Warriors"), p. 10.

58. Fr. Savo Knežević, "Extermination of Serbs—In Pictures and Words," *Serbia: Documents, Comments, Interviews* (Belgrade: Republic of Serbia Ministry of Information, Jan. 15, 1993), p. 17.

59. Andrew Borowiec, "Serbian Bishop Warns of Muslims' Gains in the Balkans," *Washington Times*, Sept. 30, 1992, p. A9. To a large extent, the threat portrayal is a function of the assumed receptivity of the intended audience. Milošević, Gen. Života Panić, and Karadžić, for example, have stressed the German danger when addressing Russian audiences, even in relation to the events in Bosnia-Herzegovina; see the interview with Milošević by Gennadiy Seleznev and Evegeniy Fadeev, "Yugoslaviya—pervaya zhertva germanskogo revanshizma" (Yugoslavia Is the First Victim of German Revanchism), *Pravda*, Feb. 20, 1993, p. 3; the interview with Gen. Panić by Col. Aleksandr Oliynik, "Sud'ba nashey armii neotdelima ot sud'by serbov i chernogortsev" (The Fate of Our Army Is Indivisible from the Fate of the Serbs and Montenegrins), *Krasnaya Zvezda*, Moscow, Feb. 9, 1993, p. 3; and Karadžić's interview with *Moscow News*, reported by Dmitry Yakushkin, "EC Wanted Balkan War, Karadžić Says," *Washington Times*, Sept. 21, 1993, p. A13.

60. Schiffer, ("Let Us Part"), p. 91.

61. Interview with Radovan Karadžić by Azcue, in *FBIS-EEU-93-013*, p. 53.

62. Tanjug Domestic Service, Oct. 26, 1992, reporting about Ćosić's interview with *Suddeutsche Zeitung*, Munich, in *FBIS-EEU-92-208*, Oct. 27, 1992, p. 35.

63. See, for example, his interview by Eric Laurent, *Le Figaro*, July 20, 1992, in *FBIS-EEU-92-141*, July 22, 1992, p. 26.

64. Quoted in John Pomfret, "Pact May Restore Utilities in Sarajevo," *Washington Post*, July 13, 1993, p. A8.

65. Radovan Karadžić, "Commentary," *Washington Times*, June 12, 1994, p. B4.

66. *NBC Nightly News*, Oct. 26, 1992.

67. Tomić, ("Europe Will Not Avoid"), p. 9.

68. Reported in S. Aleksandrić, "Srpski "Karavan Istine" u Italiji" (The Serbian "Truth Caravan" in Italy), *Evropske Novosti*, Dec. 18, 1993, p. 15.

69. Respectively, *NBC Nightly News*, Oct. 26, 1992, and quote in Michael Getler and Mary Battiata, "Serb Warns Against U.S. Entry into Bosnia," *Washington Post*, Dec. 13, 1992, p. A39.

70. Milovan Drecun, "Neprekidna drama" (Uninterrupted Drama), *Narodna armija*, May 21, 1992, p. 51.

71. Interview with General Mladić by Miloš Rajković, Belgrade Radio, Dec. 28, 1993, in *FBIS-EEU-93-248*, Dec. 29, 1993, p. 27.

72. Interview in Pogledi, Nov. 12, 1993, in *FBIS-EEU-93-228*, Nov. 30, 1993, p. 41.

73. Interview with Radoslav Stojanović, member of the Executive Council of the Democratic Party of Serbia, by Momir Djoković, "Povratak vrednostima Srbije" (A Return to Serbia's Values), *Spona*, June 10, 1993, p. 15.

74. Dragoš Kalajić, "Dzamahirijom protiv Evrope" (With a Jamahiriyya against Europe), *Duga*, Mar. 15–28, 1992, p. 18.

75. Igrić, ("The Calamity"), p. 30.

76. "Osudjen na pet godina" (Sentenced to Five Years), *Spona*, May 13, 1993, p. 32.

77. "Prvi slovenski politički azilant" (The First Slav Political Refugee), *Danas*, Oct. 22, 1991, p. 3.

78. See, for example, M. Nićiforović, "Lažima protiv svog naroda" (With Lies against Their Own People), *Evropske Novosti*, Apr. 20, 1994, p. 3.

79. Momo Kapor, "O ljudima i psima" (About People and Dogs), *Srpska stvarnost*, Sept. 11, 1993, p. 27.

80. Interview with Vojislav Šešelj by S.S., "Arkan tužio Šešelja" (Arkan Accused Šešelj), *Evropske Novosti*, Jan. 5, 1994, p. 9.

81. ("Eighth Session"), pp. 20–21.

82. Ibid., p. 22.

83. Interview with Danica Drašković by Saša Leković, "Jednog sam bosanskog srbina zviznula bocom po glavi!" (I Smashed a Bottle over the Head of a Bosnian Serb), *Globus*, Apr. 4, 1993, p. 13.

84. See an account by a former member of the Serbian Guard's staff, Vanja Bulić, "Čija je sada Srpska Garda i ko joj je najveći neprijatelj" (Whose Is the Serbian Guard Now and Who Is Its Greatest Enemy?), *Duga*, Jan. 4–18, 1992, p. 36.

85. "Srbi moraju živeti" (The Serbs Must Live), *Srpska reč*, May 24, 1993, p. 47–48.

86. The SPO's Secretary-General, Vladimir Gajić, also argued against this plan on behalf of Drašković's party: "The SPO has been opposed to the creation of a Muslim state having even a single square kilometer of land." Interview by Vesna Bjekić, "Manjinska vlada mora da padne" (A Minority Government Must Fall) *Spona,* Oct. 17, 1993, p. 14.

87. "Vuk Drašković i DEPOS u Nišu, 29. Novembar 1993" (Vuk Drašković and the Democratic Party in Niš, November 29, 1993), *Srpska reč,* Dec. 6, 1993, p. 27.

88. Interview by Vesna Bjekić, "Manjinska vlada mora da padne" (A Minority Government Must Fall), *Spona,* Oct. 17, 1993, p. 14.

89. Speech of Dec. 9, 1993, in Loznica, by Vuk Drašković, "Loznica, 9. XII 1993" (Loznica, Dec. 9, 1993), *Srpska reč,* Dec. 20, 1993, p. 19. In a speech given in November, 1993, he had insisted, on the contrary, that "no one ran away from the Serbs, no one" ("Democratic Party in Niš"), p. 27.

90. "Srbi moraju živeti" (The Serbs Must Live), *Srpska reč,* May 24, 1993, pp. 46–47.

Chapter 8

1. Interview by Soren Ostergaard Sorensen, *Berlingske Tidende,* Copenhagen, Jan. 31, 1993, in *FBIS-EEU-93-021,* Feb. 3, 1993, p. 54.

2. Aleksijević, ("Politics as the Family Fate"), p. 3.

3. ("Even We Did Not Know"), p. 20.

4. Interview with Mufti Hamdija Jusufspahić by Salwa Al-ᶜInani, "Natatallaᶜ ila bina' markaz islami fi bilgrad bi-musaᶜadat al-duwal al-islamiyya" (We Are Looking Forward to Building an Islamic Center in Belgrade with the Help of the Islamic Countries), *Al-Ahram,* Cairo, Nov. 10, 1989, p. 15.

5. Quoted, respectively, in an interview by Jelena Lovrić, "Rata neće biti" (There Will Be No War) *Danas,* Mar. 17, 1992, p. 29; and in an interview by Turki Al-ᶜUtaybi, "Ra'is jumhuriyyat al-busna wa-l-harsak li-l-madina" (The President of Bosnia-Herzegovina to *Al-Madina*), *Al-Madina,* Jeddah, Mar. 28, 1992, p. 6.

6. Peter Maass, "Serbs Strike Fear," p. A1, A25. Maass characterizes Banja Luka as "a city of daytime arrests, midnight beatings, and around-the-clock terror."

7. Filip Švarm, "Prikriveni užas" (Barely Veiled Horror), *Vreme,* Apr. 12, 1993, p. 36. Džemal Džakmić reports similar views of Muslims elsewhere in "Grad smrti i terora: Bosanska Dubica" (The City of Death and Terror: Bosanska Dubica), *BiH Ekskluziv,* June 25, 1993, p. 6, as does a representative to the Bosnia-Herzegovina Parliament, a Croatian from the Travnik area, Joško Dadić, "Vitez Doku ne pušta" (Vitez Will Not Let Doko Pass), *Nedjeljna Dalmacija,* May 7, 1992, p. 4.

8. Peter Maass, "Fleeing to Safety in a UN Convoy," *Washington Post,* July 24, 1992, p. A30.

9. Battiata, "Psychological Noose," p. A29.

10. Jevrić, ("The Guilty Ones"), p. 26.

11. Mary Battiata, "Bosnian Serb Police Unit Is Accused of Massacre of Muslim Prisoners," *Washington Post,* Sept. 22, 1992, p. A17.

12. Fadil Smajić, "Oni će pasti dolje" (They Will Fall Down), *BiH Ekskluziv,* June 11, 1993, p. 5.

13. Velizar Brajović, "Otovorena Pandorina kutija" (Pandora's Box Is Open), *Vreme,* May 10, 1993, pp. 27–29.

14. Yigal Chazan, "Bosnia's 'Loyal' Muslims Lament Their Worthless Sacrifice," *The Guardian,* Feb. 9, 1993, p. 9.

15. Tafro, ("People Die Looking On"), p. 45; and ("Drinking a Glass of Water"), p. 52.

16. Quoted by Hasan Rončević, "Evropa se vraća u srednji vijek" (Europe Is Reverting to the Middle Ages), *Ljiljan,* Dec. 15, 1993, p. 17.

17. H. Rifatbegović, "Oružje u božjem hramu" (Weapons in God's Sanctuary), *BiH Ekskluziv,* Apr. 15, 1994, p. 7.

18. "Ljudi i Vreme," *Vreme,* Nov. 1, 1993, p. 55, and R. P., "Medju članovima Stranke srpskog jedinstva su i najpoznatija imena estrade" (The Members of the Serbian Unity Party Include Some of the Best-Known Names in the Field of Entertainment), *Politika,* Nov. 9, 1993, p. 8.

19. Interview with Archdeacon Dragan Protić by M. Radetić, "Pamćenje duže od vere" (A Memory Longer than Faith), *Srpska Stvarnost,* Feb. 12, 1994, p. 6.

20. Rončević, ("Europe Is Reverting"), p. 17.

21. Interview with Vladimir Zhirinovskiy by Vlado Vurušić, "Na tlu bivše Jugoslavije nastat će četiri države" (On the Territory of Former Yugoslavia Four States Will Arise), *Globus,* Feb. 4, 1994, pp. 8, 39.

22. Testimony by Maj. Gen. Lewis MacKenzie in *Situation in Bosnia,* p. 54.

23. See Gutman, *Witness to Genocide,* p. 170, where former State Department official George Kenney is quoted.

24. Tom Gjelten, "Blaming the Victim," *New Republic,* Dec. 20, 1993, pp. 14–16.

25. See Gutman, *Witness to Genocide,* p. 170.

26. Maj. Gen. Lewis MacKenzie, *Peacekeeper: The Road to Sarajevo* (Vancouver: Douglas and McIntyre, 1993), p. 136.

27. Blaine Harden, "UN Commander in Bosnia Opposes Intervention," *Washington Post,* Dec. 13, 1992, p. A38.

28. Quoted in John Pomfret, "Sarajevo: Still No Exit," *Washington Post,* Aug. 19, 1993, p. A25.

29. See Dan Oberdorfer, "State Dept. Backtracks on Atrocity Reports," *Washington Post,* Aug. 5, 1992, pp. A1, A27.

30. Richard Johnson, "Some Call It Genocide—But Not Those Who Can Make a Difference," *Washington Post,* Feb. 13, 1994, p. C7.

31. *Larry King Live,* CNN, May 3, 1993, and U.S. House of Representatives, House Armed Services Committee, *U.S. Policy toward Bosnia,* Hearing, may 26, 1993, Federal Information Systems Corp. transcript, n. p.

32. Eagleburger and Scherf interviewed on *Panorama* documentary, BBC, Apr. 28, 1994. Significantly, Great Britain did not provide even a symbolic contribution in response to requests for financial help for the UN's Commission of Experts set up to investigate war crimes.

33. Richard Cohen, "It's Not a Holocaust," *Washington Post,* Feb. 28, 1993, p. C4.

34. Ibid.

35. Ted Galen Carpenter, "Serbia Analogy . . . and Perspective," *Washington Times,* June 12, 1994, p. B4.

36. Ibid.

37. Irving Louis Horowitz, "Genocide and the Reconstruction of Social Theory: Observations on the Exclusivity of Collective Death," in Wallimann and Dobrowski, *Genocide and the Modern Age,* p. 62.

38. Carpenter, "Serbia, Analogy," p. B4; Cohen makes a similar argument in "It's Not a Holocaust," p. C4.

39. Roy Gutman, "UN Forces Accused of Using Serb-Run Brothel," *Washington Post,* Nov. 2, 1993, p. A12.

40. Testimony by Maj. Gen. Lewis MacKenzie in *Situation in Bosnia,* p. 57.

41. Lord Owen repeated this argument often, including on the *Charlie Rose Show,* Feb. 9, 1993.

42. David Binder, "Criticized as Appeaser, Vance Defends His Role in Balkans," *New York Times,* Jan. 19 1993, p. A7.

43. Calculations based on tables 101–2, 211–4, and 211–22 from (*Statistical Yearbook of Yugoslavia, 1989*).

44. *Charlie Rose Show,* Feb. 9, 1993; Lord Owen was to return repeatedly to this erroneous portrayal of the Serbs as the only victims of World War II as a mitigating factor for their present actions. For example: "The history is one which is, of course, of intense rivalry between these three groups, of very severe massacres, which involved the Serbs [as victims] during the Second World War." Also see interview by Paula Zahn, *CBS This Morning,* Apr. 29, 1993; and interview in "David Owen in the Balkans," *Foreign Affairs* (Spring, 1993), p. 7.

45. Interview with Lord Owen by David Frost on Feb. 23, 1994, National Public Radio (NPR), Feb. 28, 1994.

46. Ibid.

47. David B. Ottoway, "Serbs Press Offensive In Bosnia," *Washington Post,* Apr. 3, 1994, p. A1.

48. Interview on NPR, Apr. 3, 1994, and Jonathan C. Randal, "UN Ordered to Stem Fighting in Gorazde," *Washington Post,* Apr. 10, 1994, p. A22.

49. Interview by Zahn, *CBS This Morning.*

50. Interview by Rose, *Charlie Rose Show,* Feb. 9, 1993.

51. Interview in *Foreign Affairs,* p. 3.

52. Interview by Zahn, *CBS This Morning.*

53. Interview with Lord Owen by Frost.

54. Interview by Zahn, *CBS This Morning.*

55. Press conference coverage, CNN, Aug. 4, 1992, New York.

56. Testimony before the U.S. House Armed Services Committee, May 26, 1993.

57. Ralph Peters, "Media Shouldn't Choose Where Troops Go to Die," *Army Times,* May 24, 1993, p. 31.

58. Jonathan Steele, Ian Traynor, and Hella Pick, "Russia Urged to Play Bigger Bosnian Role," *The Guardian,* Feb. 13, 1993, p. 12.

Chapter 9

1. Interview by Batsheva Tsur, "Croatian Defense Minister Calls for Military Aid from Israel," *Jerusalem Post*, Nov. 13, 1992, p. 4A.

2. See his interview, for example, in *Le Figaro*, Jan. 18, 1993), in *FBIS-EEU-93-012*, Jan. 21, 1993, pp. 62–63; interview by Hloverka Novak Srzić in *Danas*, Feb. 25, 1993, p. 13; and his conference of July 28, 1993, in "Iz pakla rata u blagostanje" (From the Hell of War to Press Prosperity), *Slobodna Dalmacija*, July 29, 1993, p. 17.

3. Ian Traynor, "Croat Aggression 'Seeks to Build on Peace Plan Gains,'" *The Guardian*, Feb. 3, 1993, p. 9.

4. Reported by Ivan Sabić, "Zasad bez dobrog rješenja" (No Good Solution for Now), *Danas*, July 16, 1993, p. 20; and Hrvoje Marinić, "Srednja Bosna: Ima li alternative vojnoj intervenciji?" (Central Bosnia: Is There Any Alternative to Military Intervention?), *Nedjeljna Dalmacija*, Jan. 5, 1994, p. 8.

5. See Jonathan C. Randal, "'Map War' Continues in Mostar," *Washington Post*, May 12, 1993, p. A25; Jonathan C. Randal and John Pomfret, "Serb, Croat Moves Threaten Truce Accords in Bosnia," *Washington Post*, May 14, 1993, p. A33; and Laura Pitter, "Mostar's Hungry Wait Amid the Rubble," *Christian Science Monitor*, Aug. 25, 1993, pp. 1, 4.

6. See Michael Hedges, "Croatian Women Help Halt Food Aid to Muslim Areas," *Washington Times*, May 25, 1993, p. A8; and John Pomfret, "Croatian-Muslim Battle Rages On in Bosnia," *Washington Post*, May 11, 1993, p. A12.

7. Jonathan C. Randal, "Ahmici Massacre—Bosnian Turning Point," *Washington Post*, June 20, 1993, p. A29. Also see Jonathan C. Randal, "Savage Factional Fighting Rages in Central Region," *Washington Post*, Apr. 22, 1993, p. A1; Jonathan C. Randal, "Whole Families Have Been Massacred," *Washington Post*, Apr. 23, 1993, p. A18; and Paul McEnroe, "Croats' Spree Kills 300 Muslims in Bosnian Town," *Washington Times*, Apr.27, 1993, p. A10.

8. In fact, Croatia's defense minister, Gojko Šušak, a hardliner and himself originally from Herzegovina, apparently had triggered the large-scale fighting by an inflammatory speech he gave while visiting Travnik, in Bosnia-Herzegovina in April, 1993; see Jonathan C. Randal, "Croat, Muslim Forces Turn Guns on Each Other in Central Bosnia," *Washington Post*, Apr. 20, 1993, p. A16.

9. Marko Barišić, "Uloga britanskih obavještajaca" (The Role of British Intelligence Agents), *Danas*, July 16, 1993, pp. 5–8.

10. Interview with Mate Boban in *Rossiya*, Moscow, Oct. 26, 1993), in *FBIS-Central Eurasia-93-141*, Nov. 3, 1993, p. 90.

11. Reported in an interview with Josip Manolić, president of the lower house of Croatia's Parliament, by Davor Butković, "Mate Boban pozivao je Hrvate da se masovno isele iz srednje Bosne i odu na otoke i u Istru" (Mate Boban Called on the Croatians to Leave Central Bosnia and to Go to the Islands and to Istra), *Globus*, Jan. 21, 1994, p. 6.

12. See N. Idrižović, "Presuda u rodnom listu" (Condemned by their Birth Certificate), *Oslobodjenje*, Ljubljana, Slovenia, Jan. 6–13, 1994, p. 17.

Notes to Pages 127–32

13. As reported by an Egyptian journalist, Hayfa' Khalaf Allah, "Ta'ish alam wa-amal muslimi al-busna" (Sharing the Sufferings and Hopes of Bosnia's Muslims), Al-Watan, part 3, Kuwait, Nov. 20, 1993, p. 21.

14. Alija Lizde reports this incident occurring in the Ljubuški prison, for example; see "Bliski susret s krvnicima" (Close Encounters with the Executioners), Oslobod-jenje, Dec. 3–10, 1993, p. 25.

15. Jasna Babić, "Pokolj u Stupom Dolu i rat u Varešu planirali su hrvatski ekstremisti u dogovoru sa Srbima!" (Croatian Extremists in Accord with the Serbs Planned the Massacre in Stupni Do and the War in Vareš), Globus, Nov. 12, 1993, pp. 3–4. On the massacre in Stupni Do, also see David B. Ottoway, "Bodies Bear Witness to Town's Terror," Washington Post, Oct. 28, 1993, pp. A1, A34.

16. "Osuda zločinca" (Condemnation of a Criminal), BiH Ekskluziv, July 9, 1993, p. 4; and Džanita Kamerić, "Ravnopravnost u gradu-logoru" (Equality in a Prison-Camp City), BiH Ekskluziv, July 9, 1993, p. 4.

17. Poll results published in Globus, June 26, 1992, p. 4; June 25, 1993, p. 10; Aug. 13, 1993, p. 5; Feb. 11, 1994, p. 12; and March 4, 1994, p. 10.

18. Interview with Father Tomislav Duka by Mate Bašić, "Antun Vrdoljak optužuje me da nosim pištolj a u titovoj vojsci nosio sam mitraljež!" (Antun Vrdoljak Accuses Me of Carrying a Pistol, But in Tito's Army I Carried a Machine-Gun!), Globus, Feb. 4, 1994, pp. 12, 29.

19. Roundtable reported by Davor Butković, "Državu Herceg-Bosnu treba odmah ukinuti!" (The State of Herceg-Bosna Must Be Abolished Immediately!), Globus, Feb. 11, 1994, p. 32.

20. See, for example, "Zašto će se suditi imamu Zahiragiću?" (Why Is Imam Zahiragić to Be Put on Trial?), Glas Koncila, May 3, 1987, p. 2; "Na Kosovu nema vjerskog rata" (There Is No Religious War in Kosovo); and "To nije put k rješenju" (That Is Not the Way to a Solution), Glas Koncila, Apr. 16, 1989, pp. 1, 2.

21. See Davor Butković, "Herceg-Bosna se odcijepila od Hrvatske!" (Herceg-Bosnia Has Cut Itself Off from Croatia!], Globus, June 4, 1993, pp. 3–4.

22. In one instance, a local priest told a Muslim cleric who came to him looking for help in the wake of the roundup of Muslims to be sent to camps that "they were taking Muslims in order to protect them;" see John Pomfret, "Bosnian Croats Seek to Deport Detained Muslims," Washington Post, July 18, 1993, p. A21.

23. Interview with Msgr. Ante Živko Kustić by Davor Butković, "Iz komunističke tiranije upali smo u još stariji tip primitivizma" (We have Fallen from a Communist Tyranny into an Even Older Sort of Primitivism!), Globus, Aug. 13, 1993, p. 31.

24. Interview by Ilija Ilić and Mijat Jerković, "Zbog pada Posavine sukobljavao sam se s hrvatskim političarima" (I Was in Conflict with the Croatian Politicians Because of the Fall of the Posavina Area), Posavski glasnik, Sept. 9, 1993, p. 9.

25. Ibid.

26. Randal, "Increase the Pressure," p. A14.

27. "Uz proglašenje Hrvatske Republike Herceg-Bosne" (On the Proclamation of the Croatian Republic of Herceg-Bosnia), Glas Koncila, Sept. 5, 1993, p. 2.

28. Brother Luka Markešić, "Ostvariti nemoguće" (To Achieve the Impossible), BiH Ekskluziv, Oct. 22, 1993, p. 3.

29. Quoted in Ivica Mlivončić, "Udar na fratre" (Striking at the Friars), *BiH Ekskluziv,* Aug. 27, 1993, p. 3.

30. Interview by Davor Butković and Mate Bašić, "Ako odmah ne ukine Herceg-Bosnu Bobana treba smijeniti" (Unless He Abolishes Herceg-Bosna Immediately, Boban Must Be Replaced), *Globus,* May 28, 1993, pp. 3–4.

31. Interview with Mate Boban by Josip Jović, "Mate Boban, Predsjednik Hrvatske Republike Herceg-Bosne" (Mate Boban, President of the Croatian Republic of Herceg-Bosna), *Slobodna Dalmacija,* Dec. 1, 1993, p. 8.

32. This type of balanced reporting has included *Globus,* which has published interviews with articulate critics of the Tudjman-Boban policies, among them Muslim officials. It also includes *Glas Istre* (Pula, Croatia), for example, the Dragan Ogurlić and Dražen Fligić series "Sarajevski ratni dnevnik" (Sarajevo War Diary) in early 1993 and *Tjednik Glas Istre* (Pula, Croatia), for example, Dražen Vukov Čolić, "Posljednja molitva iz Medjugorja" (Last Prayer from Medjugorje), May 22, 1993, pp. 1–2.

33. Davor Butković and Mate Bašić, "Zašto je HVO izgubio propagandni rat u Bosni?" (Why Has the HVO Lost the Propaganda War in Bosnia?), *Globus,* Aug. 20, 1993, pp. 8–9.

34. Petar Požar, "Fundamentalizam" (Fundamentalism), *Magazin Glas Slavonije,* Osijek, Croatia, Dec. 3, 1992, p. 2.

35. Ivica Mlivončić, "Livnom kontra Sarajeva" (Livno against Sarajevo), *BiH Ekskluziv,* Feb. 18, 1994, p. 3.

36. Broadcast by Zagreb Radio Croatia Network, Nov. 16, 1993, in *FBIS-EEU-93-221,* Nov. 18, 1993, pp. 26–33.

37. Alija Izetbegović, "Voljeti ono što narod voli" (To Love What the People Love), *Oslobodjenje,* Feb. 21–28, 1994, pp. 4–5.

38. Interview by Nada Al Issa, broadcast on Croatian TV, April 16, 1994.

39. Željko Garmaz, "Hoće li livanjska bomba raznijeti hrvatsko-muslimanski pakt?" (Will the Bomb in Livno Blow Up the Croatian-Muslim Pact?), *Globus,* Apr. 29, 1994, pp. 3–4.

40. Davor Butković, "Je li Dario Kordić, novi predsjednik HDZ-a BiH, kriv za ratne zločine?" (Is Dario Kordić, the New President of the HDZ for Bosnia-Herzegovina, Guilty of War Crimes?), *Globus,* July 22, 1994, pp. 2, 13; and Ivica Mlivončić, "Rascjep" (A Split), *BiH Ekskluziv,* July 29, 1994, p. 2.

41. Davor Butković, "Hrvatsko-bosanska konfederacija imat će 7 milijuna i 230 tisuća stanovnika!" (The Croatian-Bosnian Confederation Will Have a Population of 7,230,000!], *Globus,* March 4, 1994, p. 4.

42. David B. Ottoway, "Croatia Sends Its Troops Into Bosnia," *Washington Post,* Jan. 29, 1994, pp. A1, A14.

43. By mid-1993 as their position seemed to reach an impasse, some Muslims at least were becoming more prone to lash out at their non-Muslim neighbors out of frustration; reported from Sarajevo by John Pomfret, "In Sarajevo, a Lust for Vengeance Grows," *Washington Post,* Aug. 2, 1993, pp. A1, A14; and John Pomfret, "Tension Invades Bosnian Bastion of Harmony," *Washington Post,* Nov. 21, 1993, p. A30.

44. See letter by Archbishop Puljić to special UN envoy Tadeusz Mazowiecki, "Pismo nadbiskupa Vinka Puljića Tadeuszu Mazowieckom" (Archbishop Vinko Puljić's Letter to Tadeusz Mazowiecki), *Glas Koncila*, Sept. 5, 1993, p. 3; Blanka Kraljević, "Uzdol: 42 masakrirana Hrvata!" (Uzdol: 42 Croatians Massacred!], *Slobodna Dalmacija*, Sept. 16, 1993, p. 3; James Rupert, "Muslim Forces Plunder Bosnian Croat Villages," *Washington Post*, June 17, 1993, pp. A33, A34; David B. Ottoway, "Bosnian Muslims' Gains May Have High Cost" *Washington Post*, Sept. 12, 1993, p. A37; and Pero Pranjić, "Zgarišta, pustoš i jauk" (Charred Ruins, Desolation, and Lamentation), *Glas Koncila*, Sept. 19, 1993, p. 8. The Archbishop of Sarajevo reported that Muslim forces had pushed out 141,000 Croatians from their homes by August, 1993; see Agence France Presse, Aug. 31, 1993, in *FBIS-EEU-93-167*, Aug. 31, 1993, p. 42.

45. See John Sack, *An Eye for an Eye: The Untold Story of Jewish Revenge Against Germans in 1945* (New York: Basic Books, 1993).

Chapter 10

1. See, for example, Dan Oberdorfer, "U.S. Aide Resigns Over Balkan Policy, *Washington Post*, Aug. 26, 1992, pp. A1, A18. For an analysis of differing factors affecting U.S. decision making on Bosnia-Herzegovina, see Daniel Williams, "Grim Balkans Outlook Affected U.S. Position," *Washington Post*, Aug. 19, 1993, pp. A1, A24; and the insightful, although critical, assessments by George Kenney, "Good Morning, Bosnia," *Washington Post*, May 9, 1993, pp. C1, C4; "A Casualty of Level-10 Frustration," *Time*, Aug. 16, 1993, p. 22; and Patrick Glynn, "See No Evil," *New Republic*, Oct. 25, 1993, pp. 23–29.

2. Perry, "Determining Appropriate Use," p. 2.

3. Testimony by Maj. Gen. Lewis MacKenzie in *Situation in Bosnia*, pp. 59–60.

4. Quoted in Harden, "UN Commander, " p. A38.

5. Churchill Lecture, Guildhall, London.

6. Interview with Lord Owen by Caroline De Gruyter, "Oh Lord, What A Year," *Elsevier*, Amsterdam, Dec. 25, 1993, p. 56.

7. This opinion is underlined by Thompson and Quets, "Genocide and Social Conflict," p. 251.

8. Sergey Sidorov, "Radi chego 'russkie prishli' v Saraevo" (Why Did the Russians Come to Sarajevo?), *Krasnaya Zvezda*, Mar. 25, 1994, p. 3.

9. Mary Battiata, "Slayings in Bosnia Confirmed," *Washington Post*, Sept. 28, 1992, p. A1; and Battiata, "Serb Police Unit," p. A17.

10. Jovan Dulović, "At the Center of Hell," *Vreme*, May 23, 1994, *FBIS-EEU-94-113*, June 13, 1994, p. 43–44.

11. Henrik Bering-Jensen, "War Crimes: A History of Trials and Errors," *Insight*, Mar. 14, 1993, p. 30.

12. Interview by Željko Garmaz, ("The White Rose Threatens") p. 51.

13. Fox Morning News, Feb. 23, 1993.

14. Interview with Zoran Stojanović by Svetislava Stojanović, "Izručenje—kamen

spoticanja" (Extradition—the Stumbling Block), *Evropske Novosti,* Mar. 8, 1994, p. 2.

15. See Gutman, *Witness to Genocide,* pp. 168–73. Major General MacKenzie did not identify the sources of his financial backing when testifying before Congress.

16. Quoted in Anthony Lewis, "Lord Owen's Argument," *New York Times,* Feb. 5, 1993, p. 27.

17. Pascal Barollier, Agence France Presse, May 18, 1994, *FBIS-EEU-94-098,* May 20, 1994, p. 23.

18. Testimony before the U.S. House Armed Services Committee, May 26, 1993.

19. Some European Community officials, such as EC Commissioner Hans Van den Broek, were also critical of the Owen-Stoltenberg strategy, describing it as "pacifist superstition;," see Peter Michielson, "EC Commissioner Van den Broek Says Owen Played Into Hands of Bosnian Serbs," *NCR Handelsblad,* Rotterdam, Aug. 28, 1993, in *FBIS-EEU-93-167,* Aug. 31, 1993, pp. 42–44.

20. See Peter Maass, "Owen's Spokesman Denies Pressing to Divide Sarajevo," *Washington Post,* Aug. 12, 1993, p. A23; Lord Owen's letter to the editor, *Washington Post,* Aug. 13, 1993, p. A24; and Ian Traynor, "Envoy Denies Plan to Divide Sarajevo," *The Guardian,* Feb. 10, 1993, p. 7.

21. Quoted in Tony Czuczka, "Muslims Accept Talks on Splitting Sarajevo," *Washington Post,* Dec. 2, 1993, p. A44.

22. Peter Maass, "Bosnia Resists Pressure for Partitioning," *Washington Post,* Sept. 1, 1993, p. A25.

23. Interview with Gen. Jean Cot by Col. Aleksandr Oliynik, "'Golubye kaski' i voyna na Balkanakh" ("The Blue Helmets" and the War in the Balkans), *Krasnaya Zvezda,* Moscow, Nov. 2, 1993, p. 3.

24. U.S. Senate, *Situation in Bosnia,* pp. 51, 57.

25. Interview by Daniel Benjamin, "Hatred Ten Times Over," *Time,* Aug. 17, 1992, p. 28. A later commander of UN military forces in Bosnia-Herzegovina, Lt. Gen. Sir Michael Rose, also adhered to this aproach. Downplaying the prospects of the Bosnian government if it continued fighting to liberate territory, he too believed instead that the "opportunities they've [the Bosnians] got in the peace process for recovering lost territory are much better than they can envisage in the next few years [by fighting]." See Chuck Sudetic, "Bosnia Vows to Press Drive against Serbs," New York Times, Aug. 12, 1994, p. A3.

26. MacKenzie, *Peacekeeper,* pp. 159, 218, 255–56, 291.

27. Benjamin, "Hatred Ten Times Over," p. 28. One journalist, in arguing this position, repeated in his "News Analysis" all the old canards: that the Serbs "controlled" 60 percent of the land before the war, that the Muslims are only converted Serbs, and that the Muslims are responsible for the situation because they were the ones who declared independence; Andrew Borowiec, "Bosnia's Muslims Being Led Toward Winter of Death," *Washington Times,* Sept. 30, 1993, p. A14.

28. This approach appears to have been true at least for the United States, according to George Kenney, former Department of State desk officer for Yugoslavia; speech presented at the Middle East Studies Assoc., Research Triangle, N.C., Nov. 12, 1993.

29. Quoted in R. W. Apple, Jr., "Mediator Is Upset at U.S. Reluctance over Bosnia Talks," *New York Times*, Feb. 3, 1993, p. A1. Later, however, Washington reportedly also joined in exerting pressure on Izetbegović to agree to a subsequent political plan; interview with Marshall Harris, "Level-10," p. 22.

30. Interview on National Public Radio (NPR), Washington, D.C., Feb. 4, 1993.

31. Elaine Sciolino, "Aides Give Clinton Bosnia Peace Plan," *New York Times*, Feb. 9, 1993, p. A14.

32. Richard Bernstein, "Unless Situation Improves, UN Should QUit Bosnia, Mediator Says," *New York Times*, July 14, 1993, p. A3; Eugene Robinson, "EC Mediator Says U.S. 'Killed' Plan for Bosnia," *Washington Post*, Nov. 27, 1993, p. A22; and Owen, "Oh Lord," p. 56.

33. Reported by Miljenko Jergović, "Karadžić: 'Eto sada smo svi jednaki!'" (Karadžić: "There, We Are Now All Equal!"), *Nedjeljna Dalmacija*, Aug. 25, 1993, p. 5.

34. De Gruyter, "Oh Lord, What a Year," p. 55.

35. See Laura Pitter, "Bosnian Muslim Split Seen as Bolstered by Mediator, UN Troops," *Christian Science Monitor*, Oct. 8, 1993, pp. 1, 4. Also see Maass, "Bosnia Resists Pressure," p. A25.

36. See John M. Goshko, "U.S. Disputes Criticism of Bosnia Plan," *Washington Post*, Jan. 27, 1994, p. A21; William Drozdiak, "U.S. Rejects French Plea for Tougher Bosnia Action," *Washington Post*, Jan. 25, 1994, p. A14; Martin Sieff, "U.S.-French Dispute Over Troops for Bosnia Heats Up," *Washington Times*, Jan. 28, 1994, p. A16; and Thomas W. Lippman and John M. Goshko, "Gap remains in U.S.-French Dispute," *Washington Post*, Jan. 28, 1994, p. A19.

37. John Pomfret, "Two UN Officials Accuse U.S. of Prolonging War in Bosnia," *Washington Post*, Apr. 30, 1994, p. A18.

38. *Weekly Compilation of Presidential Documents* (Washington, D.C.: Government Printing Office, Jan. 31, 1994) 30, p. 144.

39. *Meet the Press*, NBC, Apr. 3, 1994.

40. Daniel Williams, "U.S. Policy Shift Puts Pressure on Muslims," *Washington Post*, Feb. 11, 1994, p. A35.

41. Daniel Williams and Ann Devroy, "Clinton Seeks 'Bottom Line' from Bosnian Muslims," *Washington Post*, Feb. 10, 1994, p. A22.

42. Daniel Williams, "Bosnian Muslims Hamper Quest for Peace," *Washington Post*, Apr. 3, 1994, p. A23.

43. Daniel Williams, "U.S. Endorses Land-Split for Bosnia Peace," *Washington Post*, June 3, 1994, p. A27.

44. See, for example, U.S. General Accounting Office, *Serbia-Montenegro: Implementation of UN Economic Sanctions*, Washington, D.C., April, 1993, and "Beating the Sanctions on Serbia," *The Economist*, July 2, 1994, p. 2.

45. William Drozdiak, "NATO Presses Bosnia's Combatants to Accept Partition," *Washington Post*, June 10, 1994, p. A24.

46. President Clinton's press conference, Apr. 15, 1994, in *Weekly Compilation*, Apr. 18, 1994, vol. 30, p. 816.

47. Interview with Douglas Hurd by Jens Schneider, in *Suddeutsche Zeitung*,

reprinted in "U ovom ratu nema pobjednika" (There are No Victors in This War), *Vjesnik,* Sept. 16, 1993, p. 17.

48. "Global Viewpoint," *Washington Times,* Feb. 8, 1993, p. E1.

49. Quoted in A. F. and C. T., "Bosnie: Les Seize ont manifesté plus de désarroi que de désaccords," (The Sixteen Have Shown Greater Confusion than Disagreement), *Le Monde,* Jan. 12, 1994, p. 3.

50. Jonathan C. Randal, "Serb Leaders Snub UN, Visit Gorazde Front," *Washington Post,* Apr. 13, 1994, p. A22.

51. Quoted in John Pomfret, "UN Looks In on Summit Seized by Serbs," *Washington Post,* Aug. 6, 1993, p. A26.

52. Quoted in "Les Serbes paraissent peu impressionés," (The Serbs Do Not Seem Very Impressed), *Le Monde,* Jan. 13, 1994, p. 5.

53. See President Clinton's remarks to North Atlantic Council in Brussels, Jan. 10, 1994, in *Weekly Compilation of Presidential Documents* (Washington, D.C.: Government Printing Office, Jan. 17, 1994), vol 30, p. 23; President Clinton's press conference, Feb. 9, 1994, in *Weekly Compilation,* vol. 30, Feb. 14, 1994, p. 254; and speech by Secretary of Defense William J. Perry to the New England Council of the American Electronics Assoc., Feb. 10, 1994, in "'Doing Something' about Bosnia," *Defense Issues* (Washington, D.C.: Dept. of Defense, 1994), 9, p. 2.

54. Interview by Charlie Rose, *Charlie Rose Show,* June 14, 1994.

Chapter 11

1. U.S. Senate, *Situation in Bosnia,* p. 58, and again before the House Armed Services Committee, May 26, 1993.

2. Interview by Ann Devroy and R. Jeffrey Smith, "Clinton Examines a Foreign Policy under Serige," *Washington Post,* Oct. 17, 1993, p. A28.

3. Ibid.

4. See Julia Preston, "UN Spurns Bid to Lift Arms Ban on Bosnian Muslims," *Washington Post,* June 30, 1993, p. A13. On the Major government's Bosnia policy, see the perceptive analysis by Branka Magas, "Bosnia: A Very British Betrayal," *New Statesman and Society,* Sept. 10, 1993, pp. 14–15; and "The War That Won't Go Away," *The Economist,* Apr. 24, 1993, p. 51.

5. An opponent of the bill, U.S. Rep. Lee Hamilton (D-Ind), reported that several Democrats had told him privately they did not really want the bill to pass, despite having voted in favor. Rather, they were "letting off steam and frustration" by their positive vote and hoped that the upcoming Senate version would weaken the initiative; interview on NPR, June 9, 1994. Also see Helen Dewar, "Senate Narrowly Backs Clinton on Bosnia," *Washington Post,* July 12, 1994, p. A8.

6. As reported by Kenneth J. Cooper, "A Firm House Tells Clinton to Lift Bosnia Arms Embargo Unilaterally," *Washington Post,* June 10, 1994, p. A24.

7. Alain Juppé, "Sarajevo: ce que je crois" (Sarajevo: What I Believe), *Le Monde,* May 21, 1994, pp. 1, 5.

8. Lt. Gen. Martin L. Brandtner, Director for Operations, Office of the Joint Chiefs of Staff, in U.S. Senate, *Current Military Operations,* p. 87.

9. *CBS Evening News,* Apr. 15, 1993. Britain's Defense Secretary, Malcolm Rifkind, echoed this belief as well; see Richard Beeston and Michael Evans, "Russian MPs Call for End to Arms Embargo on Serbs," *The Times,* May 14, 1994, p. 13.

10. Lord Owen, Churchill Lecture.

11. *Charlie Rose Show,* June 14, 1994.

12. U.S. House of Representatives, House Armed Services Committee, *U.S. Policy toward Bosnia,* Hearing, May 26, 1993, Federal Information Systems Corp. transcript, n. p.

13. Quoted in David Binder, "Criticized as Appeaser, Vance Defends His Role in Balkans," *New York Times,* Jan. 19, 1993, p. A7. Similarly, in a letter to Congressman Lee Hamilton (D-Ind), President Clinton noted that such action "would bring the peace process to an end," in Cooper, "A Firm House Tells Clinton," p. A24.

14. John Pomfret, "Bosnians Keep Faith in Fighting," *Washington Post,* July 11, 1994, pp. A1, A12.

15. Interview with Lord Owen by David Frost, NPR.

16. Interview by Željko Toth, "Nismo željeli raspad Jugoslavije" (We Did Not Want Yugoslavia's Collapse), *Večernji list,* Oct. 30, 1993, p. 15.

17. Interview on *Larry King Live,* CNN, July 20, 1993.

18. Srecko Latal, "UN May Have to Pull Out of Bosnia," *Washington Times,* July 13, 1994, p. A13; Ruth Marcus and Daniel Williams, "U.S. Moves to Lift Embargo on Bosnia," *Washington Post,* Aug. 11, 1994, p. A19; Daniel Williams, "Senate Seeks to Press Clinton on Bosnia Arms," *Washington Post,* Aug. 12, 1994, p. A13; and John M. Goshko, "Reaction to Lifting Ban on Bosnia Muslim Arms Worries Administration," *Washington Post,* Aug. 13, 1994, p. A14.

19. B. M., "Puška jača od privilegija" (The Rifle Is Stronger than Privileges), *Evropske Novosti,* Feb. 20, 1993, p. 13. Draft-dodging in Serbia, for example, had been widespread during the Serbo-Croatian War, leading to serious operational and morale problems; also see Cigar, "1991 Serbo-Croatian War," pp. 314–15, 317–19.

20. General Slavko Lisica, quoted in Dragoš Kalajić, "Lisica lavljeg srca" (Lisica [The Fox] with the Heart of a Lion), *Duga,* May 14–27, 1994, p. 31.

21. Ibid., p. 30.

22. B. Marić, "U zatvoru dezerter" (A Deserter in Prison), *Evropske Novosti,* Feb. 17, 1994, p. 10.

23. Popara, ("Seven Hundred Days"), pp. 16–17.

24. For example, in an interview by Frank Sesno, *Larry King Live,* May 3, 1993.

25. Alain Juppé, "Bosnian Crisis a Formidable Test of Old Alliances," *Washington Times,* Feb. 13, 1994, p. B4.

26. Interview by Fahrudin Radončić, Bosna će opstati" (Bosnia Will Continue to Exist), *Danas,* Apr. 9, 1991, p. 31; and interview by Milomir Marić, "Zašto je Alija Izetbegović proglasio neutralnost" (Why Alija Izetbegović Proclaimed Neutrality), *Duga,* Oct. 12–26, 1991, p. 15.

27. As found in his indictment, Sarajevo, June 17, 1983, p. 92. Typescript.

28. Interview by Halid Rifatbegović, "Vjerujem u zajednicki zivot" (I Believe in Living Together), *BiH Ekskluziv,* July 9, 1993, p. 3.

29. Interview with Bisera Turković by Samir Hasan, "Al-fahm al-khati' li-khuttat Vance-Owen wara' al-harb al-kruwatiyya al-busniyya" (The Misinterpretation of the Vance-Owen Plan Is behind the Croatian-Bosnian War), *Al-Sharq Al-Awsat,* London, May 15, 1993, p. 7. The Bosnian Army's commander, Rasim Delić, likewise did not call for an Islamic state in an interview in "Mahammati al-ula ishrak jami^c al-wataniyyin fi ma^crakat al-tahrir" (My First Task Is to Involve All Patriots in the Liberation Battle), *Al-Watan,* Kuwait, July 26, 1993, p. 20.

30. Press conference reported by Muhammad ^cArafa, "Al-^calam yafrud ^calayna al-istislam wa-lays al-salam" (The World Is Imposing on Surrender, Not Peace), *Al-Sharq,* Doha, Qatar, Mar. 11, 1993, p. 5.

31. Interview by Jamal Majayda, "Bosnia's Valiant Fight for Survival," *Emirate News,* Abu Dhabi, UAE, Dec. 28, 1993, p. 8.

32. On the situation in Tuzla, see Jonathan S. Landay, "Bosnian City Averts Ethnic Hatred and Economic Collapse, For Now," *Christian Science Monitor,* Apr. 14, 1993, pp. 1, 4.

Chapter 12

1. John Kifner, "Yugoslav Army Reported Fighting in Bosnia to Help Serbian Forces," *New York Times,* Jan. 27, 1994, pp. A1, A8.

2. Interview with Momčilo Krajišnik by Janjić, ("The State as a Little Girl"), p. 5.

3. Reported by Borislav Soleša, "Nećemo trgovati zemljom i mrtvima" (We Will Not Haggle over Land and the Dead), *Spona,* Dec. 9, 1993, p. 8.

4. Interview by M. Marković, "Mi smo država, razumete" (We Are a State, You Understand), *Srpska stvarnost,* Jan. 8, 1994, p. 20.

5. Interview with Radovan Karadžić by Vid Blagojević, Radio Belgrade Network, Feb. 1, 1994, in *FBIS-EEU-94-022,* Feb. 2, 1994, p. 19.

6. Reported by Borislav Soleša, Nećemo trgovati zemljom i mrtvima" (We Will Not Haggle over Land and the Dead), *Spona,* Dec. 9, 1993, p. 8.

7. Interview by Momčilo Karan, "Muslimanska strana ne želi kraj rata" (The Muslim Side Does Not Want an End to the War), *Spona,* Dec. 23, 1993, p. 8.

8. Interview with Gojko Djogo by J. Janjić, "Gojko Djogo, književnik" (Gojko Djogo, Writer), *Srpska stvarnost,* Jan. 8, 1994, pp. 33–34.

9. Radovan Kovačević, "Granice crtane puškama" (Borders Drawn by Rifles), *Politika,* Nov. 8, 1993, p. 9.

10. Interview by Aleksandrović, ("On the Threshold") p. 12.

11. Blagojević, *FBIS-EEU-94-022,* p. 19.

12. Borović and Tadić, ("Military Threats"), p. 9.

13. Karl von Clausewitz, *On War,* Michael Howard and Peter Paret, eds. and transls. (Princeton: Princeton University Press, 1989), p. 80.

14. O. Kesar, "Vlasti reaguju jer je i osveta zločin" (The Authorities React, for Even Revenge Is a Crime), *Politika,* Apr. 6, 1994, p. 11.

15. Quoted in an AFP report, Mar. 4, 1994, in *FBIS-EEU-94-043*, Mar. 4, 1994, p. 22.

16. Interview by Renaud Girard, *Le Figaro*, Feb. 28, 1994, in *FBIS-EEU-94-039*, Feb. 28, 1994, p. 30.

17. Interview by Toth, ("Yugoslavia's Collapse"), p. 15.

18. Pomfret, "Two UN Officials Accuse U.S.," p. A18.

19. John Pomfret, "UN Sees Hope for Sarajevo," *Washington Post*, Feb. 20, 1994, p. A31.

20. Rick Atkinson, "NATO Refining Blueprints for Peacekeeping in Bosnia," *Washington Post*, Mar. 5, 1994, p. A12.

21. Interview with Douglas Hogg by Branko Bucalo, "Britanci žude otići iz Bosne" (The British Yearn to Leave Bosnia), *BiH Ekskluziv*, Dec. 31, 1993, p. 2.

22. Interview with Mihailo Marković by Radica Momčilović, "Ko piše novo Načertanije" (Who Is Writing the New *Načertanije?*), *Evropski Ekspres*, Apr. 21, 1994, p. 5.

23. Lazukić, ("The Serbs Are a Heavenly Wonder"), p. 11.

24. See Zvonko Prijović, "Bumerang još putuje" (The Boomerang Is Still Traveling), *Vreme*, Aug. 23, 1993, p. 31.

25. Dragoljub Jenkić, "Istorijske i savremene obmane" (Historical and Contemporary Deceptions), *Vojska*, Apr.8, 1993, p. 12.

26. See M. Jelić, "A Strengthened Minority," *Pobjeda*, Podgorica, Montenegro, Sept. 23, 1992, in *FBIS-EEU-92-201*, Oct. 16, 1992, p. 55; interview with Maj. Gen. Radomir Damjanović, deputy-commander of the Second Army, by Miroslav Vukosavljević, *Vojska*, Sept. 15, 1992, in *FBIS-EEU-92-201*, Sept. 15, 1992, pp. 44–45; Velizar Brajović, "Pucanj u ledja" (Shooting in the Back), *Vreme*, May 24, 1993, p. 16.

27. Velizar Brajović, "Bitka za Nikšić" (The Battle for Nikšić), *Vreme*, June 7, 1993, p. 29.

28. Respectively, interview by D. Alempijević, "Crna Gora vodi separatističku politiku" (Montenegro Is Conducting a Separatist Policy), *Spona*, Oct. 21, 1993, p. 16; and quote in Fahrudin Radončić, "Hoće li se Sandžak otcijepiti" (Will the Sandžak Secede?), *Danas*, Mar. 26, 1991, p. 20.

29. See, for example, Jevtić, ("The Turks [Again]"), p. 62.

30. Belgrade Daily TV News, Nov. 21, 1991.

31. Milorad Pantelić, "The Threat of Flames from the Drina," *Vojska*, Sept. 3, 1992, in *FBIS-EEU-92-201*, Oct. 16, 1992, p. 41.

32. Interview with Mirko Jović by Veselin Simonović, "Svako će pokazati pravo lice" (Everyone Will Show His True Face), *Spona*, Dec. 2, 1993, p. 9.

33. Interview in *Chasa*, Sofia, Bulgaria, Nov. 8, 1993, in *FBIS-EEU-93-217*, Nov. 12, 1993, p. 45.

34. Interview by Branimir Brljević, "Da imamo vojnu silu, vratili bismo Baranju i Voljvodinu Madjarskoj!" (If We Had the Military Power, We Would Return Baranja and Vojvodina to Hungary!), *Globus*, Feb. 26, 1993, p. 8.

35. Ibid.

36. Quoted in Jovan Radovanović, "Ratoborni Slovenci" (Warlike Slovenes), *Spona*, Dec. 23, 1993, p. 21.

37. Quoted in Ana Davico, "Mi smo vaši Srbi" (We Are Your Serbs), *Vreme*, May 31, 1993, p. 41.

38. Ayatollah Musavi-Ardabili's Friday sermon, Tehran Voice of the Islamic Republic of Iran, Jan. 15, 1993, in *FBIS-Near East and South Asia-93-011*, Jan. 19, 1993, p. 84.

Index

Index

Index

Panić, Milan, 87, 89, 95–96
Panić, Gen. Života, 79
Partisans, 19
Pašalić, Ivić, 136
Pavle, Patriarch, 101–102; on anti-Islamic measures, 68; and concentration camps, 89–90; on ethnic cleansing, 87; opposes Vance-Owen Plan, 66; views of, 39, 67, 93
peacekeeping, 161, 162–63, 188–91
Perry, William, 139, 209 n3
Plavšić, Biljana, 67, 85
Pljevlja, 193
Podrinje, 185
Posavina, 128, 184
Prijedor, 48, 58, 60, 65, 84, 98, 188
Prlić, Jadranko, 125
Protić, Archdeacon Dragan, 71, 111–12
Protić, Stojan, 17
Puljić, Archbishop Vinko, 131

Ramadanovski, Džej, 111
rape, 59–60, 91–92, 93, 104; denied by Serbian Orthodox Church, 91
Rašković, Jovan, 27
Ražnatović, Željko, See Arkan
refugees, 10, 57–58; in Croatia, 125
Romanija, 44, 65
Rose, Lt. Gen. Sir Michael, 236n25; and Goražde, 120, 161; and peace enforcement, 189
Rosenfeld, Stephen S., 39
Russia: assertiveness of, 162, 164–65; and domestic politics, 144–45; and peacekeeping, 189; and Serbs, 158, 170–71; and Zhirinovskiy, 113, 186, 199
Russian Orthodox Church, 118

Saćirbey, Muhamed, 151–52
Šagolj, Smiljko, 124
Samardžić, Radovan, 77
sanctions, 140–41, 158–59
Sandžak: in Balkan Wars, 17; mosques in, 36; prospects of, 193, 194; repatriation rumors and, 29; and refugees, 138; and Serbia, 20; and Serbian Orthodox Church, 80; and World War II, 18–19
Sarajevo, 65, 83, 97, 114, 127, 151, 161, 162; and 1994 mortar attack, 94
Saudi Arabia, 80
Savović, Branimir, 47
Schwartzkopf, Gen. H. Norman, 77
Scherf, Michael, 116
SDS (Srpska Demokratska Stranka—Serbian Democratic Party), 43, 51, 192

Serbian Academy of Arts and Sciences, 23, 87
Serbian Memorandum, 23–24, 32–35, 62, 76
Serbian Orthodox Church, 101–102; anti-Islamic stance of, 30–32, 99; and Arkan, 36, 67–68; and Bosnian Serb Army, 68; and Catholic Church, 67, 69; and concentration camps, 89, 90–91; and conversion, 111–12; encourages births, 80; and ethnic cleansing, 66–69, 71; and Lord Owen, 120; and nationalists, 23; in Ottoman Empire, 15; views of, 39, 74, 78. *See also* rape; Pavle, Patriarch
Serbs, 47–48; and national will, 175; self-view of, 73–78
Šešelj, Vojislav, 47; denies war crimes, 104; on expulsion of minorities, 42; and Greater Serbia, 186; and militia, 50, 54; and rapes, 92; and war crimes tribunal, 147
Silajdžić, Haris, 108
Šipovo, 44
Slovenia, 76, 196
Smiljanić, Radomir, 92, 147
SNO (Srpska Narodna Obnova—Serbian Popular Renewal), 35
Somalia: impact of, 162–63, 189, 190, 191
South Africa, 197
SPO (Srpski Pokret Obnore—Serbian Renewal Movement), 104, 106, 193
SPS (Socijalistička Partija Srbije—Socialist Party of Serbia), 54
Srebrov, Vladimir, 103
SRS (Srpska Radikalna Stranka—Serbian Radical Party), 92
Srškić, Milan, 18
Srebrenica, 55, 94, 190, 218 n44
Stambolić, Ivan, 24
Stojanović, Lazar, 193
Stoltenberg, Thorvald, 152
Stupni Do, 126
Šušak, Gojko, 124, 130, 232 n8

Tadić, Dušan, 176
Tanasković, Darko, 29, 69, 100
Tito, 19, 35
Todorov, Nada, 70
Tomašević, King Stjepan, 29
Travnik, 146
Trebinje, 44, 53–54, 68, 82, 83, 84, 103
tribunal war crimes, 146–48; Great Britain and, 116, 230 n32; Serbian opposition to, 95
Trieste, 80

Index

Trnopolje (concentration camp), 90, 91
Tudjman, Franjo: anti-Islamic rhetoric of,
124; and domestic critics, 128; on Herceg-
Bosna, 134–36; on refugees, 125
Turkey, 29, 77
Tuzla, 58, 127

UNPROFOR (United Nations Protection
Force): and air cover, 161; behavior of,
92, 118; and Canadians, 190, 191; and
Dutch, 190; and Goražde, 120; harassment of, 190; mission of, 189; in Serbian
jokes, 72; threatened withdrawal of, 154,
191
United Nations, 98, 168, 188–90
United States: and arms embargo, 167–68,
170, 175; and commitment of forces, 162–
63, 190–91; on ethnic cleansing, 115–16;
and Goražde, 156, 160; and Lord Owen,
153; media of, 142; opinion in, 143; and
partition, 117, 156–57; Serb accusations
against, 76, 77, 94, 95, 100; threats by,
162; and war crimes tribunal, 146
Ustaše, 19, 34, 180
Uzdol, 137

Vance, Cyrus, 119, 154, 171
Vance-Owen Plan, 50, 125, 151, 152, 153

Vance, Plan, 45–46
van Hugh, Peter, 51
Vareš, 137
Vasilije, Bishop, 67, 80
Vatican, 67, 77, 101. *See also* Catholic
Church
Višegrad, 65, 88, 98
Vojvodina, 20, 41, 193, 196
Vrdoljak, Antun, 129
Vučurević, Božidar, 43
Vukovar, 45, 164, 194

Warner, John, 12
White Eagles, 35, 83
World War II, 9, 18–19, 55, 119–20, 138

Yellow Wasps (militia), 146
Yeltsin, Boris, 145
Yugoslavia: history of, 17–19; population of,
40; post-war, 19–20; rump state of, 37, 38;
and World War II, 18–19

Zhirinovskiy, Vladimir, 74–75, 79, 113, 164,
186, 198–99
Zrinski, Nikola, 26
Zrinski, Petar, 14
Zulus, 197
Zvornik, 48, 54, 71–72, 98, 102

247